In accordance with the latest syllabus prescribed by the
Council for the Indian Certificate of Secondary Education Examination, New Delhi.

A TEXT BOOK OF
ICSE COMMERCIAL STUDIES

CLASS X

AUTHORS

A. GHOSH **A. BANERJEE**

Advisory Member
Chetan Tiwari
M. Com., M.Sc., B.Ed.,
Principal St. Anthony's School, Kurseong

OSWAL PUBLISHERS
1/12 Sahitya Kunj, M. G. Road, Agra-282 002

No part of this book can be reproduced in any form or by any means without the prior written permission of the publisher.

Edition : 2021

ISBN : 978-93-89937-98-5

OSWAL PUBLISHERS

Head office	:	1/12, Sahitya Kunj, M. G. Road, Agra-282 002
Phone	:	(0562) 2527771-4, +91 75340 77222
E-mail	:	contact@oswalpublishers.com
Website	:	www.oswalpublishers.com
Printed at		

Preface

We feel immense pleasure in introducing the thoroughly revised edition of Commercial Studies text book for ICSE Class X. This edition strictly adheres to the latest syllabus prescribed by the Council for the Indian School Certificate Examination, New Delhi.

The text book has been carefully designed so as to be useful for scholars as well as for the students with preliminary knowledge of the subject. The topics have been fully explained so that each reader can acquire the relevant knowledge as per their requirements.

Philosophy of this book

The concepts have been explained in simple language, easy conversational text with familiar examples, without making any sacrifice in the depth or precision.

The subject matter dealt in this book is self-explanatory to enable the students to understand the fundamental concepts and principles of Commerce easily.

'Lesson at a Glance' given at the end of each chapter will help students in quick revision before the examination.

The Project work/Assignments given at the end of chapters have been designed specifically for ICSE students to generate a practical aptitude towards the subject.

Sufficient short questions and essay type questions, on the pattern suggested by the council, are given at the end of each chapter to enhance the ability of a students to understand the text clearly and develop the skills to answer accurately.

In spite of our best efforts, the possibilities of some errors of omission and commission cannot be ruled out. Constructive suggestions will be appreciated and thankfully acknowledged.

—PUBLISHER

SYLLABUS CLASS X
COMMERCIAL STUDIES

There will be **one** written paper of **two** hours duration carrying 80 marks and Internal Assessment of 20 marks.

The paper will be divided into **two** sections A and B.

Section A (Compulsory) will consist of questions requiring short answers and will cover the entire syllabus. There will be no choice of questions.

Section B will consist of questions, which will require detailed answers. There will be a choice and candidates will be required to answer **four** questions from this section.

1. **Stakeholders in Commercial Organisations**

    (a) Meaning of stakeholder, types : Internal (shareholder, employee and employer—meaning of each) and External stakeholders (supplier, creditor, government and society–meaning of each); difference between internal and external stakeholders.

    (b) Expectations of employers (owners and managers), employees, creditors and suppliers, government and society from a commercial organization.

2. **Marketing and Sales**

    (a) Marketing

    Meaning and objectives of marketing. Difference between marketing and sales.

    (b) Product and service

    Meaning and difference between a product and a service (with examples).

    (c) Pricing

    Meaning and objectives

    (d) Advertising and Sales promotion

    Advertising : meaning, importance of advertising, merits and demerits, difference between advertising and publicity. Advertising Agency; meaning and functions only, Social advertising media–Concept and examples only.

    Sales promotion – meaning and techniques; difference between advertising and sales promotion.

    (e) Consumer Protection

    Consumer Protection Act (2019); features of the Act, rights of a consumer, Consumer exploitation; meaning and types, Importance of consumer awareness.

    (f) E–commerce

    Introduction and benefits over traditional methods of transactions, E-tailing, E-advertising, E-marketing and E-security (meaning only). ERP and its modules (brief concept).

3. **Finance and Accounting**

    (a) Capital and Revenue

    Capital and revenue receipts, capital and revenue expenditure (meaning, difference and examples) deferred revenue expenditure (meaning and examples)

    (b) Final accounts of Sole Proprietorship

- Meaning and **preparation of Trading account, profit and Loss account and Balance sheet** based on the given trial balance with the adjustment of closing stock only.
- (Preparation of manufacturing account, profit and loss on sale of assets, intangible and fictitious assets, prepaid and accrued expenses and incomes are excluded.)

(c) Costs

Fundamental concept of Cost Classification of costs–based on behaviour (fixed, variable, semi-variable), nature (direct, indirect).

(d) Budgeting

Meaning and utility of budgeting; comparison between budgeting and forecasting; types of budgets; sales, production, cash, purchase and master–meaning only.

(e) Sources of Finance

(i) Capital Market

Meaning and functions of Capital Market.

(ii) Sources of raising capital

Long term : Meaning of shares (Types; preference and equity) and debentures, differences between the two.

Short term : loans from commercial banks (cash credit, overdraft, discounting of bills—meaning only).

4. **Human Resources**

(a) Recruitment, selection and training

(i) Recruitment – meaning; sources : internal and external; advantages and disadvantages of internal and external sources.

(ii) Selection – meaning and steps, types of selection tests.

(iii) Training – meaning, objectives and methods of training (on the job and off the job).

(b) Industrial relations and trade unions

Industrial relations : meaning and objectives; Trade Unions; Meaning and Functions.

(c) Social Security

Concept of Social Security; brief reference to Provident Fund, Gratuity, Pension, Group Insurance and Maternity Benefits. New Pension Scheme. (Acts are not required).

5. **Logistics**

Meaning of logistics and its classification

(a) Transportation

Modes of transportation : land (road and rail), air and water; merits and demerits of each.

(b) Warehousing

Meaning, importance and types (public, private and bonded– meaning only).

(c) Insurance

Meaning; Types of insurance : Life insurance, General insurance; (Fire, Health and Marine–meaning only) principles of insurance.

6. **Banking**

   (i) Central Bank

   Central Bank; Meaning and functions, Difference between the Central Bank and Commercial Banks.

   (ii) Internet Banking

   Modes of transferring money / Net Banking: NEFT, RTGS, IMPS, mobile wallets: meaning only.

   ATM, Credit & Debit cards- meaning & difference, caution to be taken while using these cards.

   (iii) Financial fraudulent practices

   Credit card fraud, false accounting, insurance fraud, intellectual property fraud, Internet and cyber fraud. A brief understanding of these types of financial fraud.

7. **Government initiatives in Environment Protection**

   (i) *Environment (Protection) Act, 1986—Features of the act.*

   (ii) *Central Pollution Control Board— Functions only.*

INTERNAL ASSESSMENT

A minimum of three assignments are to be done during the year, as assigned by the teacher.

EVALUATION

The project work is to be evaluated by the subject teacher and by an External Examiner. The External Examiner shall be nominated by the Head of the school and may be a teacher from the faculty, **but not teaching the subject in the relevant section/class.** For example, a teacher of Commerce/Accounts of Class XI may be deputed to be the External Examiner for Class X Commercial Studies project work.

The Internal Examiner and the External Examiner will assess the candidate's work independently.

Award of marks **(20 Marks)**

Subject Teacher (Internal Examiner) 10 Marks

External Examiner 10 Marks

The total mark obtained out of 20 are to be sent to the Council by the Head of the school.

The Head of the school will be responsible for the online entry of marks on the Council's CAREERS portal by the due date.

CONTENTS

1. Stakeholders in Commercial Organisations — 9–22
2. Marketing: Meaning and Objectives — 23–29
3. Product and Service — 30–37
4. Pricing — 38–41
5. Advertising — 42–51
6. Sales Promotion — 52–55
7. Consumer Protection — 56–67
8. E-Commerce — 68–74
9. Capital and Revenue — 75–79
10. Final Accounts of a Sole trader — 80–101
11. Fundamental Concept of Costs — 102–110
12. Budgeting — 111–118
13. Sources of Finance — 119–125
14. Recruitment and Selection — 126–139
15. Training of Employees — 140–151
16. Industrial Relations and Trade Unions — 152–158
17. Social Security — 159–169
18. Logistics: An Overview — 170–172
19. Transportation — 173–182
20. Warehousing — 183–189
21. Insurance — 190–201
22. Banking — 202–215
23. Banking Transactions — 216–229
24. Financial Fraudulent Practices — 230–232
25. Government Initiatives in Environment Protection — 233–236

CHAPTER-01
Stakeholders in Commercial Organisations

STAKEHOLDERS

The term 'stakeholder' has been derived from the word 'stake', which means an interest or expected benefit. Stakeholders, therefore, refer to all those individuals, groups and institutions which have a stake in the functioning and performance of a commercial organisation or a business enterprise. A person is said to be a stakeholder when that person has an interest in the organisation, especially because he/she has invested money in it.

- Meaning of Stakeholders
- Internal Stakeholders— employers, employees and shareholders
- External Stakeholders— suppliers, creditors, distributors, society and government.
- Difference between internal and external stakeholders.
- Expectations of Stakeholders— employers, employees, creditors, suppliers, government and society from a commercial organisation.

Thus, stakeholders are the individuals or groups that are directly or indirectly affected by an organisation's decisions and actions. Stakeholders include owners/shareholders, employees, suppliers, distributors, general public, labour unions, financial institutions and government. Conventionally, the customers also come into the purview of stakeholders but in the contemporary competitive environment, the customers have the option to switch over to other organisations, thereby, remaining unaffected from organisation's action and decisions.

The primary task for any business today is to define its stakeholders and their expectations. Conventionally, most business organisations primarily thought of their owners/shareholders, *i.e.*, they were concerned only about the profits, applying the traditional rule of minimum investment and maximum return. In today's competitive business scenario, however, no business organisation can grow until and unless its stakeholders, *i.e.*, employees, suppliers, distributors, general public, labour unions, creditors, financial institutions and government are satisfied. Thus, if these stakeholders of an organisation, *e.g.*, Reliance Industries, are unhappy, Reliance cannot earn large profits for shareholders. Hence, it becomes rather mandatory for any business organisation today to atleast satisfy the minimum expectations of its stakeholders.

The organisation can deliver to any stakeholder a minimum level, a performance level or an extraordinary level of satisfaction. In setting these levels, the organisation must be careful not to violate the sense of fairness among stakeholders about the relative treatment they are getting.

There is a dynamic relationship connecting the stakeholder groups. A growing organisation caters to high level of employee satisfaction which leads employees to direct their energies towards continuous improvements, look for new breakthroughs and innovate. Consequently, higher quality services and products are produced which deliver higher degree of customer satisfaction. Customer satisfaction leads to repeated business which means growth and profits. This in return gives higher satisfaction to owners/shareholders. This cycles back and permits building a qualitative environment for employees. The same can be applied for suppliers, distributors, financial institutions, government, labour unions and general public.

The dynamic relationship mentioned above is shown below through diagram:

DISTINCTION BETWEEN STAKEHOLDERS AND SHAREHOLDERS

It should be understood that, stakeholder is a much wider term than shareholder. In a joint stock company, the persons and groups who have the shares of the company are known as shareholders. They contribute to the company's share capital and assume risk of loss. In addition to shareholders; customers, creditors, employees, government and others also have a stake in the company. All these are known as stakeholders.

The term shareholders is used only in connection with a joint stock company but the term stakeholders is used in connection with all business enterprises—sole proprietor-ship, partnership, joint stock company, etc.

DISTINCTION BETWEEN STAKEHOLDERS AND CUSTOMERS

As mentioned in the beginning of this chapter, if we look from conventional point of view, even the customer constitutes the stakeholders group. Any individual/group who is affected by the decisions of the organisation is a stakeholder. The customer is also affected by the decisions of the organisation but unlike other stakeholders, customer has wide options and can switch over to other product or organisation the very moment his/her interest is affected adversely, which is not very pleasing for suppliers, distributors, etc.

Basis of Distinction	Stakeholders	Customers
Financial Stake	As per meaning, stakeholders have a financial stake in a business firm.	Customers do not have financial stake in a business firm.

Basis of Distinction	Stakeholders	Customers
Supply of Capital	Human as well as financial capital is supplied by the stakeholders.	They do not supply any kind of capital to the organisation.
Risk Taking	They bear the risks of the organisation.	They do not bear the risk of the organisation.
Product and Market Orientation	Tastes of stakeholders do not influence the manufacturing of the products.	Products are manufactured according to the tastes of the customers. Therefore, market orientation is necessary to satisfy customers.
Sharing of Profits	They share profits in the form of interest, dividend, wages, salaries etc.	They do not share profits.
Participation in Management	Stakeholders, such as owners, participate in the management of an organisation.	They do not participate in the management of an organisation.

INTERNAL AND EXTERNAL STAKEHOLDERS

Stakeholders can be grouped as internal stakeholders and external stakeholders. Internal stakeholders are those groups or individuals which form the organisation themselves and these include employers, shareholders, owners, managers and employees. External stakeholders are those individuals or groups which are outside the organisation, such as suppliers, distributors, labour unions, creditors, general public and government.

Internal Stakeholders

1. Employers:
This group of stakeholders is constituted by the shareholders/owners and managers/board of directors. The decisions taken by the managers can affect the shareholders/owners and the managers themselves too. If the managers of any organisation decide to add a product to their range of products, it requires more money and it may prove fruitful or it may not. If it does not, definitely it will affect the profits of the organisation which will result in the loss to owners of the organisation and will also have a negative impact on other stakeholders. Similarly, the governing structure of public limited companies allows shareholders to influence a company by exercising their voting rights which again can affect the various stakeholders.

2. Employees:
An employee is an individual who is hired by an employer to do a specific job. The level of satisfaction of employees must be taken due care of, because it generates high morale and motivation. If the employees do not get proper remuneration, have poor working conditions or have inadequate social security; it will affect the

profitability of the organisation and can also create distress amongst employees which can be harmful for the public image of any organisation and can adversely affect the stakeholders including employees themselves.

3. Shareholders:
Shareholder is an individual who owns one or more equity shares of a particular company. Basically shareholders are partial owners of the company and hence, they are entitled to a certain share of the profit. This share of the profit is given to them on the pre-existing agreement depending on the increased valuation of the company's stock. As owners, shareholders can also incur losses when the company does. They may also have voting rights equal to the percentage of their ownership.

External Stakeholders

1. Suppliers:
Every organisation buys inputs, raw materials, services, energy, equipments and labour and uses them to produce output. What the organisation brings in from outside and what it does with what it brings in, will determine both the quality and the price of its final product. Organisations are, therefore, dependent upon suppliers and also, the suppliers are dependent upon organisations for orders. Any decision taken by the organisation can demotivate indigenous suppliers, deregulate the supply schedule, block their money and can affect them. On the other hand, any decision taken by the suppliers can affect the production process of an organisation.

2. Creditors and Financial Institutions:
Creditors and financial institutions disburse loans and advances to earn interest and hence, generate profit. These loans are given to the organisation keeping in view its past performance and future prospects. Any decisions taken by the organisation which reduces its cash flow, definitely affect the repayment of loans and payment of interest to creditors and financial institutions.

3. Distributors/Retailers:
Organisations require channels to distribute their product to the end user. This work is done by distributors and retailers. Any decision taken by the organisation can affect them. *For example*, if an organisation decides to open more outlets for its products or services in the same locality, it will adversely affect the existing retailers because their sales would be reduced. The same thing is true for the distributors.

4. Society:
Activities of organisations affect the society also, hence, every organisation has social responsibilities too. Organisations should not misuse natural resources. They should help in avoiding class conflicts, protect natural environment and should not engage in any kind of activity which proves detrimental to the interest of the general public. Taxes and duties paid by these organizations form a major part of government revenue, which is spent on public in providing basic amenities, social projects, etc. Thus, any decision taken by organisation can affect the society also.

5. Government:
It becomes the duty of any organisation to obey the rules laid down by the government, pay taxes and duties timely to the government and not to enter into

contracts with enemy countries through illegal channels. Hence, any decision taken by organisation can affect Government also.

From the above discussion, it is evident that any decision taken by the organisation can affect the stakeholders, which in turn affects the growth and profitability of the organisation itself. Due care should be taken of the expectations of internal as well as external stakeholders as they affect the growth, profitability and public image of an organisation.

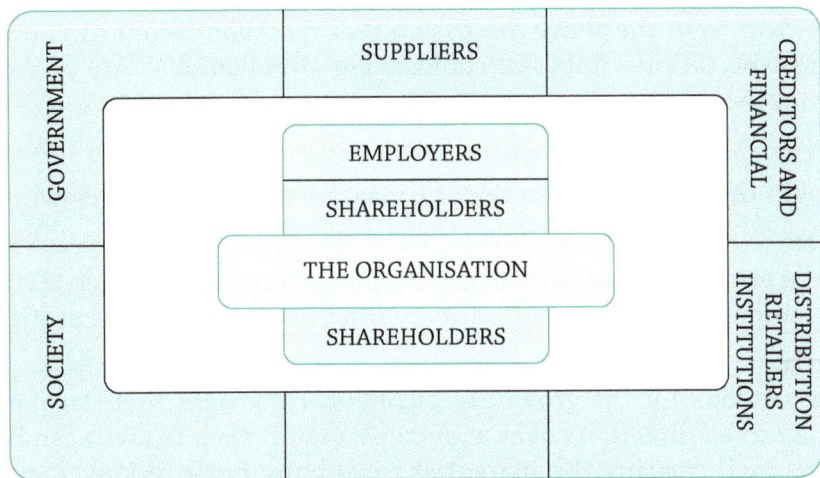

DIFFERENCE BETWEEN INTERNAL AND EXTERNAL STAKEHOLDERS

Owing to complexity of the business environment it is sometimes difficult to differentiate between an internal and an external stakeholder. However, the following table points out to the differences in detail:

Basis of Distinction	Internal Stakeholders	External Stakeholders
Nature	The individuals who are directly a part of the organisation are called internal stakeholders.	The parties or the groups who are not a part of the organisation but are affected by its activities, are called the external stakeholders.
Nature of Impact	Internal stakeholders have direct impact on the company.	External stakeholders have indirect impact on the company.
Who are They?	The people who serves the company.	The people who are affected by the functioning of the company.
Employed by the Entity?	Yes.	No.
Responsibility of the Company towards them	The company has primary responsibility towards internal stakeholders.	The company has secondary responsibility towards external stakeholders.

Basis of Distinction	Internal Stakeholders	External Stakeholders
Example	Employees, Owners, Board of Directors, Managers, etc.	Suppliers, creditors, customers, competitors, government and the society in general.

EXPECTATIONS OF STAKEHOLDERS

It is quite clear from the above discussion that no organisation can grow and earn profits if the expectations of its stakeholders are not taken due care of. Expectations of various stakeholders are discussed as follows:

(A) Expectations of Employers

Expectations of employers from the organisation are discussed below:

1. Profit:
Profit is the primary expectation of any business owner or manager. It is the reward of an entrepreneur. Every owner wants to run business and make profits.

2. Growth:
All employers look for the growth of business. They want their business to grow and prosper in all directions over a given period of time. Growth can be achieved in business by increasing the market share, adding more products, expansion of markets, cutting down of costs and increasing the productivity.

3. Market Leadership:
To become the leader of the market, is another expectation of employers. To attain a niche in the market, innovation is an important factor. Innovation may be in the field of advertising, finance, product etc.

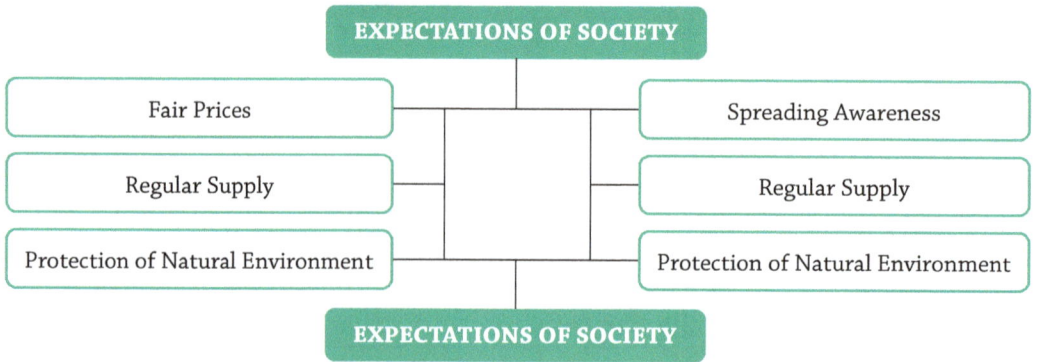

4. Expectations from Suppliers:
Owners and managers expect their suppliers to supply the goods regularly or whenever required, so that the production process is not hindered. They also expect suppliers to charge reasonable prices and sell goods to them (employers) on easy terms of credit.

5. Expectations from Employees:
Employers expect employees to be faithful to the organisation, so that the secrets of the organisation are not disclosed to the competitors. Employers expect serious and

devoted efforts from employees towards their work in return for the remuneration and services/amenities provided to them.

6. Expectations from Government:
Employers, *i.e.*, owners and managers expect government to formulate such policies which are favorable for the business environment. They expect that domestic industries be given cover in form of loans, subsidized technological import etc. to face the threat and competition from foreign companies or organisations. They expect the government to levy taxes in a manner which is not too harsh for the employers.

7. Expectations from Creditors:
Owners and managers expect creditors and financial institutions to grant loans and advances at reasonable rate of interest, *i.e.*, creditors should not take undue advantage of situation at the time of crisis of cash inflow.

(B) Expectations of Employees
Expectations of employees from the organisation are discussed below:

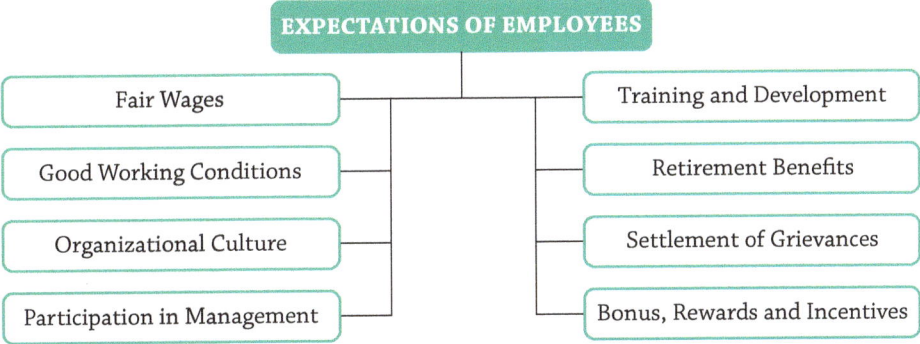

1. Fair Wages:
Employees of an organisation expect fair remuneration for the work done by them. If the workers or employees do not get salaries or wages proportionate to work done by them, their efficiency will be affected which in turn would result in lower product quality and disloyalty to the organisation in terms of continuity with the job. The moment the employee gets proper and better remuneration in some other organisation, he will leave his job from the present organisation.

2. Good Working Conditions:
Employees of an organisation expect their working conditions to be proper. It means, that the environment in which the employees work, should be such that they are able to work with their full potential. For example, the employee working in a shoe unit during summers with fan or cooler will have higher efficiency than the employee working without fan or cooler. Similarly, proper sitting place, canteen and water facilities should be provided to the employees. Employees also expect that immediate and proper treatment should be given to them at the time of accidents.

3. Organizational Culture:
Employees expect that the organizational ambiance and culture should be amicable. They expect that the relationship between boss and subordinate should not be

autocratic and imposed. If it is imposed, employees will work unwillingly and this will definitely affect their efficiency and quality of work.

4. Participation in Management:
Employees expect that their demands should be considered favorably. To communicate their demands to top level management or Board of Directors, they expect that a person (employee) representing them should hold a post on top level management.

5. Training and Development:
Employees dislike remaining stuck to the same position forever. Instead, they want themselves to go on to the superior position for which they require proper training. Employees expect the organisation to look into this need and make proper arrangements for their training and development. They also expect to get their due promotions.

6. Retirement Benefits:
Employees expect that once they are old and are retired from the job, there should be sufficient income for them in the form of pension, provident fund and gratuity to comfortably live the rest of their life. It is not only in case of retirement, but also in case of premature death of an employee. They expect that job on compensatory ground should be provided to their dependent so that the family members of deceased do not starve.

7. Settlement of Grievances:
Grievance means 'cause for complaints or annoyance'. Employees expect that their grievances are handled immediately with sincerity of purpose and an intention to resolve it. They expect that their grievances are resolved at the lowest admissible level so that it does not take far too long a time to get resolved.

8. Bonus, Rewards and Incentives:
Employees expect that any extra work will be properly rewarded by the organisation. Additionally, if organisation earns some extra profits, it would be shared with them as bonus.

(C) Expectations of Suppliers
Expectations of suppliers from the organisation are discussed below:

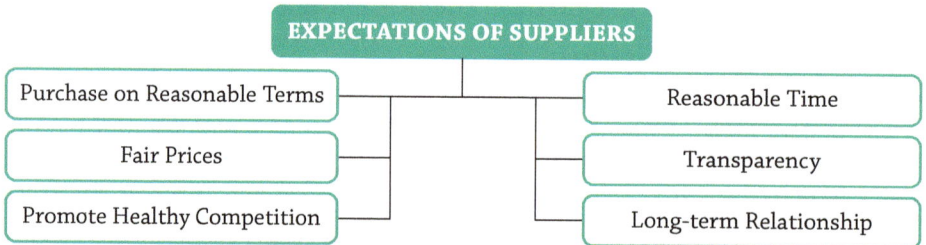

1. Purchase on Reasonable Terms:
Suppliers expect that the organisation is going to make purchases from them on reasonable terms, *i.e.*, if the supplier is new to the organisation he would not be exploited in terms of prices, proper time will be given to him to deliver the goods and favorable treatment will be given to the supplier during period of shortages.

2. Fair Prices:

Seller always expect cost plus profit from the buyer, same is the case with suppliers. They expect that any organisation purchasing goods from them will pay fair price and will not take any undue advantage due to the competition prevailing in the market amongst suppliers.

3. Promote Healthy Competition:

The primary objective of any business organisation is to earn profit. Profit can be increased either by cutting down the costs or by increasing the selling price. Later is not possible in today's competitive environment, thus, every business organisation wants to purchase at minimum price. To buy at the lowest price, every organisation negotiates with the different suppliers available in the market and opts for the one who supplies the required quality and quantity of goods at minimum price and on reasonable terms. At the same time, the suppliers expect that the organisation is going to promote healthy competition amongst different suppliers and does not mislead any supplier for their own advantage.

4. Reasonable Time:

The processing of order consumes time as the goods have to be given finishing touch and packed, before they are delivered to the buyer. Sometimes, in period of shortages, supplier has to arrange for the goods too. Thus, supplier expects that reasonable time should be given to them by the organisation for the supply of goods.

5. Transparency:

Suppliers want that the dealings between them and the organisation should be clear in terms of payment, time of the delivery of goods, quality of goods, quantity of goods and treatment of defective material, etc., so that no dispute arises later at the time of payment.

6. Long-term Relationship:

Suppliers expect long term relationship with the organization, so that they can have business for the longer period with them. Good relations with the organisation also help suppliers in avoiding any disputes regarding defective goods, financial matters or otherwise.

(D) Expectations of Creditors or Financial Institutions

Expectations of creditors or financial institutions from the organisation are discussed below:

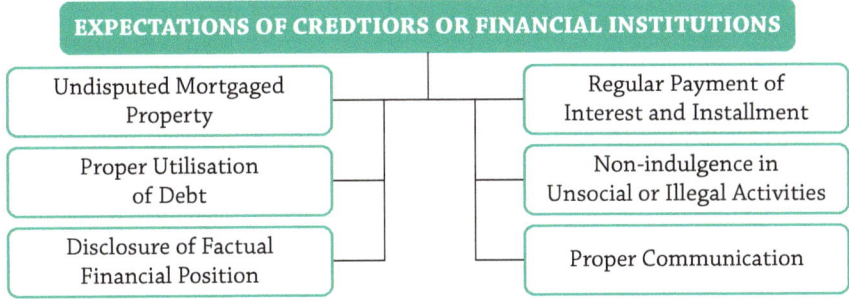

1. Undisputed Mortgaged Property:
Loan or credit given by the creditors or financial institutions is secured by some asset of the organisation. In other words, if organisation is unable to repay the loan to the creditor, creditor can sell out the pledged property and recover the dues. Thus, creditors expect that the property or assets pledged with them by the organisation does not have any dispute regarding its ownership.

2. Proper Utilisation of Debt:
Creditors or financial institutions expect that the debts raised by them will be used for the purpose stated. If it is misutilised, *i.e.*, it is used for some other or personal purposes, it would have an adverse impact on the business of organisation which would in turn affect the repayment schedule, which is not in favour of creditors or financial institutions.

3. Disclosure of Factual Financial Position:
Creditors expect that any organisation approaching them for credit, is going to disclose its factual financial position and is not going to portray fake image with the help of vague documents for the purpose of obtaining loan or credit. Thus, the documents or account statements submitted by the organisation should be real and not manipulated.

4. Regular Payment of Interest and Installment:
Creditors expect that the organisation to whom they have given credit, will make payment of interest and installment on due date so that regularity of cash inflows is maintained and they can further rotate that money.

5. Non-indulgence in Unsocial or Illegal Activities:
Creditors or financial institutions who lend the money to the organisation expect that the organisation is not going to engage in any unsocial or illegal activities because if it does so, it will have an adverse impact on business and it will not be in favour of creditors and financial institutions.

6. Proper Communication:
Financial institutions and creditors expect that the financial position of the organisation will be communicated to them periodically so that they can plan for the future credits and repayments accordingly.

(E) Expectations of Society
Expectations of society from the organisation are discussed below:

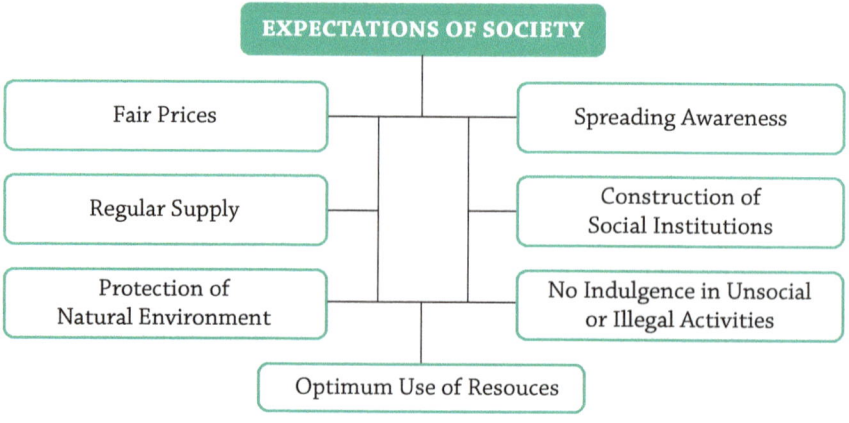

1. Fair Prices:
Society expects that goods will be supplied to them at fair prices. They expect that organisations producing the same product will not make a pool and charge higher prices from the customers.

2. Regular Supply:
Hoarding of goods leads to black marketing. Thus, public expects that the goods will be supplied to them regularly and no artificial shortage will be created in the market.

3. Protection of Natural Environment:
Profit maximisation is the primary objective of any organisation but public expects that during the attainment of their primary objectives, organisations do not destroy the natural environment and rather work for the protection of the environment.

4. Spreading Awareness:
Society expects that the organisation should spread awareness about its product amongst public and also inform public about the advantages and disadvantages of using that particular product. They should also inform public for whom their product is useful and for whom it is not.

5. Construction of Social Institutions:
Although profit maximisation is the primary objective of any business organisation but the society expects that organisations who are earning heavy profits will construct social institutions, such as old age homes, orphanages and rehabilitation centers for the use of public.

6. No Indulgence in Unsocial or Illegal Activities:
Unsocial or illegal products and activities will have negative impact on the growth of nation and its citizen. Thus, society expects that business organisations do not manufacture such products which are harmful for the society and refrain from engaging themselves in such activities which are detrimental to the health and image of society, for example, drug trafficking.

7. Optimum Use of Resources:
Society expects that the organisation is going to make optimum use of resources and will promote the research environment so that better quality goods at cheaper rates will be made available to the public.

(F) Expectations of Government
Expectations of government from the organisation are discussed below:

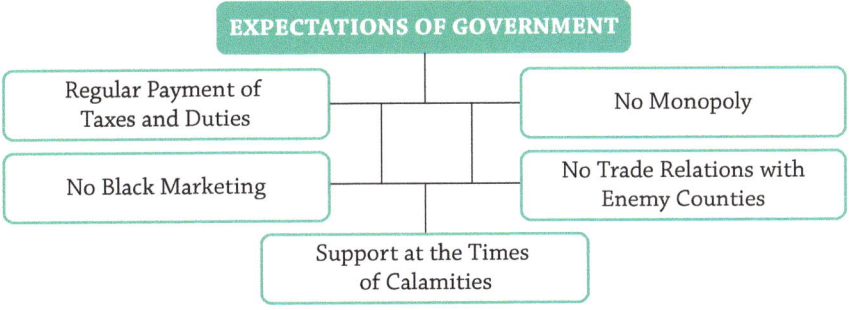

1. Regular Payment of Taxes and Duties:
Revenue generated by the government in form of taxes and duties is spent by it on the social welfare and defence of the country. Thus, government expects that business organisations pay the taxes and duties regularly and do not try to evade them.

2. No Black Marketing:
Many organisations stock the goods and do not supply to the public at normal prices, due to which an artificial shortage is created in the market. These goods are supplied to consumers at higher prices through black markets, which is an illegal activity. Thus, government expects that organisations do not themselves indulge in such black marketing of goods.

3. No Monopoly:
Government expects that any business organisation in the course of its business should not gain monopoly and exploit the customers. Although government has established Competition Commission of India to check unfair and monopolistic trade practices, it expects organisations not to concentrate economic powers which are detrimental to social interests.

4. No Trade Relations with Enemy Countries:
Government expects that business organisation should not engage themselves in trade with the enemy countries through any channel. Developing trade relations with enemy countries is neither desirable nor expected.

5. Support at the Times of Calamities:
At the time of natural calamities, government expects organisation to join hands with it and help the residents of the affected area to overcome the disaster. Earthquake of Gujarat is a recent example where many business and social organisations joined hands with the government and helped the people of affected areas.

Lesson at a Glance

- **Stakeholders:** Stakeholders are the individuals or groups that are directly or indirectly affected by an organisation's decisions and actions. They include owners/shareholders, employees, suppliers, distributors, general public, labour union, creditors, financial institutions and government.
- **Internal and External Stakeholders:** Internal stakeholders are the individuals or groups which themselves form the organisation and include (i) Employers (shareholders, owners, managers); (ii) Employees, (iii) Shareholders. The external stakeholders are the individuals or groups which are outside the organisation and include : (i) Suppliers; (ii) Creditors and Financial institutions; (iii) Distributors / Retailers; (iv) Society; (v) Government.
- **Distinction between Internal and External Stakeholders:** (i) Nature; (ii) Nature of Impact; (iii) Who are they ?; (iv) Employed by the entity; (v) Responsibility of the company towards them; (vi) Examples.

- **Expectations of Stakeholders:**
  - **Expectations of Employers:** (i) Profit; (ii) Growth; (iii) Market leadership; (iv) Expectations from suppliers; (v) Expectations from employees; (vi) Expectations from government; (vii) Expectations from creditors.
  - **Expectations of Employees:** (i) Fair wages; (ii) Good working conditions; (iii) Organisational culture; (iv) Participation in management; (v) Training and development; (vi) Retirement benefits; (vii) Settlement of grievances; (viii) Bonus, rewards and incentives.
  - **Expectations of Suppliers :** (i) Purchase on reasonable terms; (ii) Fair prices; (iii) Promote healthy competition; (iv) Reasonable time; (v) Transparency; (vi) Long-term relationship.
  - **Expectations of Creditors or Financial Institutions:** (i) Undisputed mortgaged property; (ii) Proper utilisation of debt; (iii) Disclosure of factual financial position; (iv) Regular payment of interest and installments; (v) Non-indulgence in unsocial or illegal activities; (vi) Proper communication.
  - **Expectations of Society:** (i) Fair prices; (ii) Regular supply; (iii) Protection of natural environment; (iv) Spreading awareness; (v) Construction of social institutions; (vi) No indulgence in unsocial or illegal activities; (vii) Optimum use of resources.
  - **Expectations of Government:** (i) Regular payment of taxes and duties; (ii) No black marketing; (iii) No monopoly; (iv) No trade relations with enemy countries; (v) Support at the times of calamities.

Project Work

Visit a manufacturing organisation in your nearby area. Choose two persons each from employers, employees, suppliers, creditors, general public and taxation authorities and find out their expectations from the organisation. Prepare a report and justify whether their expectations are worth consideration or otherwise. Give suitable reasons to explain, how these expectations are beneficial to organization, if same are duly cared for.

Assignments

1. Your friend was absent on the day when your teacher taught you the meaning of term stakeholder and its importance. Now your friend is asking you to explain the same to him. How are you going to do it?

2. Your neighbour argues on the point that customer is also a stakeholder. How will you explain to him the basic difference between stakeholder and customer?

3. You have studied the various expectations of internal and external stakeholders. How will you explain the same in the class?

QUESTIONS

A. Short Answer Type Questions:
1. Distinguish between internal and external stakeholders.
2. What do you mean by stakeholders?
3. Name two types of internal stakeholders.
4. State any two types of external stakeholders.
5. Give any three expectations of employers from the organisation.
6. Give any three expectations of employees from the organisation.
7. Give any three expectations of creditors from the organisation.
8. State any three expectations of society from the organisation.
9. Give any three expectations of government from the organisation.
10. Distinguish between stakeholders and customers.
11. Mention any two expectations of suppliers from a business organisation.
12. State any two expectations of shareholders from a business concern. [ICSE 2017]
13. Distinguish between internal and external stakeholders. [ICSE 2020]

B. Essay Type Questions:
1. Discuss the various types of Internal and External stakeholders.
2. State any five expectations of employers from a business enterprises. [ICSE 2019]
3. State any five expectations of employees from a business organisation. [ICSE 2020]
4. Explain the various expectations which creditors have from the organisation.
5. "With profits, social welfare should also be considered." Enumerate this statement with reference to the expectations of society.
6. Describe in detail the difference between the internal and external stakeholder.
7. Explain the conflicting needs of the stakeholders of a company.
8. Explain any five expectations of Suppliers from a business organisation. [ICSE 2018]
9. Explain expectations of the Government from a business organisation. [ICSE 2017]

CHAPTER-02
Marketing: Meaning and Objectives

MARKET

The term market appears to have its origin from the Latin word 'Marcatus', which means a place where business is conducted, buyers and sellers come together to facilitate exchange and by means of which the prices of goods tend to be equalized easily and quickly.

Traditionally market has been expressed from the point of view of a specific place, but with time the concept of market has evolved. Following are the various concepts on which, a market can be defined:

- *Meaning of Market*
- *Meaning of Marketing*
- *Definitions of Marketing*
- *Traditional and Modern View of Marketing*
- *Features of Marketing*
- *Objectives of Marketing*
- *Meaning of Sales*
- *Difference between Marketing and Sales.*

Place Concept:
To any common person a market means a specific place where buyers and sellers meet and complete the transactions of goods and services in exchange of a certain price. The buyer gets both ownership and physical possession of the products once the payment is being made to the seller.

Area Concept:
A market may be viewed as a geographical region where buyers and sellers can establish continuous business relations for the exchange of goods and services through various means of communication. It is because of the availability of fast means of communication that the price of a commodity tends to be same throughout the entire area or region.

There is free interplay of the forces of demand and supply throughout the region leading to almost the same price in all places in the particular region. The region may be small or large. For instance, the entire world is a market for BMW cars, whereas India is the market for Tata Nano.

Demand Concept:
According to the demand concept the mere existence of demand for a product or service constitutes a market. This viewpoint emphasizes the demand of consumers. The size of the market is determined by consumers' demand and their willingness to pay. The greater the demand for a product, the larger will be its market. Consequently if the demand, for certain product, shrinks, then the market also shrinks.

- *"A market means any body of persons who are in intimate business relations and can carry extensive transactions in any commodity."* —Prof. Jevons
- *"In fact the market must be thought of not as a geographical meeting place but as any getting together of buyers and sellers in person by Mail, Telephone, Telegraph or any other means of communication."* —H.E. Mitchell

- "It is a center about which, or an area in which the forces leading to exchanges of titles to a particular product operate and towards which and from which the actual goods tend to travel."
  —Clark and Clark
- "A market is the set of all actual and potential buyers of a product." —Philip Kotler

Thus, based on these definitions, it can be said that, market is the sum total of the situation or environment in which the resources, activities and attitudes of buyers and sellers affect the demand for products in a given area. It should be clearly understood that the term market means a place where buyers and sellers come together in person by mail, telephone, telegraph, cable, fax or any other means of communication.

MARKETING

Marketing is a process of buying and selling of products and services in exchange of consideration to satisfy the consumer's needs. It consists of all those activities that a seller undertakes, in order to ensure that a company is able to sell the product at a price that gives them adequate profit in returns.

Today, marketing is regarded as the most important of all management functions in any business organisation. Goods and Services cannot be sold by merely producing them, but they have to move from place of production to customers for consumption. In the modern world, producers are bound to be consumer oriented because customers have a wide range of products and brands to which they can switch which gives them the utmost satisfaction, *i.e.*, the product has to be developed according to the needs and wants of the customer. Thus, marketing involves development of products or services according to the needs of the customer and then moving them from place of production to place of consumption profitably, to satisfy customer wants.

- "Marketing includes all activities involved in the creation of place, time and possession utility." —Converse, Huegey and Mitchell
- "Marketing consists of those activities which effect transfers in ownership of goods and care for their physical distribution." —F.E. Clark
- "Marketing is the performance of business activities that direct the flow of goods and services from producer to consumer or user". —American Marketing Association
- "Marketing is the economic process by means of which goods and services are exchanged and their values are determined in terms of money prices." —Dudhey and Reizan

There are two approaches to marketing–traditional (product oriented) and modern (consumer oriented).

TRADITIONAL AND MODERN VIEW OF MARKETING

Traditional View

In olden time, marketing was defined as the flow of goods from the producers to the consumers. This is a product-oriented definition of marketing. The process of marketing began after the process of production. The producers concentrated on what they could produce and sell. The needs of the customers were not taken into consideration. The product-oriented definition is based on the assumption that whatever is produced is bound to be sold.

Modern View

Consumer-Orientation is the modern concept of marketing. It analyses the needs of the customers and then produce goods that strive to meet their needs. According to J.F. Pyle,"Marketing is that phase of business activity through which human wants are satisfied by the exchange of goods and services." This definition takes into consideration the satisfaction of human wants. It emphasises the determination and the satisfaction of the requirements of potential customers which take precedence over production.

The customer oriented marketing involves 'selling of satisfaction' rather than 'selling a product'.

Business must produce what the consumers want, in the quantity and quality they desire, at a price they are willing to pay, at the time they need and through the channels most convenient to them.

- *"Marketing is a total system of interacting business activities designed to plan, price, promote and distribute wants satisfying products and services to present and potential customers."* —Stanton

FEATURES OF MARKETING

1. Customer Oriented:
Marketing is a customer oriented activity. Every business depends on human needs. It identifies the need of the customers and then produce accordingly. In a competitive market, the goods that are best suited to the customer are the ones that are well-accepted. Hence, marketing focuses on customer-orientation.

2. Consumer Satisfaction:
Customer satisfaction is one of the main features of marketing. The aim should be maximization of profit through customer satisfaction. The consumers get pleased when product performance matches with customer expectation. When product performance is below customer expectation, the customers are dissatisfied. When product performance exceeds customer expectation, the customers are delighted.

3. Marketing is both Art and Science:
Science is the systematic body of knowledge, based on fact and principles and Art is the application of that knowledge. The concept of marketing includes both. The principles of marketing are based on certain facts and the application of those principles is an art.

4. Objective-Oriented:
All marketing activities are objective-oriented. The main objective is to earn profit through satisfaction of consumers' needs and wants.

5. Continuous and Regular Activity:
Marketing is a continuous and regular activity which starts with identification of human wants. It does not merely end on sales. Its demand to be continued after the selling process in the form of after sales services. It addresses both the actual and potential consumers. Thus, it is a continuous process.

6. Exchange Process:
Marketing is an exchange process. Exchange takes place between sellers and buyers. Buyer gets goods and services in exchange of money and seller gets money in exchange of goods and services.

7. Marketing Mix:

A marketing mix is a combination of 4 Ps *i.e.*, product, price, place and promotion. It is the flexible combination of variables influenced by consumer behavior, trade cycle, government and other important factors.

OBJECTIVES OF MARKETING

The objectives of marketing can be discussed as below:

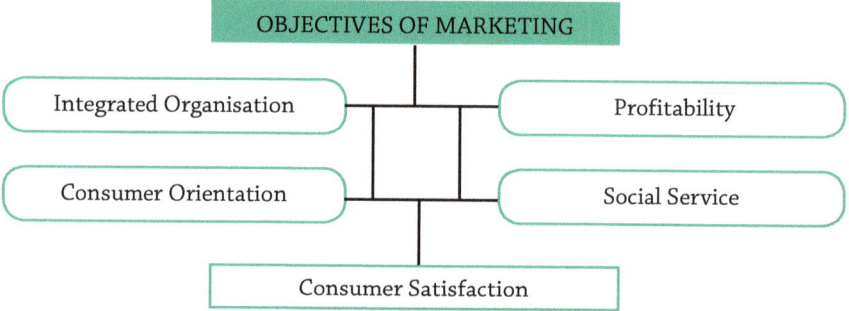

1. Integrated Organisation:

Integrated organisation means that all the different departments of organisation, *i.e.*, production, finance, purchase and planning must be tightly integrated with each other, keeping marketing at the centre. This is important because every function of organisation has an impact on customer and the objective should be to see that all the functions lead to a favourable impression on customer. For this to happen, all the departments have to be integrated and consequently orient themselves towards customer satisfaction.

2. Consumer Orientation:

In the words of Peter F. Drucker, "The purpose of any business is to create a customer. It is the customer who determines what a business is. It is the customer and he alone, who being willing to pay for a good or service, converts economic resources into wealth and things into goods. What a business thinks it produces is not of first importance—especially not to the future of the business and to its success. What the customer thinks he is buying–what he considers value, is decisive; it determines what a business is, what it produces and whether it will prosper." Thus, it can be concluded that a customer does not buy whatever the producer produces but the producer produces whatever the consumer needs. Therefore, the first objective of marketing is consumer orientation.

3. Profitability:

Business organisation is an economic institution which is set up for earning profits and not for charity. Thus, one of the main objectives of marketing is to maximise profits with minimum investment but it should not be carried out at the expense of consumer satisfaction. Therefore, marketing seeks both–obtaining commitment and building relationships.

4. Social Service:

The other objective of marketing is social orientation. Only those goods and services should be marketed which are environment friendly, useful to the consumer and enhance the standard of living. Reasonable prices should be charged for qualitative goods and services. Marketing should also provide opportunities for employment and should not deceive by carrying restrictive, monopolistic and unfair trade practices.

5. Consumer Satisfaction:

Mere consumer orientation does not fulfill the objective of marketing. Consumer orientation along with an integrated organisation leads to consumer satisfaction. This is also one of the most important objectives of marketing. In today's market, no organisation can even think to ignore the satisfaction of consumers.

SALES

'Sale' is a direct transaction happening between two parties–the buyer and the seller. The buyer receives the goods, which can be either tangible or intangible (in case of a service) and in exchange he/she offers the seller an agreed price. Sale is nothing but a contract between the buyer and the seller.

While both sales and marketing are aimed at increasing the revenue of the firm, there are certain basic differences which demarcate the concepts. In certain small or medium scale companies, it is usually the same group of employees who manage sales and marketing functions. However, the underlying concepts of both marketing and sales are quite different.

Selling Concept

According to the selling concept, customers would not act upon by themselves if not persuaded to purchase. The idea behind the concept is that the companies, no matter how much marketing they do, need to give the final push of sales to make the customers buy the product or the service. Despite producing good quality of products and providing good service many companies fail to generate substantial profit. For that reason selling concept is being created. The concept believes that the customers will only buy the products by means of sales promotion efforts. Or to put it simply, consumers will not make the final purchase with their own initiative. The company needs to make the final push to convince the customers to buy the products or services.

Features of Selling

1. Selling Orientation:
Here the focus is not on the consumers but rather on the seller. It believes that the product or service should be sold at any cost.

2. Aggressive Selling and Promotion:
The selling concept encourages the use of aggressive selling strategies to encourage the customers to buy the product.

3. Not Focused on Consumers:
The selling concept is not focused on the consumers' needs and wants and rather they concentrate on the number of products that needs to be sold.

4. Consumer Persuasion:
The selling concept only focuses on persuading the customers to make the purchase. It does not necessarily take into account customer's needs and wants.

Difference Between Marketing and Sales

Basis of Difference	Marketing	Sales
Definition	Marketing is the process of systematic planning and implementation of the business activities aimed at increasing sales.	Sales is just the transaction happening between two parties in the form of buyer and seller.
Approach	Marketing encompasses a wide range of approaches including product design, pricing, sales promotion, advertising, understanding consumer need and many more.	Sales include the interactions and the transactions happening at the end of the marketing cycle.
Focus	The entire focus of marketing is to deliver the product or service in demand at a competitive price and generate maximum revenue from it.	The focus of sales is to achieve as many transactions as possible, in a given time period.
Process	The process of marketing involves the analysis of market needs, understanding the consumer behaviour, and setting up price for the product along with many other things.	It only involves a one-to-one interaction between the sales person and the buyer.
Scope	Scope of marketing is very wide which includes, Market research; Advertising; Sales; Public relations; Customer service and satisfaction.	Persuading the customers to buy the product or service and help them fulfill their requirements.
Horizon	Long Term	Short Term
Strategy	Pull	Push
Priority	Priority of marketing is to reach out to more and more consumers and maintain a healthy relationship.	Sales is the ultimate result of marketing.
Creations	Marketing creates specific brand identity for the product/service or for the company as a whole.	Sales does not necessarily create brand identity but it focuses on meeting the customer requirement at a given point of time.

LESSON AT A GLANCE

- **Market:** Market is the whole or any region in which buyers and sellers are brought into contact with one another and by means of which the prices of goods tend to be equalized easily and quickly.

- **Marketing:** Marketing involves development of products or services according to the needs of the customer and then moving them from the place of production to the place of consumption profitably to satisfy the wants of the customer. According to William J. Stanton, "Marketing is a total system of interacting business activities designed to plan, price, promote and distribute want satisfying products and services to present and potential customer."

There are two approaches to marketing–traditional approach (product-oriented) and modern approach (consumer oriented).

- **Features of Marketing:** (i) Customer oriented; (ii) Consumer satisfaction; (iii) Marketing is both art and science; (iv) Objective oriented; (v) Continuous and regular activity; (vi) Exchange Process; (vii) Marketing Mix.
- **Objectives of Marketing:** (i) Integrated organisation; (ii) Consumer orientation; (iii) Profitability; (iv) Social service; (v) Consumer satisfaction.
- **Sale:** Sale is any transaction taking place between two parties the buyer and the seller, where the buyer receives the goods or services in exchange for money.
- **Difference between Marketing and Sales:** (i) Definition; (ii) Approach; (iii) Focus; (iv) Process; (iv) Scope; (vi) Horizon; (vii) Strategy; (viii) Priority; (ix) Creations.

Project Work

Select a company of your own choice and find out the marketing activities performed by that company to promote its products.

Assignment

Your friend was absent in class when your teacher taught objectives of marketing. Explain to him/her the same.

Questions

A. **Short Answer Type Questions:**
   1. Define marketing.
   2. Give any three objectives of marketing.
   3. State any four features of marketing.
   4. How does marketing ensure consumer satisfaction?
   5. State two differences between marketing and sales?
   6. Define the word 'Sales'.
   7. How are Marketing and Sales related?
   8. Distinguish between marketing and sales. [ICSE 2019]

B. **Essay Type Questions:**
   1. What do you mean by marketing ? Give its definitions.
   2. Define marketing and state its main objectives.
   3. Discuss social service as one of the main objectives of marketing.
   4. Give at least six points of difference between marketing and sales.
   5. Explain any five objectives of marketing. [ICSE 2020]
   6. Briefly explain the importance of marketing. [ICSE 2018]

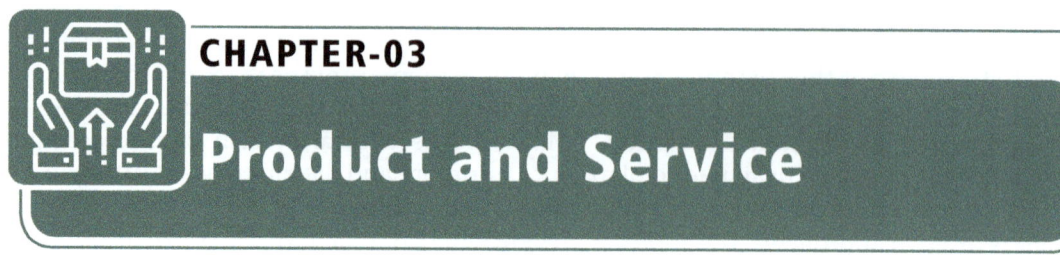

CHAPTER-03
Product and Service

PRODUCT AND ITS CLASSIFICATION

The term "product" refers to any object or service that is capable of being created and sold at a price and which serves human need or satisfies a want. In short, a product is any commodity or service, offered for sale. It can be in physical or virtual form. Thus, a product has a combination of tangible and intangible benefits, features, functions, and uses. It is because of these attributes that the customer buys the product. Examples of tangible products are bathing soap, shirt, a can of soft-drink, etc. Intangible products or better known as "services" can be in the form of medical advice from a doctor, or legal advice from a lawyer.

- Meaning of Product
- Classification of Products
- Characteristics of Product
- Meaning of Service
- Classification of Services
- Characteristics of Service
- Difference between Product and Service

A product can range from being a high-end customized offer like Ferrari Cars to very generic merchandise like detergent soap. From the sophisticated patio furniture set to the toothpaste you use–everything falls under the definition of a product. Services are also sometimes highly customized to individual needs, like a legal service or a doctor treating a patient. But just like products, in many other occasions it is generic and catering to the need of the mass. Movies shown in a movie theatre is a good example of generic services or for that matter, electric supply provided at your home.

The products can broadly be classified on the basis of three factors which are as follows:
(A) Durability, (B) Consumer Products, (C) Industrial Products.

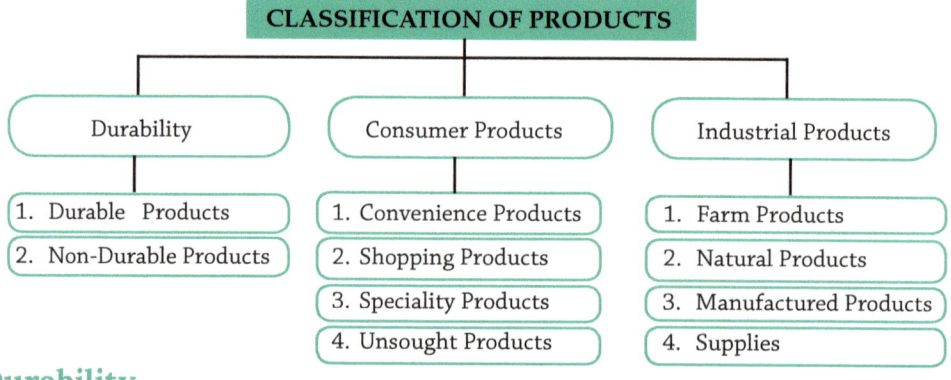

(A) Durability

According to durability, products can be classified into two categories:

1. Durable Products:

The products which are tangible and can be used repeatedly many a times, are termed as durable goods. For example, television, refrigerator, clothes, machines etc.

2. Non-Durable Products:
The products which are tangible and perish within one or few uses, are termed as non-durable products. For example, salt, pepper, soap etc.

(B) Consumer Products
According to consumer's shopping habits, products can be classified into following categories:

1. Convenience Products:
These products which are purchased frequently, and immediately and with minimum efforts, are known as convenience products. For example, newspaper, toothpaste, washing detergent, cigarette, tobacco etc.

2. Shopping Products:
The products which customer purchases less frequently and after careful comparison, on the basis of suitability, quality, price and style, are known as shopping products. For example, major appliances, clothing, furniture, cars etc.

3. Speciality Products:
Those products that have brand identification or unique characteristics are known as specialty products. Buyers for these goods generally spend more time seeking the product they want than on comparing brands. For examples, cars, stereos, television etc.

4. Unsought Products:
Those consumer products that are either not known to the consumers or even if they are known, customers generally do not have compelling impulse to buy them, are known as unsought products. For example–Life insurance, blood donation etc.

(C) Industrial Products
Those products that are purchased for further processing or for use in operating a business are called industrial products. They can be classified as :

1. Farm Products:
Products which are produced on farms and supplied as raw material to different organisations, are termed as farm products. For example, wheat, cotton, livestock, vegetables, fruits etc.

2. Natural Products:
Products which are gift of nature, are termed as natural products. For example, crude oil, fish, timber, iron-ore etc.

3. Manufactured Products:
The products which have been manufactured but still, are used as products for further industrial use, are known as manufactured products. For example, pig-iron is converted in steel and then steel is further used for making bars, utensils etc.

4. Supplies:
Any short-term good or material which is necessary for the day-to-day operations of a business is termed as supplies. Supplies are of two types–operating (*e.g.*, lubricants, coal, typing paper, etc.) and maintenance (*e.g.*, paint, nails, brooms etc.).

CHARACTERISTICS OF PRODUCT

From the categories mentioned above, we now know that the products can be of different shapes and sizes, catering to the different needs of the consumers. However, some of the features are generic for all the products and are listed below:

Physical configuration | Mobility | Associated Services | Packaging and Branding | Life-Cycle | Storability | Medium of Communication | Exchange Value

1. Physical Configuration:
A product can be seen, has bulk or mass and can be felt. These features define the dimension of a product and it is one of the most basic features all products have, irrespective of the usage it possesses.

2. Mobility:
A product has to be manufactured, can be stored and physically transported from the point of production to the point of sale. Thus it acquires utility of place.

3. Associated Services:
Products are often associated with certain services. Starting from simpler services like providing a "user manual" (before-sale service) to the consumer to actual installation of the product, (after-sale service) all fall under the concept of associated service. For instance the periodical and maintenance service of a water purifier can be cited as a good example.

4. Packaging and Branding:
The packaging is considered as a part of a product. It is packaging and branding that differentiates a product from its competing products. The packaging also determines the size of each unit to be sold along with the price of the product. We can determine and differentiate the price of a 500 gm Amul butter packet from a 500 gm of Britania butter packet on the basis of packaging and branding.

5. Life-Cycle:
Every product has its life cycle, which can be determined at some stage of its existence. The life-cyle of a product consists of introduction in the market, growth, maturity and decline (*i.e.*, a fall in its sales). Life-cycle has its own importance for the manufacturers and customers.

6. Storability:
All tangible goods can be stored over a period of time. However, this feature is only applicable for non-perishable products. Though perishable products can also be stored but only for a limited time period.

7. Medium of Communication:
Every product speaks about itself, what it is made up of, what uses it can be put to, who has manufactured it, where it is available etc. Thus, a product is a medium of communication also.

8. Exchange Value:
Each product has a exchange value, which means its value can be measured in terms of money.

SERVICE AND ITS CLASSIFICATION

A service is any act or performance that one party can offer to another. It is essentially intangible and does not result in the ownership of anything. Its production may or may not be tied to any physical product. Products themselves sometime do not satisfy customer's need but it is the service which they render that provides satisfaction to the customer. For instance, if you have to go to school by bicycle, bicycle, being a product, does not provide you the desired satisfaction by itself. Rather, it is the service of transportation, which it renders, provides satisfaction to you.

Services can be broadly classified into four categories, which are as follows:

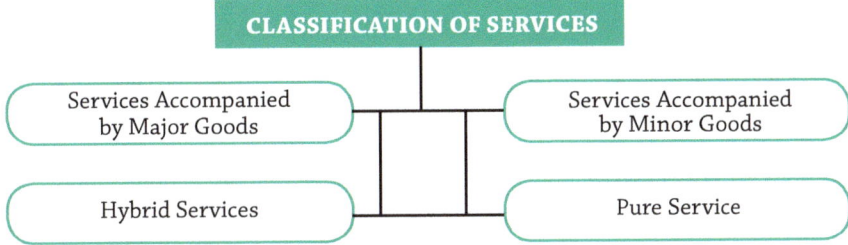

1. Service Accompanied by Major Goods:
When tangible product is accompanied by one or more services to enhance its consumer appeal, it is known as service accompanied by major goods. For example, when Maruti Ltd., along with the car, promises three free services and one year warranty, these free services and one year warranty are the services which are accompanied by the major product, i.e., car.

2. Hybrid Services:
These types of services are not separable from the product itself, i.e., they consist of equal part of goods as well as the services. For example, if one goes to the Restaurant, he gets both product (food) and service (waiters etc.).

3. Service Accompanied by Minor Goods:
When tangible minor product is supplied along with the service, it is known as service accompanied by minor goods. For example, when a passenger travels through aeroplane, he buys transportation services but the service include provision of food, drinks and magazines which are the minor products.

4. Pure Service:
A service in which no tangible product is given along with, is known as pure service. For example, in psychotherapy, the psycho-analyst only provides service, no product is accompanied along with it.

Characteristics of Service
Following are the characteristics of service:

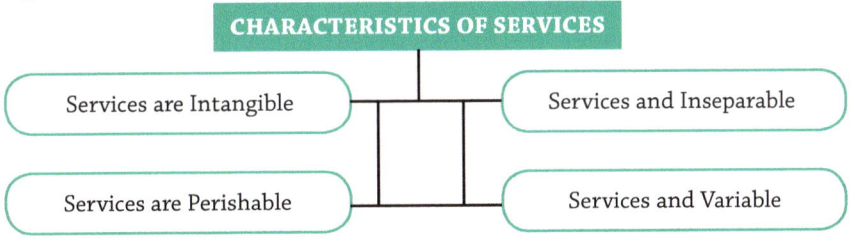

1. Services are Intangible:
This means they cannot be felt, seen, or heard before they are purchased. They are abstract and invisible.

2. Services are Perishable:
Services cannot be produced and kept in inventory. Thus, they are perishable, they cannot be produced ahead of time and stocked for the periods of peak load of demand. They can only be delivered at the time of consumption.

3. Services are Inseparable:
With customer participation in the process, services are typically produced and consumed at the time of its production. That means services are produced and consumed at the same time. Products are first produced and then they are sold, whereas, services are generally first sold and then they are produced and consumed at the same time.

4. Services are Variable:
Services are not always standardised and uniform in very clear terms. It is often impossible to assure consistencies in the services provided by a seller or to standardise offerings among the sellers of the same service while it is possible to offer consistencies and uniformities in case of products.

DIFFERENCE BETWEEN PRODUCT AND SERVICE
Product can be differentiated from services on the following grounds:

1. Tangibility:
Products are tangible, *i.e.*, they can be felt, seen, tasted, heard or smelled before they are purchased, whereas, services are intangible, *i.e.*, they cannot be felt, seen, tasted or smelled before they are purchased. For example, a person wants to purchase a car. He/she can feel, and see the car before purchase but a person going for a massage to the parlour, cannot feel the result before getting the massage done.

2. Separability:
Products are separable, *i.e.*, products are manufactured, put into inventory, then through channel of distribution they reach the ultimate consumer. Thus, product is separable but this is not true in case of services, they are produced and consumed simultaneously. For example, a car is manufactured, put into inventory, distributed through their showrooms and then it is purchased by the customer but when a person travels by aeroplane, services of aeroplane (transportation) can only be taken while it is flying, thus, it is inseparable.

3. Variability:
Services are highly variable but products are not. Quality of service depends on the quality of the service provider, the place where the service is provided and the time. These factors cause variation in the quality of service provided. This, however, is not the case with tangible products. For example, if a patient wants to get his liver transplanted, the services given by a hospital situated in Delhi, which is equipped with all modern amenities for doing so, will be quite different from a hospital situated in rural areas of India.

4. Perishability:

Products can be stored whereas, services cannot be stored. Thus, products are not immediately perishable but services are. If a showroom keeps twenty scooters for sale during one month and they are not sold, they don't perish. But if a passenger bus has to carry fifty passengers at one time and it carries only 30 then the service meant for 20 passengers perishes, for the single ride.

5. Homogeneity:

Products are homogeneous in many respects. In case of standardized products, a product is a perfect substitute for another where it is impossible for an individual to distinguish one from another. Thus, if a person has to buy a Gillette shaving gel, he can pick any one lying at the store. But services are not homogeneous, they are heterogeneous. For example, when you go to a same restaurant every time and order a snack then you will find the difference in the taste each time you visit, even the cook is same which suggests that services are heterogeneous in nature.

6. Participation:

Customers do not participate in the production of a product. But in case of service, service cannot be performed in absence of the customer's active participation. For example, when a car is manufactured, customer does not stand there when the production process is on, but when a person goes for a hair cut or massage, he has to participate in the process.

7. Transferability:

When a transaction of a product takes place, the title of ownership moves from the seller to the buyer. In case of services, there is no transfer of title of ownership from the seller to the buyer. For example, if a person purchases a car the ownership of car is transferred from the seller to the purchaser. When a patient goes to doctor for treatment, he has to pay fees every time he visits the doctor. He cannot take the doctor for granted after paying the doctor's fees only once. Next time when he goes for treatment, he will have to pay the fees again.

Difference between product and Service

	Product	Service
Tangibility	Products are tangible: (a) They can be felt and seen. (b) They can be fully standardised.	Services are Intangible: (a) They cannot be touched. (b) They cannot be standardised.
Separability	Products are separable.	Services are inseparable.
Variability	Products are not variable.	Services are highly variable.
Perishability	Products are not perishable.	Services are perishable.
Homogeneity	Products are homogeneous in many respects.	Services are heterogeneous.
Participation	While manufacturing a product customers do not participate.	Customers participate in the process of production to consume a service.

| Transferability | When a transaction of a product takes place, the title of owner moves from the seller to the buyer. | In case of services, there is no transfer of title of ownership from the seller to the buyer. |

LESSON AT A GLANCE

- **Product:** A product is any object or service, that is offered for sale in the market and can satisfy human needs and wants.
- **Classification of Products:** Products can be classified on the basis of :
  - *(A) Durability:* (i) Durable products; (ii) Non-durable products.
  - (B) Consumer Products: (i) Convenience products; (ii) Shopping products; (iii) Speciality products, (iv) Unsought products.
  - *(C) Industrial products:* (i) Farm products; (ii) Natural products; (iii) Manufactured products; (iv) Supplies.
- **Characteristics of Product:** (i) Physical configuration; (ii) Mobility; (iii) Associated service; (iv) Packaging and branding; (v) Life-cycle; (vi) Storability; (vii) Media of communication; (viii) Exchange value.
- **Service:** A service is any act or performance that one party can offer to another. It is intangible and does not result in ownership of any thing.
- **Classification of Services:** (i) Services accompanied by major goods; (ii) Hybrid; (iii) Services accompanied by minor goods; (iv) Pure services.
- **Characteristics of Services:** (i) Services are intangible; (ii) Services are perishable, (iii) Services are inseparable; (iv) Services are variable.
- **Difference between Product and Service:** Product can be differentiated from services on the grounds of : (i) Tangibility; (ii) Separability; (iii) Variability; (iv) Perishability; (v) Homogeneity; (vi) Participation; (vii) Transferability.

Find out five types of consumer products and industrial products. Give their names, company's name and use/uses of those products to their customers.

You have to explain to your class the difference between product and service. How would you do the same with the help of examples ?

Questions

A. **Short Answer Type Questions:**
   1. Define product.
   2. Name different types of products.
   3. Give four examples of durable products.
   4. Give four examples of non-durable products.
   5. Give four types of consumer products. Give two examples of each.
   6. Give four types of industrial products. Give two examples of each.
   7. Give four main characteristics of products.
   8. Define service.
   9. Give four types of services. Also give two examples of each.
   10. Give four differences between product and service.
   11. Distinguish between a product and a service. [ICSE 2019]
   12. Distinguish between a consumer goods and an industrial goods. [ICSE 2018]
   13. What are convenience products? Give any two examples. [ICSE 2017]

B. **Essay Type Questions:**
   1. Define product and discuss different types of products.
   2. Discuss the characteristics of product.
   3. Define services and discuss different types of services.
   4. Discuss the main types of consumer products.
   5. Discuss the main types of industrial products.
   6. Discuss the characteristics of services.
   7. State the differences between product and service.

CHAPTER-04
Pricing

Pricing is a mechanism by means of which a business sets a specific price for a unit of its product or servicing sold in the market. The price of the product or service is a predefined agreement between the seller and the buyer. Once the company or the business sets a price of a unit of the product or the service sold, it cannot alter it without informing the buyers in advance. This is part of the overall marketing strategy of a company where they determine the cost of manufacturing a product or delivering a particular service to the customers. In order to determine the price of the product, a profit margin is added to the cost of producting the product.

- Meaning of Pricing
- Objectives of Pricing

For example, the manufacturing cost of a tube of toothpaste is INR 30 and the company wants to sell 10,000 units of toothpaste tubes at a certain price INR 200,000. In order to achieve this goal, they will determine the profit they earn from one tube of toothpaste. In this case it would be 200000/10000= INR 20. Hence, the price of the product will be set to INR (30 + 20) = INR 50. Where INR 30 is the manufacturing cost of the product and INR 20 is the profit margin per unit. Several other factors such a machinery expenses, factory expenses, electricity expenses, labour cost, are also taken into account while determining the price of a product.

The price of the product is depending on the cost of raw materials, cost of manufacturing the product, demand for the product, purchasing power of the consumers, price of the competing firms, government regulations, intended profit margin of the business etc. Price is also influenced by the marketing method used by the company *e.g.*, commission, which is to be paid to the middlemen for sale of the goods.

OBJECTIVES OF PRICING

The objectives of pricing can be classified into five major segments, *i.e.*, profit-related objectives, sales-related objectives, competition-related objectives, customer-related objectives, and other objectives.

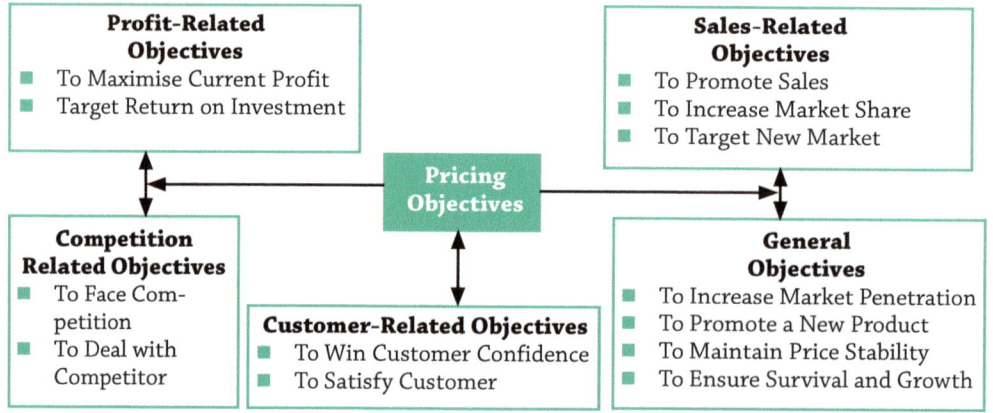

Profit Related Objectives

As aforementioned one of the major objectives of pricing is to gain profit. A company fulfills several profit related objectives by setting up a price for its product.

(a) To Maximise Current Profit:
One of the core objectives of setting up a price is to maximize profit. Companies set that price for their product or service that will maximize their current profit margin.

(b) Target Return on Investment:
Pricing is also set with an objective of gaining a specific return on the investment made in the production of product or service.

Sales Related Objectives

At times, a company sets up that price for its product that will boost its sale. Offering discounted pricing is one example of how companies try and achieve their sales related objectives. Below are the sales related objectives of setting up a price.

(a) To Promote Sales:
Companies tend to set up price in a way that more sales occur in the long run. In this way the pricing strategy also involves an objective of increasing sales volume for the organization.

(b) To Increase Market Share:
Increasing the market share of the firm is also a major objective of determining the price of a product. The company captures more share in the market when a consumer gets attracted to purchase a product because of its pricing.

(c) To Target New Market:
Sometimes innovative pricing enables a company to target unexplored markets. In that way, one of the objectives of pricing is to attract new customers and earn more profit from them.

Competition-related Objectives

Competition is a powerful factor which determines how companies price their products. Competitive brands like Pepsi or Coke always price their products in a similar manner to negate the chances of any competitive advantage to their competitors.

(a) To Face Competition:
One of the major objectives of pricing is to make the product or service competitive in the market. Pricing provides major competitive advantage to the companies.

(b) To Deal with Competitors:
Pricing often keeps competition away. Especially for a bigger company it is easier to achieve a price leadership which would help them to differentiate itself from local competitors. Price leadership can be gained when a firm produces the same quality and quantity of a product at a much lesser price. For example potato chips company Lay's achieved price leadership by introducing INR 5/pack offer thereby keeping the local and unbranded potato chips company out of competition.

Customer-related Objectives

Pricing also helps companies attract more customers. The customer related objectives of pricing are given below:

(a) To win Consumer Confidence:
Good pricing strategy often helps in winning customer's confidence. Appropriate pricing, keeps the customers happy and satisfied. The customers should be satisfied with the benefits they get from the product or the service at a particular price set by the company. The company should also be satisfied with the profit they earn from selling its product.

(b) To satisfy the Customers:
One of the prime objectives of pricing is to satisfy the customers. That is why pricing is such an important part of the entire marketing strategy of a company. The companies aim to design pricing in such a way that the customer satisfaction level remains maximum.

General Objectives

Apart from the specific objectives of pricing there are also some general objectives which are as follows:

(a) To increase Market Penetration:
Companies adopt competitive pricing strategies to penetrate unexplored markets. Reliance Communication's 'Jio' offer is a recent example of how the company ventured into untapped markets through a competitive pricing policy.

(b) To promote a New Product:
Whilst introducing a new product in the market the company must price the product very carefully. One of the major objectives of pricing is to make the new product attractive to the customers.

(c) To maintain Price Stability:
Companies who offer a stable price throughout the year are preferred by the customers. Seasonal variation of prices sometimes confuses and irritates the customers when they suddenly have to pay a higher price for the same product. To avoid annoying consumers, Supermarkets selling vegetables often maintain similar prices throughout the year, unlike the local markets.

(d) To ensure Survival and Growth:
Finally, pricing also aims to ensure survival of the company. Throughout the entire life cycle of the product, the company must alter the pricing strategy so that profit is earned at every stage of the cycle.

LESSON AT A GLANCE

- **Pricing:** Pricing is a mechanism by means of which a business sets a specific price for a unit of its product or service being sold in the market.
- **Objectives of Pricing:**
  (1) Profit-Related Objectives: (a) To Maximise Current Profit, (b) Target Return on Investment.

(2) **Sales-Related Objectives:** (a) To Promote Sales, (b) Increase Market Share, (c) To Target New Market.
(3) **Competition-Related Objectives:** (a) To Face Competition, (b) To Deal with Competitors.
(4) **Customer-Related Objectives:** (a) To Win Customer Confidence, (b) To Satisfy the Customers
(5) **General Objectives:** (a) To Increase Market Penetration, (b) To Promote a New Product, (c) To Maintain Price Stability, (d) To Ensure Survival and Growth.

PROJECT WORK

Find out how pricing of different packages of Coke is made differently. Compare it with Pepsi and write a report on that.

ASSIGNMENT

With the help of proper examples explain Customer-Related Pricing objective of few companies. Cite examples of firms who give heavy discounts and promotions to win consumer confidence.

QUESTIONS

A. **Short Answer Type Questions:**
   1. Define Pricing.
   2. State the five segments of pricing objectives.
   3. State two Profit-related Objectives.
   4. State two Sales-related pricing objectives.
   5. Mention two competition-related pricing objectives.
   6. Mention two customer-related pricing objectives.
   7. How is market penetration a pricing objective?
   8. Describe how maintaining price stability is a pricing objective.
   9. Mention any two objectives of Pricing. [ICSE 2019]

B. **Essay Type Questions:**
   1. What is pricing? Describe with examples.
   2. What are the major categories of pricing objectives? Explain with examples.
   3. What are the profit-related objectives of Pricing?
   4. What are the sales-related objectives of pricing?
   5. How can pricing aid in giving competitive advantage to a firm?
   6. What are the customer-related pricing objectives?
   7. 'Pricing helps in gaining customer confidence.' Explain the statement.
   8. Describe how pricing can help a company to penetrate new markets.

CHAPTER-05
Advertising

Advertising is a combination of actions taken in order to draw public attention towards any particular product or service. It is a kind of 'paid announcement' which the company creates in order to inform, educate and tempt the public to purchase their products or services.

- Meaning of Advertising
- Features of Advertising
- Importance of Advertising
- Merits and Demerits of Advertising
- Meaning and Definition of Publicity
- Distinction between Advertising and Publicity
- Advertising Agency
- Functions of Advertising Agency
- Social Media Advertising

The word 'advertising' has been derived from the Latin term 'advertere' which means 'turn to' or turning the attention towards the product. Goods are always produced in anticipation of demand. Success of a business depends upon fast sales and repeated orders. Every businessman, therefore, tries to increase the sales. In order to obtain high turnover, business enterprises now use various methods of persuading the people to buy their products. Advertisement is the art of making yourself and your product known to the world in such a way that a desire for buying that product is created in the hearts of the people. It has been rightly pointed out that in order to fly the aeroplane of sales, advertisement acts as fuel. Advertising in fact, is a salesmanship in print. It is inevitable for increasing the volume of sales.

- *"Advertising is a means of communicating information pertaining to product or ideas by other than direct personal contact and on an openly paid basis with an intent to sell or otherwise obtain favourable consideration."* —R. V. Zacher
- *"Advertising consists of all the activities involved in presenting to a group, a non-personal, oral or visual, openly sponsored message regarding a product, service or idea; this message called an advertisement, is disseminated through one or more media and is paid for by the identified sponsor."* —William J. Stanton
- *"Advertising is any paid form of non-personal presentation or promotion of ideas, goods or services of an identified sponsor."* —American Marketing Association

FEATURES OF ADVERTISING

1. Non-personal Form of Presentation:
Advertising is non-personal because no face to face contact is involved between the advertiser and customers. The messages that are disseminated are for public at large. It is often described as non-personal selling by creating awareness among the prospective customers.

2. Paid Form of Communication:
Advertisement can be made through any medium, but the advertiser has to pay for the use of space or time utilized by him to convey his message to the prospective customers.

3. Presence of Sponsor:
Advertising is issued by an identified sponsor. The name of the advertiser is mentioned in the advertisement itself. Its sponsor can either be the seller or the producer of that product or service.

4. Presence of Medium:
Advertising takes place through some media or medium. For example, newspaper, radio, television, etc.

5. Variety to Consumers:
Advertising provides the consumers with a wide range of products to choose from. This enables them to make an informed choice and enhances their knowledge about various products available in a specific product line.

IMPORTANCE OF ADVERTISING
Advertising has become inevitable in the contemporary business environment. It is necessary for producers, consumers as well as the society.

(A) Importance of Advertising to Producers:

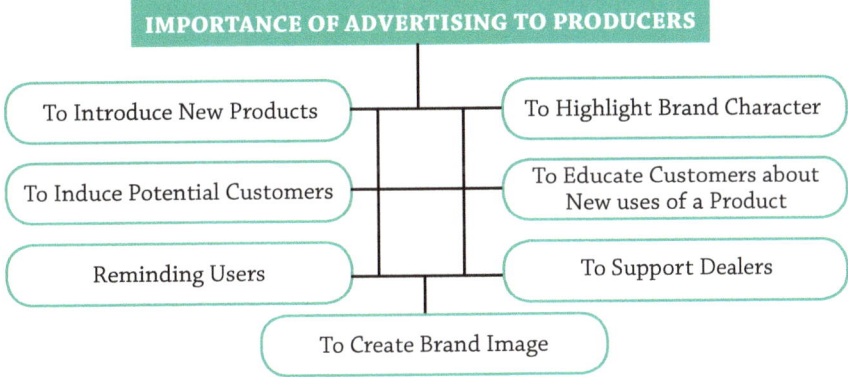

1. To Introduce New Products:
Advertisement of the new product is necessary so that consumers become aware about the product, its availability, its utility, its price etc., thus, advertising is crucial to promote the sale of a new product.

2. To Induce Potential Customers:
Advertising is one of the best means by which the sale of an existing product can be increased. For this purpose, the advertisement should emphasize the usefulness of the product, its quality, price advantages, etc., so as to win over the potential buyers and make them actual buyers.

3. Reminding Users:
In a competitive market, new products are introduced frequently. All these products are advertised in the market. As a result, old brands are likely to be forgotten by

the consumers. To offset this possibility, manufacturers continue to advertise their products to maintain the buyers' interest. Thus, advertisements are also designed to serve as a reminder to existing customers.

4. To Create Brand Image:
Business firms very often advertise for establishing an image for the product and creating customers' loyalty for that product. When customers develop brand loyalty, they are unlikely to switch to other brands easily.

5. To Highlight Brand Character:
For certain products, consumers feel that a particular characteristic is very important. Its existence determines the buyer's choice of a particular brand out of several brands. If the product has that feature, advertising is used to stress it and demonstrate its advantages.

6. To Educate Customers about New Uses of a Product:
Advertising is sometimes, used to convey new uses of an existing product to the customers or to draw their attention to some new features of the product. The basic objective of advertising in this case is to convince the customers about the superiority of a product in comparison with other products in the same line.

7. To Support Dealers:
Sometimes, the aim of advertisement is to provide support to dealers and distributors. Thus, there are many advertisements in newspapers in which the list of dealers and distributors is given along with the particulars of the product.

(B) Importance of Advertising to Consumers

1. Improved Quality of the Product:
It is absolutely essential to improve the quality of the product to maintain confidence of the customers and ensure brand loyalty. Hence, advertised goods are usually of good quality.

2. Protect Consumers from Exploitation:
Advertising also acts as an information service and educates the consumer. It enables him to know exactly what he wants and where to get it.

3. Reduction in Price:
Advertising stimulates production and reduces the cost per unit. This reduction in the cost is generally passed on to the consumer and that is why price of well-advertised goods is found to be generally lower than other goods of the same quality which are not so well advertised.

4. Facilitates Direct Selling:
Advertising also makes it possible to sell direct to the consumer by Mail Order Business. Thus, consumers from remote areas can also enjoy the comforts and luxuries available only in the cities or towns. In this way advertising improves social welfare.

5. Improved Consumer Satisfaction:
As manufacturers control the price of well-advertised goods, price-cutting is not available to the retailers and the shopkeepers as they try to attract customers by giving better and more satisfactory service.

6. Enables Comparison:
Advertising helps consumers find best product for themselves by facilitating comparison among various products available in the market. When consumers are aware about the range of products, they are able to compare the price, quality and characteristics and pick up the best from among them.

(C) Importance of Advertising to Society
1. Advertising helps in increasing awareness among people. Advertising dealing with social issues such as child labour, liquor consumption, female foeticide, smoking, family planning etc. and promotes social welfare.
2. Advertising provides direct employment to large number of people engaged in designing, writing and issuing advertisements. Indirectly, advertising increases employment opportunities by increasing the volume of production and distribution.
3. Advertising helps in improving the standard of living of people by promoting variety and quality in consumption. It educates people about new uses of a product and provides information for developing better ways of leading life.

MERITS OF ADVERTISING
Advertising is beneficial to manufacturers, traders, consumers and society as a whole:

1. Promotion of Sales:
Advertising helps the producer to increase his sales. A form attempts to increase the demand for its product, either by reducing the price or by inducing buyers to purchase more of its product; even at the constant price. The latter involves the use of sales promotion and hence advertising.

2. Expansion of Production:
Increased demand brought about by advertising has to be met by a corresponding increase in production. In this way, advertising causes production to expand in order to cater to an increased demand.

3. Enhances Goodwill:
Advertising is instrumental in increasing the goodwill of the company (advertises). It introduces the manufacturer and his product to the people. Repeated advertising and better quality of products strengthens manufacturers reputation and enhances his goodwill.

4. Large Turnover and Huge Profits:
An increased demand, generated through advertisements can create a larger turnover for the company and eventually resulting in more profits.

5. Information about Different Options and Comparative Prices:
Advertisement keeps the buyers well informed by providing information about the different products and their relative prices. This helps the consumer to take adequate decision regarding the features they want and the amount they want to spend, even before physically going to the shops.

6. Creates Employment Opportunities:

Advertising is capable of providing employment to large section of the society including the professionals like painters, photographers, singers, cartoonist, musicians, models and people working in different advertising agencies.

7. Higher Standard of Living:

Advertisement promotes larger consumption, increased production and greater employment. This further reflect on lower prices, better quality and greater variety of goods to the consumers. Advertising, thus, ensures better and happier living.

DEMERITS OF ADVERTISING

Despite of being regarded as the life-blood of modern business advertising has the following disadvantages:

1. Adds to the Cost of Production and Product:

Advertising increases the cost of the advertised product, as the expenses on advertisement add to the total cost of the product. To mitigate the cost incurred during advertising of the product or the service, the advertiser adds the cost of advertisement to the total price of the product or the service. So, the advertising cost is actually being borne by the consumers.

2. Leads to Price War:

Large scale competitive advertising by prominent competing firms can possibly lead to advertising wars with the consumers being made to pay for it. It leads to a situation of price war and that makes the production activity unduly wasteful. The entire industry has to suffer a setback.

3. Deceptive Advertising:

Sometimes, advertising is used as an instrument of cheating. Unscrupulous firms defraud the consumers by misrepresenting their products through advertising. In order to induce people to purchase their product, firms issue false statements with regard to different virtues of a products; this undermines public confidence in advertising. As a result we have the Advertising Code of Conduct that regulates advertising and ensures commercial honesty.

4. Leads to Unequal Competition:

The producers spend a huge amount of money for the advertisement of their products and services. Small local firms cannot match the big advertising budgets of multinational companies. Therefore, the scales are always tilted in favour of the bigger producers leading to unequal competition.

5. Creates a Monopolistic Market:

Larger firms by virtue of their larger advertising budgets drive the smaller firms out of the market. This leaves the market open to just a few large producers. In this way the bigger firms win competition and monopolize the market.

6. Promotes Unnecessary Consumption:

Advertising promotes the consumption of goods and services which are not even required by the people. Hence it is wastage of national resources.

7. Decline in Moral Values:
In order to attract attention of the people, many times advertisers use indecent, vulgar language and obscene photographs.

All these reasons together justify the statement that "Advertising is Social Waste", because it does not add any real value to the society.

PUBLICITY

Publicity, in its simplest form, means conveying information to the general public through the media. The information being publicised could be news, awareness about a product and service etc. Publicity is not paid for by the organisation. According to Definition Committee (1948) of the American Marketing Association, "Publicity can be defined as any form of commercially significant news about a product, an institution, a service or a person published in space or radio time that is not paid for by the sponsor." Publicity media include posters, pamphlets, films, radio, television, direct mailing demonstrations, fairs and exhibitions, meetings, conferences, social media like Face book, Twitter and blogs etc. These may be arranged all together or one by one as the case may be.

The words 'Advertising' and 'Ability' are often used interchangeably. But following distinctions must be kept in mind:

Basis of Distinction	Advertising	Publicity
Nature of Communication	Communication of only commercial information to the public.	Publicity may or may not be related with the communication of commercial information.
Decisions Regarding Format	The content, style, format, etc. of the advertising message are decided by the sponsor, *i.e.*, the advertiser.	The content, style, and other matters, such as space and timings of dissemination of the message, are controlled by the media owners.
Payment	The advertisers have to pay to the advertising agencies and media owners for conveying message to the public.	Sponsor does not pay for the use of space or time to convey the message to the public.
Inter-dependability	Advertising is just a part of publicity.	Publicity includes advertising.
Identity and Purpose	The identity and purpose of the sponsors of an advertisement are clearly known.	The identity and purpose of the sender of the message are unknown in many cases.
Party which Suffers	The sponsor of the advertisement suffers the loss.	The public which ignore or disregard the message, suffers.

ADVERTISING AGENCY

Advertising agencies are third-party vendors who conceptualize, design and actually make the advertisement on behalf of the company. Thus an advertising agency is involved in various forms of activities like planning, preparing the adverts and choosing when and on which media should the advertisement appear. These agencies take all the efforts for promoting the product of the clients (Advertisers). For this purpose, they have a team of different people for difference functions like copywriters, art directors, planners etc. The agencies make optimum use of these people, their experience and their knowledge.

Functions of Advertising Agency

Functions of an Advertising agency are listed below:

1. Advertising Planning:

One of the primary functions of the advertising agencies is to plan for the advertising. After analysing the clients' products or the service, the prevailing competition and the market conditions the agency makes the entire advertising plan and executes the plans after obtaining clients' approval.

2. Creative Function:

An advertising agency also performs creative functions. The creative functions include copy writing, drawing photographs, preparing illustrations and layouts and write effective advertisement taglines and dialogues. These functions are performed by copywriters, artists, designers, who are highly skilled in their respective fields. This function makes an advertisement more appealing and helps increase sales of a product.

3. Media Selection:

Advertising agency assists an advertiser in selecting a proper media (advertising platform) to promote his advertisement. Media selection is the most critical function of an advertising agency as it must select the most suitable media for its client's advertisement which has the potential to give best results at lowest costs. It must also select more than one media for the advertisement. This function determines the effectiveness of the advertisement and the impact it will have on the targeted audience.

4. Determining Advertising Budget:

The advertising agencies also help the advertisers to decide on the advertising budget. That is the entire cost of advertising. The advertising agencies need to give a proper estimation of the cost of the plan and wait for the advertiser to approve it.

5. Coordination and Connection:

Advertising agency maintains close coordination among the Advertiser itself, media houses and distributors. This is a crucial function because proper coordination helps in boosting the sales of a product.

6. Market Research:

Many advertising agencies conduct market research on behalf of their clients (advertisers) and consult them on the kind of advertising that needs to be done.

7. Non-Advertising Functions:
Advertising agencies often provide consultations regarding the pricing and design of the products. They also help the companies in designing the packaging, trade marks, tables etc.

SOCIAL MEDIA ADVERTISING
Social Media's Advertising often create and deliver messages with an aim to educate the public about certain social issues including the impact of global warming, stopping child abuse, the importance of vaccinating your child, ill effects of smoking, curbing female foeticide etc. Social advertisements contain strong and direct messages and they do not generally talk about any particular product or service but the message itself is paramount to any other objective.

For example :
1. Tata Tea "Jago re" campaign was a kind of social advertisement.
2. Havell's: "Hawa Badlegi" ad is also a social advertisement campaign which has gained popularity in India.
3. Fastrack: The Closet-based on theme of queer rights.
4. Kaun Banega Crorepatis' Kohima ad highlights racial discrimination faced by people from North-Eastern states of India.

Social Issues like child marriage, dowry, corruption etc. are being highlighted by means of these adverts.

Lesson at a Glance

- **Advertising:** According to William J. Stanton. "Advertising consists of all the activities involved in presenting to a group, a non-personal, oral or visual, openly sponsored message regarding a product, service or idea. This message called an advertisement, is disseminated through one or more media and is paid for by the identified sponsor."
- **Features of Advertising:** (i) Non-personal form of presentation; (ii) Paid form of communication; (iii) Presence of sponsor; (iv) Presence of medium, (v) Variety to consumers.
- **Importance of Advertising:**
  - **(A) To Producers:** (i) To introduce new products; (ii) To induce potential customers; (iii) Reminding users; (iv) To create brand image; (v) To highlight brand character; (vi) To educate customers about new uses of a product; (vii) To support dealers.
  - **(B) To Consumers:** (i) Improved quality of the product, (ii) Protects consumers from exploitation; (iii) Reduction in price; (iv) Facilitates direct selling; (v) Improved consumer satisfaction; (vi) Enables comparison.
  - **(C) To Society:** (i) Helps in increasing awareness in public; (ii) Provide direct employment; (iii) Helps in improving standard of living.
- **Merits of Advertising:** (i) Promotion of sales; (ii) Expansion of production; (iii) Enhances goodwill; (iv) Larger turnover and huge profits; (v) Information about different options and their comparative prices; (vi) Creates employment opportunities, (vii) Higher standard of living.

- **Demerits of Advertising:** (i) Adds to the cost of production and product; (ii) Leads to price war; (iii) Deceptive advertising; (iv) Leads to unequal competition; (v) Creates a monopolistic market; (vi) Promotes unnecessary consumption; (vii) Decline in moral values.
- **Publicity:** Publicity can be defined as any form of commercially significant news about a product; an institution, a service or a person published in space or radio time that is not paid for by the sponsor.
- **Distinction between Advertising and Publicity:** Basis of distinction are: (i) Nature of communication; (ii) Decisions regarding format; (iii) Payment; (iv) Inter-dependability; (v) Identity and Purpose; (vi) Party which suffers.
- **Advertising Agency:** Advertising agency is a third party vendor who conceptualise, design and actually makes the advertisement on behalf of the advertiser.
- **Function of an Advertising Agency:** (i) Advertising planning; (ii) Creative function; (iii) Media selection, (iv) Determining advertising budget; (v) Coordination and connection; (vi) Market Research, (vii) Non-advertising functions.
- **Social Media Advertising:** Social Media Advertising often create and deliver messages with an aim to educate the public about social issues.

Project Work

Collect 20 punch lines of various advertisements and explain what they convey to public.

Assignment

If a head of advertising agency has to give a speech on the advantages of advertising, how and what he will tell people about these concepts.

Questions

A. **Short Answer Type Questions:**
   1. Define advertising.
   2. Mention two importance of advertising.
   3. Give two differences between advertising and publicity.
   4. Write two disadvantages of advertising.
   5. What is an advertising agency?
   6. State two functions of an advertising agency.
   7. What is social media advertising? [ICSE 2019]
   8. "Advertising encourages unhealthy consumption." Explain.
   9. Advertising is a social waste.
   10. Distinguish between Advertising and Publicity. [ICSE 2020]

B. Essay Type Questions:
   1. What is advertisement? Explain briefly its features and importance.
   2. "It pays to advertise." Do you agree? Give reasons.
   3. Explain the importance of advertising.
   4. Discuss the role of advertising in modern business.
   5. What is an advertising agency? Explain any two of its functions. [ICSE 2019]
   6. What is a Social Media Advertising? Provide examples of Social Advertising in India.
   7. "Advertising encourages artificial living." Do you agree with this statement? Why?
   8. Briefly explain any five benefits of advertising to producers. [ICSE 2020]
   9. Advertisement is a social waste. In this context explain the demerits of advertisement. [ICSE 2017]

CHAPTER-06
Sales Promotion

Sales promotion is a set of marketing activities under-taken to boost sales of a product or service, by persuading or giving incentive to a potential customer, to buy that product or service.

- Meaning of Sales Promotion
- Techniques of Sales Promotion
- Difference between Advertising and Sales Promotion

According to American Marketing Association (AMA) sales promotion can be defined as, "sales activities that supplement both personal selling and advertising and coordinate them and help them effectively, through displays, shows and expositions, demonstrations and other non-recurrent selling efforts not in the ordinary routine." The definition implies that sales promotions are different from advertising, personal selling and publicity but complement personal selling and advertising. For instance, advertising and personal selling can be used to inform potential customers about the incentives offered for sales promotion. Thus, sales promotion consists of all activities other than advertising and personal selling that helps to boost sales of a particular commodity.

Sales promotion adopt short term, non-recurring methods to increase sales. These offers are not available to the customers throughout the year and are generally found during festivals, end of the seasons and some other occasion.

Sales promotion is important for producers and manufacturers because it helps to increase sales in a competitive market and thus, increases profits. It also helps to introduce new products and to communicate new uses of an existing product to the customers. It is often used to maintain sale of seasonal products like air conditioners, refrigerators, cooler etc. by offering off-season discount. Sales promotion measures have also become essential to retain the market share of the seller, in the era of intense competition.

Sales promotion is important for consumers as well because they get the product at a cheaper rate. Sales promotion also enables the consumers to get all information about the quality, features and uses of different products, helping them to raise their standard of living. By exchanging their old items, they can use latest items available in the market.

TECHNIQUES OF SALES PROMOTION

To increase sales of any product, producers adopt different measures like distributing samples, gifts, coupons, bonus, etc. They are known as techniques of sales promotion. Some of the commonly used tools of sales promotion are as follows:

1. Coupons:
Coupons are issued by producers of packaged goods or by retailers that enables customers to buy the product next time at a reduced price. These coupons are either

advertised by producers/retailers in newspapers or distributed in weekly flyers via mail across households. For examples, Big Bazaar issues coupons for selected items in their weekly flyers that are distributed via mail or along with newspapers.

2. Free Samples:
Free samples are small and packaged portion of the (main) merchandise distributed for free. Free samples are developed for introducing new products. These samples may be distributed door-to-door (through personal selling) or retail stores. For examples, Sensodyne Toothpaste meant for relieving tooth sensitivity is unique product introduced in India. The manufacturer of Sensodyne has been reaching out to local dentists of Mumbai who have been distributing free sample of these toothpastes to create awareness among their patients.

3. Price-off offer:
This involves offering products to consumers at discounted or reduced prices by a certain percentage from the regular price of the product. This activity aims at attracting consumers to other or newer brands, seasonal and unseasonal goods. For example, a 15 to 60 percent off on clothes before some festive season in retail shops are examples of sales or sales promotion.

4. Fairs and Exhibitions:
Fairs and exhibitions may be organised at local, regional, national or international level to introduce new products, demonstrate the products and to explain special features and usefulness of the products. For example, 'International Trade Fair' held in New Delhi in November every year.

5. Free Gifts:
Producers may distribute a free gift along with their product as a incentive to the consumers for purchasing the product. For example, milkshaker along with Nescafe, toothbrush along with a toothpaste.

6. Competitions or Contests:
Producers can organise competitions or contests among salespersons to encourage them to generate more sales from new customers. Companies can offer a car or consumer durables for generating a certain percentage sales in a particular month or quarter.

7. Free Service:
Producers/retailers may promise free service to consumers for a specified period of time after sales. For example, few car retailers offer free servicing for the first 6 months if certain car components are damaged or are under performing.

8. Special Rebate:
Rebate is a partial refund to someone who has paid more or extra on purchase of a specified quantity or value of goods within a specified period. Unlike, price cut off or discounts, rebates are provided after the full payment of full invoice amount.

9. Full Finance @ 0%:
Under this method, the product is sold and money is received on installment basis at 0% or without interest rate. The seller determines the number of installments in which the price of the product will be recovered from the customers.

10. Scratch and Win Offer:
Under this scheme, a customer scratches a specific marked area on the package of the product and gets the benefit according to the message written therein.

11. Money-back Offer:
Under this scheme customers are given assurance that full value of the product will be returned to them if they are not satisfied after using the product. This creates confidence among the customers with regard to the quality of the product.

12. Exchange Schemes:
It refers to exchange of old product for a new product at a price less than the original price of the product. This is useful for drawing attention to product improvement.
Example : "Exchange your black and white television with a colour television."

Difference Between Advertising and Sales Promotion

Basis of Difference	Advertising	Sales Promotion
Meaning	One-way communication of a persuasive message by an identified sponsor, whose purpose is non-personal promotion of product/services to potential customers.	Sales Promotion involves an immediate incentive for a buyer (intermediate distributors or end consumer). It can also involve disseminating information about a product, product line, brand or a company.
Objective	It is done to build brand image and boost sales.	It is done to push short term sales.
Time-Frame	Long term.	Short term.
Nature of Appeal	Emotional in nature.	Unemotional and rational in nature.
Directness	Advertising uses indirect and subtle methods to create a brand image.	Sales promotions are more direct.
Results	Slow, can be seen over time.	Instant.
Cost Involved	Expensive.	Cost-effective (Less expressive)
Frequency	Recurrent.	Mostly non-recurrent.
Contribution to Profit	Moderate.	Medium to high.
Focused Ideas/ Products	Current and new.	Current.
Suitable for	Medium to large companies.	Small to large companies.
Communication	One way process.	To way process.
Strategy	Promotional.	Marketing.

| Employed Tools for Interaction | Mass media such as television, hoarding, newspapers, social media handles like facebook, twitter etc. and Retail stores. | Free gifts, coupons, exhibitions and fairs, price-off offers, exchange offers etc. |

Lesson at a Glance

- **Sales Promotion:** It is a set of marketing activities undertaken to boost sales of a product or service, by persuading or giving incentive to a potential customer, to buy that product or service.
- **Techniques of Sales Promotion:** (i) Coupons; (ii) Free Samples; (iii) Price-off Offer; (iv) Fairs and Exhibitions; (v) Free Gifts; (vi) Competitions or Contests; (vii) Free Service; (viii) Special Rebate; (ix) Full Finance @ 0%; (x) Scratch and Win Offer; (xi) Money-back Offer; (xii) Exchange Schemes.
- **Difference between Advertising and Sales Promotion:** (i) Meaning; (ii) Objective; (iii) Time-Frame; (iv) Nature of Appeal; (v) Directness; (vi) Results; (vii) Cost involved; (viii) Frequency; (ix) Contribution to Profit; (x) Focused Ideas/Products; (xi) Suitable for; (xii) Communication; (xiii) Strategy; (xiv) Employed Tools for Interaction.

Make a visit to any departmental store and consult with its marketing manager or sales manager. Ask him the techniques adopted for sales promotion of his products in different departments. Also, ask him the results of methods adopted and evaluate which one is the best for boosting sales.

You have to explain, to the class, the importance of sales, promotion from the point of view of the manufacturer.

A. Short Answer Type Questions:
    1. What do you mean by sales promotion?
    2. Name two methods of sales promotion.
    3. What do you mean by coupons?
    4. Distinguish between advertising and sales promotion.

B. Essay Type Questions:
    1. What do you mean by sales promotion?
    2. Describe in detail the difference between sales promotion and advertising.
    3. Suggest five techniques used in sales promotion.   [ICSE 2018]

CHAPTER-07
Consumer Protection

CONSUMER (UNDER CONSUMER PROTECTION ACT 2019)

A person who has indicated his or her willingness to obtain goods and/or services from a supplier with the intention of paying for them is termed as consumer.

- Meaning of Consumer
- Consumer Exploitation
- Meaning and Types
- Consumer Awareness
- Importance of Consumer Awareness
- Consumer Protection Act (COPRA), 2019—Features of the Act
- Consumer Rights

The word "consumer" has been defined under Consumer Protection Act of 2019 as follows:

"consumer" means any person who:

1. Buys any goods for a consideration which has been paid or promised or partly paid and partly promised, or under any system of deferred payment and includes any user of such goods other than the person who buys such goods for consideration paid or promised or partly paid or partly promised, or under any system of deferred payment, when such use is made with the approval of such person, but does not include a person who obtains such goods for resale or for any commercial purpose, or

2. Hires or avails of any service for a consideration which has been paid or promised or partly paid and partly promised, or under any system of deferred payment and includes any beneficiary of such service other than the persons who hires or avails of the services for consideration paid or promised, or partly paid and partly promised, or under any system of deferred payment, when such services are availed of with the approveal of the first mentioned person, but does not include a person who avails of such service for any commercial purpose. It should be noted that:

    (a) The expression "commercial purpose" does not include use by a person of goods bought and used by him exclusively for the purpose of earning his livelihood, by means of self-employment;

    (b) The expressions "buys any goods" and "hires or avails any services" includes offline or online transactions through electronic means or by teleshopping or direct selling or multi-level marketing;

Thus, a person is not a consumer if he purchases goods for commercial or resale purposes. However, the word "commercial" does not include use by consumer of goods bought and used by him exclusively for the purpose of earning his livelihood, by means of self-employment and his purchase (goods or services) Includes both offline and online transactions.

A consumer is supposed to be the 'king of the market' *i.e.* all the production brought about by the producers should be carried keeping the needs of the consumers in mind and consumer satisfaction should be of prime importance in all these activities, but in practical scenario it has been witnessed that the needs of most important component of business, the consumer, are actually neglected and the obligation every business holds towards the consumer remains unfulfilled. This results in exploitation of the consumers.

CONSUMER EXPLOITATION

Consumer exploitation is a process by which business intentionally cheat or deceive consumers in order to gain profit. This takes place either because of limited information on the part of consumers about the product, such as guarantees and terms of purchase, quality and price, or because of lack of awareness about consumer rights. Illiterate consumers are especially vulnerable; consequently they are likely to be cheated into paying more and even purchasing a counterfeit product. Also, it is very difficult for an ordinary consumer to distinguish between a genuine product and its imitations. Since consumers are large in numbers and are segregated, they often find themselves in a weak position, when there is a complaint regarding goods and services. Sellers, on the other hand, leverage this situation and never accept responsibility of selling bad quality goods or any other misappropriation.

Consumers have to act responsibly to avoid getting exploited. They should beware of misleading advertisements. They should be quality conscious and inspect a variety of goods before making selection. A Consumer should insist on a valid documentary evidence (cash memo/invoice) relating to purchase of goods or availing of any service. They should be aware of their rights and exercise them while buying goods and services. Most importantly, a consumer should complaint for genuine grievances in the redressal forums and consumer protection councils.

Ways In Which A Consumer Gets Exploited

Some common ways by which consumers are exploited by manufacturers and traders are given below:

1. Underweight and Under-measurements:
The goods being sold in the market are sometimes not measured or weighed correctly.

2. Sub-standard Quality:
The goods sold are sometimes of sub-standard quality. Selling of consumable beyond their expiry dates and supply of deficient or defective home appliances are generally the regular grievances of consumers. This also includes the sales of medicines after expiry date, and selling spurious drugs (sub-standard drugs).

3. High Prices:
Very often the traders charge a price higher than the prescribed retail price.

4. Duplicate Articles:
In the name of genuine parts or goods, fake or duplicate items are being sold to the consumers.

5. Adulteration and Impurity:
Costly edible items such as oil, *ghee* and spices are adulterated in order to earn higher profits. Adulteration of foods causes heavy loss to the customers; they suffer from monetary loss as well as spoil their health.

6. Lack of Safety Devices:
Electronic goods, electrical devices or other appliances produced locally, lack the required inbuilt safeguards. This poses health risks to the consumers.

7. Artificial Scarcity:
In order to make illegitimate profit, businessmen often create artificial scarcity by hoarding. They sell the products at a later stage at higher prices.

8. False or Incomplete Information:
Sellers easily mislead consumers by giving wrong information about a product, its price, quality, reliability, life cycle, expiry date, durability, its effect on health, environment, safety and security, maintenance costs involved, and terms and conditions of purchase. Cosmetics, drugs and electronic goods are common examples where consumers face such problems.

9. Unsatisfactory After-sale Service:
Many of the high cost durable items, such as electrical or electronic equipments, home appliances and cars, need adequate after-sale care. The suppliers do not provide the satisfactory after-sale services despite the necessary payments made by the consumer.

10. Rough Behaviour and Undue Conditions:
In matters related to procuring LPG gas connection, fixing of a new telephone line, procurement of licensed items etc. consumers are often harassed and subjected to undue conditions in order to obtain the desired service.

11. Hidden Price Component:
A lot of companies give offers that invites the consumers to buy products at very low prices or make exchange offers or offers like buy one get one, which are good enough to lure the innocent consumers initially but have some or the other hidden price component attached to it which the consumer is forced to fulfill later, leading to his exploitation.

12. Environmental Hazards:
The producers may cause ecological and environ-mental hazards for the consumers and society by causing water, air and noise pollution.

13. Other Ways:
There are few other ways by which consumers are cheated, like:
(a) Variations in the content filled in the packaged goods.
(b) Illegal fixation of maximum retail price (MRP) and selling above MRP.
(c) Non-compliance with the terms and conditions of sales and services.

Reasons or Factors Causing Exploitation of Consumers

Limited Information:
Producers provide incomplete and incorrect information about various products.

Limited Supplies:
When goods and services are hoarded by producers/suppliers with an intention to create short supply, then prices shoot up.

Limited Competition:
Single producer may manipulate the market in terms of price and stocks *i.e.*, when seller enjoys monopoly in the market.

Low Literacy:
Illiteracy leads to exploitation. Lack of consumer awareness is the root cause for exploitation.

Lack of Bargaining Power:
This results among consumers due to lack of market information.

Irregular Prices Offered:
Sellers often manipulate the pricing of the product in absence of government control and there is price discrimination by the seller.

Misleading Advertisements:
Form a basic reason causing exploitation of a consumer. They have been designed and projected in such a way that the consumer gets carried off and gets trapped in the mesh of hidden costs, etc.

For example:
The producers may advertise a low price for the goods on offer. But when one goes to purchase the goods, he ends up paying more than the advertised price because it did not include the price of accessories or other things that are necessary to use the goods.

Lack of Unity:
Consumers lack courage and unity to voice against the exploitation, irrespective of the rights issued to them by our government.

Cumbersome and Time Taking Legal Proceedings:
Our legal procedures are critical and cumbersome. This puts off the courage in people to file any complaint against exploitation.

According to the Consumer Protection Act 2019, a consumer can complaint against any exploitation by seller. Here, "complaint" means any allegation in writing, made by a complainant for obtaining any relief provided by or under this Act, that:

(i) An unfair contract or unfair trade practice or a restrictive trade practice has been adopted by any trader or service provider;

(ii) The goods bought by him or agreed to be bought by him suffer from one or more defects;

(iii) The services hired or availed of or agreed to be hired or availed of by him suffer from any deficiency;

(iv) A trader or a service provider, as the case may be, has charged for the goods or for the services mentioned in the complaint, a price in excess of the price:

    (a) Fixed by or under any law for the time being in force;

(b) Displayed on the goods or any package containing such goods; or
  (c) Displayed on the price list exhibited by him by or under any law for the time being in force; or
  (d) Agreed between the parties;
(v) The goods, which are hazardous to life and safety when used, are being offered for sale to the public:
  (a) In contravention of standards relating to safety of such goods as required to be complied with, by or under any law for the time being in force;
  (b) Where the trader knows that the goods so offered are unsafe to the public;
(vi) The services which are hazardous or likely to be hazardous to life and safety of the public when used, are being offered by a person who provides any service and who knows it to be injurious to life and safety;
(vii) A claim for product liability action lies against the product manufacturer, product seller or product service provider, as the case may be.

CONSUMER AWARENESS

Consumer awareness is the knowledge that a consumer should have about his/her legal rights and duties.

Broadly, it refers to the combination of the following:

(1) The knowledge of the product purchased by the consumers in terms of its quality and its impact on their lives.
(2) The education about the bad effects of an advertisement and its contents.
(3) The knowledge about the consumer rights. A consumer should know that he/she has the right to get the right kind of product and he/she also has the right to claim compensation, if the product is found out to be faulty.
(4) The knowledge about consumers' responsibilities: This implies that consumers should not indulge in wasteful and unnecessary consumption.

Importance of Consumer Awareness

Following facts list the need of making consumers aware:

(1) To Achieve Maximum Satisfaction:
A consumer wants to buy maximum goods and services with his limited income. Therefore, it is necessary that he should get the goods which are measured appropriately and he is not cheated in any way, to maximise his satisfaction. For this, he should be made aware.

(2) Protect Against Exploitation:
Producers and sellers exploit the consumers through under weighing, charging more price than the market price, selling duplicate goods, misleading advertisement etc. Consumer awareness shields the buyer from getting exploited.

(3) Control over Consumption of Harmful Goods:
There are several goods available in the market which cause harm to consumers, for example—Cigarette, tobacco, liquor etc. Consumer education and awareness inspire people not to purchase such goods which are injurious to their health.

(4) Motivation for Saving:
Consumer awareness motivates people to keep away from wastage of money and extravagancy and inspire them to take the right decision. Such consumers are not attracted by sale, concession, free gifts, attractive packing etc. which means, people can use their saved income in a productive manner.

(5) Knowledge Regarding Solution of Problems:
Consumers are cheated due to illiteracy, innocence and lack of information. Therefore, it is important that consumers are made aware of their rights and the procedure for claiming compensation in the grievance redressal forums and the consumer court.

(6) Construction of healthy society:
Every member of the society is a consumer. So, if a consumer is aware and rational, then the complete society becomes alert towards their rights.

CONSUMER PROTECTION ACT, 2019 (COPRA)

The Consumer Protection Act was passed in 2019 and it came into force on 20 July, 2020. The main objectives of the Act are to provide better protection of the interests of the consumers and effective safeguards against different types of exploitation such as defective goods, deficient services and unfair trade practices. It also lays down the provisions for a simple, speedy and inexpensive machinery for redressal for consumers' grievances.

Objectives of the Consumer Protection Act, 2019

1. To conduct investigations into violations of consumer rights and institute complaints/prosecution.
2. Order recall of unsafe goods and services.
3. Order discontinuance of unfair trade practices and misleading advertisements.
4. Impose penalties on manufacturers/endorsers/publishers of misleading advertisements.
5. Act includes trade carried out through e-commerce and direct selling under its ambit. It defines e-commerce as buying or selling of goods or services including digital products over digital or electronic network and online market place or online auction sites
6. The CPA 2019 also provides for the settlement of disputes by way of mediation in case there is a likelihood of compromise at the acceptance point of the complaint or at some further date, provided the parties consent. For accelerated settlement, a mediation cell would be attached to each city, state, and national commission and its regional benches.

Scope of the Act

1. The Consumer Protection Act extends to the whole of India except the state of Jammu & Kashmir.
2. Unless otherwise provided by the Central Government by notification, this Act shall apply to all goods and services.

3. It covers all sectors whether private, public or cooperative.
4. The provisions of this Act are compensatory in nature.

Salient Features Of Consumer Protection Act, 2019

The salient features of Consumer Protection Act (COPRA) 2019 are as follows:

(1) It applies to all goods, services and unfair trade practices, unless specifically exempted by the Central Government.

The term 'goods', under this Act, covers all types of movable property other than money and includes stocks and shares, growing crops, etc. The term 'service' means service of any description made available to potential users and includes banking, financing, housing construction, insurance, entertainment, transport, supply of electrical and other energy, boarding and lodging, amusement, etc. It also includes the services of doctors, engineers, architects, lawyers etc.

(2) It covers all sectors whether private or public.

(3) It provides for establishment of consumer disputes redressal agencies at the district, state and national levels for resolution of consumer grievances and complaints. These are know as District commission, State Commission and National Commission.

CONSUMER PROTECTION COUNCILS

The Act provides for the establishment of a Central Protection Council by the Central Government and a State Consumer Protection Council in each state by the respective State Governments.

The Central Consumer Protection Council/Central Council:

This council will be established by the Central Government by notification and it will consist of the following members:

(a) The Minister-in-charge of the Department of Consumer Affairs in the Central Government, who shall be the Chairperson; and

(b) Such number of other official or non-official members representing such interests as may be prescribed.

The Central Council shall meet as and when necessary, but at least one meeting of the Council shall be held every year.

The objects of the Central Council shall be to render advice on promotion and protection of the consumers' rights under this Act.

The State Consumers Protection Council / State Council:

This council will be established by the State Government by notification. The State Council shall consist of the following:

(a) The Minister-in-charge of Consumer Affairs in the State Government who shall be the Chairperson;

(b) Such number of other official or non-official members representing such interests as may be prescribed;

(c) Such number of other official or non-official members, not exceeding ten, as may be nominated by the Central Government.

The State Council shall meet as and when necessary but not less than two meetings shall be held every year.

The objects of every State Council shall be to render advice on promotion and protection of consumer rights under this Act within the State.

District Consumer Protection Council /District Council:
The State Government establish by notification, for every District, a District Consumer Protection Council or the District Council.

The District Council shall be an advisory council and consist of the following members, namely:

(a) The Collector of the district (by whatever name called), who shall be the Chairperson; and
(b) Such number of other official and non-official members representing such interests as may be prescribed.

The District Council shall meet as and when necessary but not less than two meetings shall be held every year.

The objects of every District Council shall be to render advice on promotion and protection of consumer rights under this Act within the district.

CONSUMER DISPUTES REDRESSAL AGENCIES

The Consumer Protection Act provides for a three tier redressal system comprising of the following:

There is a proper method which has to be followed by a consumer to produce his complaint to the consumer protection council.

Where to file the complaint (depends upon the cost of the goods or services or the compensation)

- **A. District Commission:** If any of the above is less than ₹ 1 Crore.
- **B. State Commission:** If any of the above more than ₹ 1 Crore but less than ₹ 10 crore.
- **C. National Commission:** If any of the above more than ₹ 10 crore.

A. District Commission:

The State Government shall, by notification, establish a District Consumer Disputes Redressal Commission, to be known as the District Commission, in each district of the State:

The State Government may establish more than one District Commission in a district, if it deems fit.

Each District Commission shall consist of:
(a) A President; and
(b) Not less than two and not more than such number of members as may be prescribed, in consultation with the Central Government.

Jurisdiction:

Subject to the provisions of this Act, the District Forum will have Jurisdiction to entertain complaints where the value of goods or services and the compensation of any claim does not exceed ₹ 1 Crore.

(B) The State Commission (Consumer disputes redressal agency at state level)

Composition:

Each state commission shall consist of:

(a) A President; and (b) not less than four or not more than such number of members as may be prescribed in consultation with the Central Government.

Jurisdiction:

Subject to the provision of the Act, the State Commission has the jurisdiction:

- To entertain complaints where the value of goods or services or compensation claimed is between ₹ 1 Crore and ₹ 10 crore.
- To entertain appeals against the orders of any District Forum within the state, and
- To call for the records and pass appropriate orders in any consumer dispute that is pending before or has been decided by any District Forum within the State, where it appears to the State Commission that such District Forum has exercised jurisdiction not vested in it by law or has failed to exercise a jurisdiction so vested or has acted in exercise of its jurisdiction illegally or with material irregularity.

(C) The National Commission (Redressal commission at the national level)

Composition:

The National Commission will consist of:

(a) A President; and (b) Not less than four and not more than such number of members as may be prescribed.

Jurisdiction:

The National Commission shall have Jurisdiction:

- To entertain complaints where value of the goods or services and the compensation if any claimed exceeds ₹ 10 crore.
- To entertain appeals against the orders of any State Commission, and
- To call for the records and pass appropriate orders in any consumer dispute which is pending before or has been decided by any State Commission where it appears to the National Commission that such State Commission has exercised a jurisdiction not vested in it by the law, or has failed to exercise a jurisdiction so vested or has acted in the exercise of its jurisdiction illegally or with material irregularity.

COMPLAINTS BEFORE THE DISTRICT FORUM AND STATE COMMISSION

A complaint in relation to any goods sold or delivered or any service provided may be filed with a District Forum or State Commission as the case may be, by:

Consumer Protection

- The consumer to whom such goods are sold or delivered or such service provided.
- Any recognised consumer association, whether the aggrieved consumer is a member of such association or not, or
- The Central or State Government.
- One or more consumers on behalf of consumers having same interest, and
- A legal heir or representative of a deceased consumer.

Remedial Action:
If after the conduction of the proceedings any of the consumer redressal agencies is satisfied that the goods complained against suffer from any of the defects specified in the complaint or that any of the allegations contained in the complaint about the services provided, it will issue an order to the opposite party directing him to take any or more of the following actions namely:

- To remove the defects and deficiencies pointed out by the appropriate laboratory from the goods and services in question.
- To replace the goods with new goods of similar description which should be free from any defect.
- To return to the complainant the price or as the case may be, the charges paid by the complainant.
- To pay such amount as may be rewarded by it as compensation to the consumer for any loss or injury suffered by the consumer due to the negligence of the opposite party.
- To withdraw hazardous goods.
- To take steps to discontinue unfair or restrictive trade practices.

If a trader or person against whom a complaint is made, fails or omits to comply with any order made by a redressal agency, he shall be punishable with imprisonment upto three years or with fine not less than 25,000 extendable to 1 lakh, or both.

CONSUMER RIGHTS

To deal with cases of consumer exploitation, government of India has provided the following rights to all the consumers under the Consumer Protection Act, 2019:

1. Right to Safety:
Means right to be protected against the marketing of goods and services, which are hazardous to life and the property. This right not only meets their immediate needs but also fulfills their long term interest. Before purchasing, consumers should be informed of the products and services. They should preferably purchase quality marked products, such as ISI, AGMARK etc.

2. Right to be Informed:
Means the consumer has the right to be informed about the quality, quantity, potency, purity, standard and price of goods or services so as to protect the consumer against the abusive and unfair practices. The consumer should insist on getting all the information about the product or services before making a choice or a decision. This will enable the consumer to desist from falling prey to high pressure selling techniques.

3. Right to Choose:
Means right to be assured, wherever possible, of access to variety of goods and services at competitive price, of satisfactory quality and service at a fair price. It also includes right to basic goods and services. This is because of denial to the majority of their fair share. This right can be better exercised in a competitive market where a vast variety of choices are available to the consumer at competitive prices.

4. Right to be Heard:
Means that consumer interests will receive due consideration at appropriate forums. It also includes the right to be represented in various forums formed to consider the consumers' welfare. The consumers should form non-political and non-commercial consumer organisations and other bodies to give them unity and a platform to voice their problems.

5. Right to Seek Redressal:
Means right to be redressed against unfair trade practices or unscrupulous exploitation of consumers. Consumers must make complaint for their genuine grievances. Many a times their complaint may be of small value but its impact on the society as a whole may be very large. They can also take the help of consumer organisations for getting redressed of their grievances.

6. Right to Consumer Awareness:
Means the right to acquire the knowledge and skill to be an informed consumer throughout life. Ignorance of the rights is responsible for their exploitation. They should know their rights and must exercise them. Only then consumer exploitation will be prevented.

Thus, the concern of consumer protection is to ensure fair trade practices; maintain quality of goods and efficient service quantity, potency of the product, composition and price for their choice of purchase. Such a consumer protection policy would enable satisfaction from the delivery of goods and services needed by them.

LESSON AT A GLANCE

- **Consumer:** Is a person who has indicated his/her willingness to obtain goods or services from a supplier with the intention of paying for them.
- **Consumer Exploitation:** When producers cheat consumers of their hard earned money and hurt them physically, mentally or financially, it is called consumer exploitation.
- **Ways in Which a Consumers gets Exploited:** (i) Under-weight and under-measurements; (ii) Sub-standard quality; (iii) High prices; (iv) Duplicate articles; (v) Adulteration and Impurity; (vi) Lack of safety devices; (vii) Artificial scarcity; (viii) False or incomplete information; (ix) Unsatisfactory after sale services; (x) Rough behaviour and undue conditions; (xi) Hidden price component; (xii) Environmental hazards; (xiii) Other ways.
- **Consumer Awareness:** It is the knowledge of rights and duties of a consumer; so that he/she does not get exploited. Consumer awareness can be promoted through consumer education.

- **Importance of Consumer Awareness:** (i) To achieve maximum satisfaction; (ii) Protect against exploitation; (iii) Control over consumption of harmful goods; (iv) Motivation for saving; (v) Knowledge regarding solution of problems; (vi) Construction of healthy society.
- **Consumer Protection Act, 2019:** The consumer protection act, 2019 was enacted to promote and protect the rights of the consumer. The Act provides for simple, speedy and inexpensive redressal of grievances and is compensatory in nature.
- **Consumer Rights:** (i) Rights to safety; (ii) Right to be informed; (iii) Right to choose; (iv) Right to be heard; (v) Right to seek redressal; (vi) Right to consumer awareness.

Project Work

Your mother intends to purchase an automatic washing machine. Explain her the ways by which she may be exploited by the sellers/ manufacturers. Also explain her the rights which she enjoys as a consumer. In case, she is exploited, educate her where she should appeal for redressal of grievances and ways by which she may be protected.

Assignment

Explain to your class the importance of consumer protection and why it is necessary.

Questions

A. **Short Answer Type Questions:**
1. Who is a consumer?
2. What is consumer exploitation?
3. How does false and incomplete information be a way for exploiting the consumers?
4. What is meant by hidden price component?
5. How do advertisement cause consumer exploitation?
6. Write a short note on consumer awareness.
7. "Consumer education is an important method to eliminate consumer exploitation." Explain.
8. What is COPRA 2019 and when did it come into force?
9. What are the two features of Consumer Protection Act 2019?
10. Explain the Right to Consumer Awareness under the Indian Consumer Protection Act 2019.

B. **Essay Type Questions:**
1. 'Consumer is the king of market', still he is exploited. Discuss the reasons.
2. What are the various ways by which consumers are exploited. [ICSE 2020]
3. Explain the factors causing 'consumer exploitation'.
4. What is consumer awareness and how has it grown in recent times?
5. What is the need for consumer awareness in the modern days world?
6. Enumerate six consumer rights conferred upon the consumers by COPRA, 2019.

CHAPTER-08
E-Commerce

E-commerce is a means of conducting business, where the buying or selling of goods and services or the transmitting of funds or data, occur via electronic medium. There is no physical market place and the entire process of marketing and selling of goods, takes place on-line or electronically. This means, the buyer and the seller do not often meet face to face. It is a replica of a physical market place in the virtual world.

E-commerce, also called e-trading, operates in all four major market segments: Business to Business, Business to Consumer, Consumer to Consumer and Consumer to Business. Examples of E-commerce include on-line shopping, electronic payments, on-line auctions, Internet banking, on-line ticketing, etc.

- Meaning of E-Commerce
- Benefits over traditional means of transactions
- E-Tailing
- E-Advertising
- E-Marketing
- E-Security
- ERP and its Modules

BENEFITS OF E-COMMERCE OVER TRADITIONAL MEANS OF TRANSACTIONS

The key benefits of e-commerce revolve around the fact that it eliminates limitations of time and geographical distance, encountered while conducting business in a conventional manner. The advantages of e-commerce over traditional commerce are listed below:

(1) Overcomes Geographical Boundaries:
The reach of a physical store is limited to the area of its location. Even if it has several branches throughout the city or the country, the constraints of the physical space remains. However, an e-commerce web site can reach to customers beyond borders. This enables it to expand its market to national and international level with minimum capital investment.

(2) Wider Customer Reach:
E-commerce businesses can get new customers more easily than traditional businesses. This is due to the fact that e-commerce has a wider reach than traditional marketing networks. They can promote their business on the Internet, on various social networking sites as well as on television, newspapers etc., to reach their target audience.

(3) Lowers Cost:
Setting up an e-commerce network is cheaper as compared to a traditional business set-up. The cost of labour, personnel management, infrastructure, advertising and marketing is comparatively less. A part of these lowered costs is passed on to customers in the form of discounted prices.

E-commerce also lowers the cost for consumers by eliminating travel time and costs incurred in commuting to the physical store. E-commerce allows them to access desired products and services, with just a few mouse clicks.

(4) Remains Open all the Time:
E-commerce provides the option for the consumers to shop any time, as per their convenience. Unlike traditional shops, the e-commerce sites never shut down and that allows the businesses to thrive.

(5) Enables Comparative Shopping:
E-commerce facilitates comparison shopping. A customers can compare between various brands and prices, which helps him in making the best choice.

(6) Customer Care and Feedback:
E-commerce facilitates quick redressal of consumer's grievances. These web sites provide users an opportunity to write down their feedback through which they can identify needs and demands of customers. Most of the traditional and local form of businesses have failed to establish good relationship with consumers and customer service is slow.

E-TAILING

E-Tailing is the abbreviation of electronic retailing. It is the sale of goods and services through the Internet. E-tailing involves business-to-business or business-to-customers transactions. It can be regarded as the Internet front of any traditional retailer.

E-tailing shops believe in building strong brands. The web sites they create are easily understood by the visitors. They also provide discounts and offers to engage the customers. The pricing, in E-tailing shops, is generally lower than that of a traditional shop. In this way the e-tailing shops lure the customers to make purchases on-line. The customers also get benefited from the fact that he/she does not need to physically visit the shop for making the purchase. The customers are free to make their own decisions regarding the purchase, at their own leisure time.

However, e-tailing shops need to have a strong distribution network in order to secure the delivery of the products. Otherwise, the purpose of the e-tailing site will be defeated. Big e-tailing sites like Ebay.com and Amazon.com are making great business in this country.

Advantages of E-Tailing
1. No requirement of physical infrastructure.
2. Order completion is smoother than that of physical shops.
3. Customers might get addicted to on-line shopping, which in turn boost sales and increase revenue.
4. It is easy to review the product before, actually, purchasing it.
5. Most items available on-line are cheaper with quick and easy shipping and returns.

Disadvantages of E-Tailing

1. Creating and maintaining an e-tailing web site is an expensive process.
2. Customers do not often get to check the actual dimensions of the products and the quality displayed there.
3. Customers may have trust issues before providing their personal details and credit card details.

E-ADVERTISING

E-Advertising is the mechanism of promoting products or services on-line. It is the process of gaining attention of the customers, through the digital media.

The main purpose of e-advertising is to reach out to a wider range of customers. It is more cost effective when compared to the traditional forms of advertising. E-advertising also enables you to target the specific customers.

On safeguard to be taken regarding E-advertising is that advertisements have to be consistently monitored and controlled because if it is done poorly, it can severely damage the image of the company.

Features

1. E-advertising will only be published on the Internet.
2. Sometimes e-advertising will provide hyper links to the company's web site.
3. Can include image, texts, and even animations within the advertisements.

Types of E-Advertising

There are various types of e-advertising.

(a) Wallpaper Advertising:
It changes the background of the web site to the chosen promotion.

(b) Pop Up Advertising:
It pops up a new screen upon clicking on a certain link on the web site, that itself advertises the product.

(c) Floating Advertising:
The floating e-advertising is a kind of a floating banner on the web site, which tempts the visitor to click on it.

(d) Ad Sense Advertising:
This refers to companies' paying major search engines (such as Google) to promote their business within the first three links that appear when a search is entered.

E-MARKETING

Electronic Marketing (e-marketing) is also known as Internet marketing, web marketing, digital marketing on on-line marketing. It is the process of marketing a product or service using the Internet, e-mail and wireless media. Unlike e-advertising, e-marketing is very subtle. It is not always a direct message of persuasion but rather it is something which will educate the customers and convince them to buy the product or service.

Digital marketing techniques include Search Engine optimization (SEO), Search Engine Marketing (SEM), content marketing, e-commerce marketing, social media marketing, display advertisement, marketing through SMS and on-hold mobile ring tones, etc.

When compared to the means of traditional marketing, e-marketing offers several advantages.

Advantages of E-Marketing

1. E-marketing provides much better return on the investment made by the marketer.
2. It reduces the cost of marketing campaign.
3. The marketer can easily monitor and track the results of the campaign.
4. The results are often easily measurable and quickly obtained.
5. E-marketing allows marketers to create viral content, allowing viral marketing.

Disadvantages of E-Marketing

1. Devising a strong online marketing campaign involves spending money, the cost of which is ultimately borne by the customer. The cost of website design, software, hardware, maintenance of website, online distribution cost and invested time, are also factored in, while deciding the cost of providing a service or a product online.
2. Website of the company has to be constantly updated, which required research and skills and thus timing of updates is also critical.
3. Digital marketing is not suitable for marketing of industrial goods and pharmaceutical products making it useful for only specific categories of products, namely consumer goods.

Types of E-Marketing

There are several options through which the e-marketers can promote their product and services:

1. Article Marketing:
Writing articles about products and services often helps in the process of educating the customers.

2. Affiliate Marketing:
It is a kind of referral marketing where reference of any product will be provided on the other websites and when the customer buy's the product based on the recommendation this website owner with gets commission.

3. Video Marketing:
In this kind of e-marketing, a video will be shared describing the usage and benefits of the product or a service. It is often similar to television commercials.

4. Email Marketing:
Direct emails are being sent to potential customers describing benefits of the product or service.

5. Blogging:
Publishing blogs about similar products is also a very subtle way of marketing some business.

6. Social Media Marketing:
This form of marketing means promoting company's products and service on social media handles like facebook, Twitter and instragram. It is cost-effective because these platforms allow business to create profiles for free.

E-SECURITY

E-security is the process of securing the data and information, adopted by a website, from the external attacks. It involves protection of e-commerce assets from unauthorized access, use, alteration or destruction. Various e-marketing and e-tailing websites follow strict e-security measures in order to protect their sensitive information, from getting hacked.

Many customers provide their personal and financial information on these sites, which makes e-security crucial for the e-shopping websites.

Harms Caused by the Lack of E-Security
1. Data about customers being stolen.
2. Bank account details can be hacked and used for malicious purposes.
3. Blocking of real time financial transactions between the customer and the website and steal the customer's money.
4. Steal business information.
5. Hack and modify the website.

Ways to Minimize E-Security Threats
1. Preventing unauthorized data modification.
2. Protection against unauthorized data disclosure.
3. Authentication of data source.
4. Developing security policy, listing what data has to be protected, from whom and by whom.
5. Creating a security organisation to implement and administer security policy.
6. Performing a security audit regularly.

ENTERPRISE RESOURCE PLANNING AND ITS MODULES

Enterprise Resource Planning or ERP is a kind of software which is used to manage various functions of an organization. Right from the inventory management to payment done to the employees, every aspect of the business can be monitored and managed by the system.

ERP manages business processes of various departments and functions and helps the top management to have a better sense and control over the business. The centralized software system is divided into some basic modules, based on which the performance of the various departments can be checked. The following are the basic modules of ERP:

1. Human Resource:
This module helps in managing and tracking employees' performance. It also helps the management to decide on the pay hike and performance bonus.

2. Inventory:
This module helps the inventory system to keep track of the items and trace their current location in organization.

3. Sales & Marketing:
It tracks the sales process starting from the queries made by the customers to the dispatch of the orders.

4. Purchase:
It keeps track of all the purchases made by the organization.

5. Finance & Accounting:
Whole inflow & outflow of money/capital is managed by the finance module.

6. Customer Relationship Management (CRM):
CRM module helps to manage and track detailed information of the customer.

7. Engineering/Production:
This module consists of functionalities like production planning, machine scheduling, raw material usage, Bill of material preparation, track daily production progress, production forecasting and actual production reporting.

8. Supply Chain Management (SCM):
SCM module manages the flow of product items from manufacturer to consumer and consumer to manufacturer.

Lesson at a Glance

- **E-Commerce:** E-Commerce is the means of conducting business where the buying or selling of goods and services occur via electronic medium.
- **Benefits:** (i) Overcomes geographical boundaries, (ii) Wider customer reach, (iii) Lowers Cost, (iv) Remains Open all Time, (v) Enables comparative shopping, (vi) Customer care and feedback.
- **E-Tailing:** E-Tailing is the abbreviation of E-Retailing. E-tailing can involve business-to-business or business-to-customers transactions. It can be regarded as the Internet front of any traditional retailer.
- **E-Advertising:** E-Advertising is the mechanism of promoting products or services online. It is the process of gaining the attention of the customers through the digital media.
- **E-Marketing:** E-Marketing is also known as Internet Marketing and it comprises of a whole array of activities on the Internet in order to create awareness about a certain product or a service.
- **E-Security:** E-Security is the process of securing the data and information, adopted by a website, from the external attacks.

- **ERP:** Enterprise Resource Planning or ERP is a kind of software which is used to manage the various functions of an organization.
- **ERP Modules:** (i) Human Resource, (ii) Inventory, (iii) Sales and Marketing, (iv) Purchase, (v) Finance and Accounting, (vi) CRM, (vii) Engineering (Supply chain management) Production, (viii) SCM.

Project Work

Study the promotional offers given in a e-shopping website and write a report on the kind of discounts and offers they provide.

Assignment

Explain to your class the concept of e-security in online shopping and why it is necessary.

Questions

A. Short Answer Type Questions:
1. What is e-commerce?
2. State two advantages of e-commerce.
3. State one disadvantage of e-tailing.
4. What is e-advertising?
5. State two features of e-advertising.
6. State two types of e-advertising.
7. What is e-marketing?
8. State and describe one form of e-marketing.
9. What is e-security?
10. State one reason for ensuring e-security.
11. What is ERP?
12. What does the production module of ERP do?
13. What is the function of the SCM module of ERP?
14. What is e-tailing? [ICSE 2020]
15. What do you mean by e-security? [ICSE 2020]

B. Essay Type Questions:
1. What is e-tailing? What are the advantages of e-tailing?
2. Describe in details the shortcomings of e-tailing.
3. What is e-advertising? What are the different types of e-advertising?
4. What is e-marketing? What are the different forms of e-marketing?
5. What is e-security? What are the downsides of not having e-security?
6. What is ERP? Explain any three modules of ERP system. [ICSE 2020]
7. Briefly discuss any five advantages of e-commerce over traditional methods of transactions. [ICSE 2019]

CHAPTER-09
Capital and Revenue

- Meaning of Capital Receipts
- Meaning of Revenue Receipts
- Difference between Capital and Revenue Receipts
- Meaning of Capital Expenditure
- Meaning of Revenue Expenditure
- Difference between Capital and Revenue Expenditure
- Deferred Revenue Expenditure

CAPITAL RECEIPTS

Capital receipts are the receipts which are not received in the ordinary course of business. These are non-recurring receipts and their benefit is enjoyed over a long period of time.

Examples of capital receipts include:
(i) Money obtained from the sale of fixed assets or investments.
(ii) issue of shares or debentures
(iii) Loans raised
(iv) Additional capital introduced the proprietor etc.

Capital receipts are shown on the liabilities side of the Balance Sheet.

REVENUE RECEIPTS

Revenue receipts are the receipts which are obtained in the normal course of business. They are a receipt against supply of goods or services. These receipts help a business to carry out its day-to-day activities and are recurring in nature.

Examples of revenue receipts include:
(i) income received from sale of goods
(ii) interest earned on investments,
(iii) rent received from leasing out business property,
(iv) commission received,
(v) dividend received from shares etc.

Revenue receipts are credited to profit and loss account.

Difference Between Capital and Revenue Receipts

Basis of Difference	Revenue Receipts	Capital Receipts
Meaning	Revenue Receipts are the incomes that are generated from the operating activities of the business.	Capital Receipts are the incomes that are generated from investment and financing activities of the business.
Effect	They have a short term effect. The benefit of these receipts is derived for one accounting period only.	It has a long term effect. The benefit of these receipts is derived over many accounting periods.

Basis of Difference	Revenue Receipts	Capital Receipts
Nature	They are obtained repeatedly over the course of business, *i.e.*, they are recurring in nature.	They are non-repetitive and non-recurring in nature.
Generation of Capital and Revenue Receipts	Revenue receipts do not generate capital receipts.	Capital receipts generate revenue receipts when capital is invested by the owner of the business.
Value of Asset or Liability	These receipts increase the value of assets and decrease the value of liabilities.	These receipts increase the value of liability and decrease the value of asset.
Shown in	These receipts are shown in the Profit and Loss account.	These receipts get reflected in the Balance Sheet.
Nature of Expenses Incurred to Generate Receipts	Sometimes, expenses of capital nature have to be incurred to gene-rate revenue receipts, *e.g.*, purchase of shares of a company is capital expenditure but dividend received on shares is a revenue receipt.	Sometimes, expenses of revenue nature have to be incurred to generate capital receipts, *e.g.*, on obtaining loan (which is a capital receipt), interest is paid until its repayment which is a revenue expenditure.
Received in exchange of	Income	Source of income

CAPITAL EXPENDITURE

The expenditure incurred for acquiring a fixed asset or which results in increasing the earning capacity of the business is called capital expenditure. These expenditures are 'non-recurring' in nature and the assets which are acquired by incurring capital expenditure are used in the business and are not for sale. The benefit of these expenditures is derived over several accounting periods.

Capital expenditures aid the process of production of goods and services and helps in reducing costs and in increasing the profits of a business.

Examples of capital expenditure include:
(i) Purchase of land, building, machinery or furniture
(ii) Cost of acquisition of long term rights and benefits (*e.g.*, Patents , copyrights),
(iii) Cost of addition or extensions to existing asset.
(iv) Cost of overhauling second hand machine.
(v) Preliminary expenses incurred before the commencement of business such as legal charges paid for drafting the memorandum and articles of association of a company or brokerage paid to brokers, or commission paid to underwriters for raising capital.

REVENUE EXPENDITURE

The expenditure incurred for conducting the day-to-day business of a firm is called the revenue expenditure. These expenditures are incurred on a regular basis and the benefits from these expenditures are obtained over a relatively short period of time. These expenditures are also known as "expired costs".

These expenditures are incurred on items or services which are useful to the business but are used up in less than one year. Therefore, they amount to temporary increase in profit.

Examples of revenue expenditure include:

(i) Salaries and wages paid to employees.
(ii) Rent paid for the factory or office premises.
(iii) Depreciation on plant and machinery.
(iv) Expenditure on consumable items, on goods and services for resale either in their original or improved form such as on purchase of raw material.
(v) Expenditure incurred on purchase of goods meant for sale such as carriage inwards, octroi, import duty etc.

Difference Between Capital Expenditure and Revenue Expenditure

Basis of Difference	Revenue Expenditure	Capital Expenditure
Purpose	This expenditure is incurred in acquiring a fixed asset or improving the capacity of an existing one, resulting in the extension of its life years.	This expenditure is incurred in regulating day to day activities of the business.
Effect	The effect is temporary and the benefits are derived during one accounting year only.	The effect is long term. The benefits are availed over many accounting periods.
Acquisition of Assets	No assets are acquired.	An asset is acquired or the value of an existing asset is increased.
Occurrence of Expenditure	It is a recurring expense	It is a non-recurring expense.
Nature of Expense	This expense is incurred in order to maintain the business.	This expense is incurred in order to improve the position of the business.
Earning Capacity	It does not increase the earning capacity of a business.	It increases the earning capacity of a business.
Placement in Financial Statements	It appears in the trading or profit and loss account and is shown on the debit side of the either of the two accounts.	It appears in the balance sheet on the asset side.

| Amount Involved | The amount involved in revenue expenditure is relatively small. | Capital expenditures tend to involve larger monetary amounts than revenue expenditures. |

DEFERRED REVENUE EXPENDITURE

Deferred Revenue Expenditures are those expenditures which are incurred in one accounting period and they do not create any assets but their benefit is spread over more than one accounting period. It is a kind of revenue expenditure and is incurred during a particular accounting period but is applicable either wholly or in part to future accounting periods. These expenses are usually large in amount.

A proportionate amount is charged to profit and loss account of each year and the balance is carried forward to subsequent years as deferred revenue expenditure. It is shown as an asset in the balance sheet.

Examples of Deferred Revenue Expenditure include:
(i) Discount on issue of shares and debentures,
(ii) Heavy initial advertising expenditure incurred for introducing a new product in the market,
(iii) Expenditure incurred on research and development,
(iv) Repairing and painting of building,
(v) Expenditure incurred in shifting business to more convenient premises.

LESSON AT A GLANCE

- **Capital Receipt:** Capital receipts are the receipts which are not received in the ordinary course of business. These are non-recurring receipts and their benefit is enjoyed over a long period of time.
- **Revenue Receipt:** Revenue receipts are the receipts which are obtained in the normal course of business. They are receipts against supply of goods or services.
- **Capital Expenditure:** The expenditure incurred for acquiring a fixed asset or which results in increasing the earning capacity of the business is called capital expenditure.
- **Revenue Expenditure:** The expenditure incurred for conducting the day-to-day business of a firm is called the revenue expenditure.
- **Deferred Revenue Expenditure:** Deferred Revenue Expenditures are those expenditures which are incurred in one accounting period and they do not create any assets but their benefit is spread over more than one accounting period.

Analyze balance sheets of a firm for 5 consecutive years and find out the change in the capital investments made. Try and find out the reasons for the change in capital investments.

Capital and Revenue

 **ASSIGNMENT**

Try and find out 10 examples of deferred revenue expenditure of a business firm and explain the benefits derived from those expenditures.

 **QUESTIONS**

A. **Short Answer Type Questions:**
   1. Define Capital Receipt.
   2. What is revenue receipt?
   3. State two differences between capital and revenue receipt.
   4. What is capital expenditure?
   5. What is meant by revenue expenditure? [ICSE 2017]
   6. State two differences between capital and revenue expenditure.
   7. What is meant by deferred revenue expenditure? [ICSE 2019]
   8. Distinguish between capital and revenue expenditure. [ICSE 2020]
   9. What is meant by 'Capital Receipt'?

B. **Essay Type Questions:**
   1. What is capital receipt? Describe with examples.
   2. What is revenue receipt? Describe with examples.
   3. State the differences between capital and revenue receipts.
   4. What is capital expenditure? Describe with examples.
   5. What is revenue expenditure? Describe with examples.
   6. What are the differences between capital and revenue expenditure?
   7. Explain the concept of deferred revenue expenditure and how it is entered in the books of accounts.

CHAPTER-10
Final Accounts of a Sole Trader

FINAL ACCOUNTS

Mathematical accuracy of account books is ascertained by trial balance. After ascertaining mathematical accuracy of account books, every businessman wants to know whether he has earned a profit or suffered a loss during the accounting period and what is the financial position of his business at the end of the said accounting period. To obtain this information, final accounts are prepared with the help of the trial balance which include the following:

(A) Trading Account; (B) Profit and Loss Account; and (C) Balance Sheet.

Trading account reveals gross profit or gross loss for the accounting period while profit and loss account portrays net profit or net loss. Balance Sheet discloses financial position of the business on the last day of the accounting period. Since these accounts or statements are prepared at the end of the accounting period and in the last stage of accounting process and books of the business are closed after the preparation of these, so they are known as 'Final Accounts'. These are also termed as 'Financial Statements'.

- *Meaning of Final Accounts*
- *Meaning of Sole Proprietorship*
- *Preparation of Final Accounts*
- *Trial Balance*
- *Trading Account*
- *Main Items of Trading Account on Debit and Credit Side*
- *Determining Gross Profit or Gross Loss on Trading*
- *Profit and Loss Account*
- *Main Items of Profit and Loss Account on Debit and Credit Side*
- *Some specific items which are not shown in Profit and Loss Account*
- *Balance Sheet*
- *Preparation of Balance Sheet*
- *Items included in Balance Sheet on Liability Side and Asset Side*
- *Format of a Balance Sheet*

Final accounts are of great need and importance, not only for the owner of the business but also for other parties related to the business, such as creditors, lenders, employees, etc. On the basis of final accounts, creditors and lenders take decisions relating to credit sales and loan facility, respectively. Employees estimate the stability of their employment, increments in salary and promotions on the basis of profit/loss and financial position of the business. Final accounts of large companies are also important for Government, investors and public at large. Government receives revenue from these companies, in form of taxes while investors receive return on their investment. Public at large is also affected by these companies because their failure causes loss to national property.

SOLE PROPRIETORSHIP

A sole proprietor, also known as a sole trader, is a person who owns the business and is personally responsible for its debts. He can conduct a business under his own

Final Accounts of a Sole Trader

name or under a fictitious name. He pays personal income tax, based on the profit he earns. He typically signs contracts in his own name because sole proprietorship has no separate legal entity.

PREPARATION OF FINAL ACCOUNTS

For the preparation of final accounts of a business, it is essential that proper accounts of transactions during the accounting period should be maintained and while maintaining these accounts, adherence to basic concepts, conventions and assumptions of accounting be ensured. From this point of view, the following points are worth mentioning :

1. Since business and businessman are separate entities and final accounts are prepared to disclose profit or loss and financial position of business, personal incomes and expenses of the businessman should be separated from business incomes and expenses.
2. Capital and revenue incomes and expenses should be differentiated.
3. Incomes and expenses of the accounting period should be separated from the incomes and expenses related to other period.

(A) Trial Balance

The starting point for preparing final accounts is the trial balance prepared by the book-keeper. It is a list of all balances standing in the ledger accounts and cash book of a firm, at any given time. It is the shortest method of verifying the arithmetical accuracy of entries made in the ledger. If the trial balance agrees, it is an indication that the accounts are correctly written up but it is not a conclusive proof. All the figures recorded in the trial balance helps to prepare the, Trading A/c, Profit & Loss A/c and Balance Sheet.

Preparation:

There are two methods for preparing the trial balance:

First Method:

In this method, ledger accounts are not balanced, they are totaled. The debit totals of and the credit side are entered in a separate sheet. The grand total of debit column will be equal to the grand total of the credit column.

Second Method:

This method is more widely used. In this method, ledger accounts are balanced. The brought down balances are then brought to a sheet as given below:

Firm's Books

Trial Balance as on.........20.........

S. No.	Name of Account	L.F.	Debit Balance (in rupees)	Credit Balance (in rupees)

Assets, Sundry Debtors, Losses, Expenses and Drawings are debit balances. Capital, Liabilities, Sundry Creditors, Gains, Incomes and Capital, Revenues are credit balances. Debit and credit balances should match, which would be an indication that accounts have been correctly prepared.

(B) Trading Account

Trading account, in nature, is a nominal account. It is also called Goods A/c. It provides information about the gross result of trade (*i.e.* purchase and sale of finished goods) during the accounting period which is known as gross profit or loss. For this, net sale value of goods sold, generally known as 'net sales', during the accounting period is compared with the cost of goods sold. If the former exceeds the later, excess is termed as 'gross profit'. In the reverse case, *i.e.*, if the former is less than the later, the deficit is known as gross loss. This gross profit or loss is transferred to profit and loss account. Net sales means the amount derived by subtracting sales return from the total of cash and credit sales while cost of goods sold is calculated as follows :

Cost of Goods Sold = Opening Stock + Net Purchases – Closing Stock + Direct Expenses

Direct expenses are all those expenses which are incurred in bringing the purchased goods to the godown or trading place of the trader.

For example, if the opening stock of the year is ₹ 50,000, net purchases during the year is ₹ 4,00,000 and closing stock at the end of the year is ₹ 30,000, then cost of goods sold will be ₹ 50,000 + ₹ 4,00,000 – ₹ 30,000 = ₹ 4,20,000. If net sales during the year is ₹ 6,00,000, amount of gross profit will be ₹ 6,00,000 – ₹ 4,20,000 = ₹ 1,80,000.

Format of Trading Account

Trading Account

Dr. For the year ended............ Cr.

Particulars	Amount (₹)	Particulars	Amount (₹)
To Opening Stock	....	By Sales	
To Purchases		Cash	
Less: Purchases Returns		Credit	
on Return Outwards		*Less*: Sales Returns	
Less: Goods used as :		or Return Inwards	....
Charity		By Closing Stock	....
Drawings		By Profit & Loss A/c	....
Donation		(Gross Loss transferred to	
Loss by fire theft		P & L A/c)	
Free Sample			
To Wages/Wages on Purchases	....		

To Wages and Salaries	....		
To Carriage/Carriage Inward	....		
To Inward Expenses	....		
To Custom Duty	....		
To Import Duty	....		
To Freight/Freight on Purchases	....		
To Railways Freight	....		
To Dock Charges	....		
To Brokerage & Commission on Purchases	....		
To Cartage/Cartage on Purchases	....		
To Royalty on Purchases	....		
To Other Direct Expenses	....		
To Profit & Loss A/c (Gross Profit transferred to P & L A/c)			
	....		....

Main Items to be shown on debit side of trading account

1. Opening Stock:
Closing stock of the previous accounting year is opening stock for the current year, which is shown on the debit side of the trading account. There is no opening stock in the first year of a business. Opening stock includes opening stock of raw material, opening stock of semi-finished goods and opening stock of finished goods.

2. Purchases:
It includes purchases of goods during the accounting year in cash and on credit for the purpose of sale. It is shown on the debit side of trading account. But assets purchased during the year and goods received on consignment are not included in purchases. Amount of net purchases is shown on the debit side of the trading account for which the following items are subtracted from the total purchases: (i) Purchases return, (ii) Donation of goods, (iii) Drawings of goods by the owner of the business, (iv) Theft of goods, (v) Loss of goods by fire, (vi) Goods distributed as free sample, and (vii) Goods used as advertisement material etc.

3. Direct Expenses:
All the expenses incurred in bringing the purchased goods to the godown of the trader or trading place are known as direct expenses, *e.g.*, carriage inward, brokerage and commission on purchases, wages, import duty, octroi, etc. If such expenses are related to the purchase of an asset, then these will not be debited to trading account. Rather, these will be added to the cost of that asset.

Main items to be shown on credit side of trading account

1. Sales:
Aggregate of cash and credit sales of goods during the accounting year is termed as total sales. Net sales is ascertained by deducting the amount of sales return from total sales which is shown on the credit side of trading account. Here, it is pertinent to note that sale of assets is not shown in trading account.

2. Closing Stock:
Goods remaining unsold at the end of the accounting year are known as closing stock. A single account is not sufficient to open in account books to show inflow and outflow of goods, rather several accounts are opened for this purpose, viz. opening stock account, purchases account, purchases return account, sales account, sales return account, etc. Therefore, closing stock account generally does not exist in trial balance. To ascertain the amount of closing stock, goods remaining unsold at the end of the year are physically counted and evaluated. The amount thus ascertained is shown on the credit side of trading account and on the assets side of balance sheet. If closing stock already exists in the trial balance, it is shown only on the assets side of balance sheet and not on the credit side of trading account.

3. Sales Returns:
Sales returns must be deducted from total sales and to be shown on the credit side of the trading account. Sales returned are the sold goods which are returned by the customers.

Determining Gross Profit or Gross Loss on Trading account

When all the necessary balances have been transferred to the Trading Account, the balance of this account will represent Gross Profit (if it is a credit balance, *i.e.*, if the credit total of Trading Account exceeds its debit total) or Gross Loss (if it is a debit balance, *i.e.*, if the debit total of the Trading Account exceeds its credit total). If there is no balance, it would mean the absence of Gross Profit or Gross Loss. The balance of the Trading Account will then be transferred to the Profit and Loss Account.

If the Trading Account has a credit balance implying Gross Profit, Profit and Loss Account would be credited and Trading Account will be debited. If the Trading Account has a debit balance implying Gross Loss, Profit and Loss Account would be debited and the Trading Account credited with the amount thereof.

(C) Profit and Loss Account

After ascertaining the Gross Profit, the next stage is to prepare the Profit and Loss Account. Besides the normal purpose for helping the management in understanding the performance of business, this Profit and Loss Account is necessary for two other purposes also.

Firstly, the profits can be distributed to the owners only out of net profit. Secondly, the tax liability is computed after ascertaining the net profit. The profit and Loss Account is an account which shows the net result of the operations of the enterprise during the financial year. The main feature of a Profit and Loss Account is that it contains indirect gains (*i.e.*, gains or incomes not directly connected with the routine business activities *e.g.*, rent received, sale of old newspapers, commission from agency etc.) and indirect expenses (connected with selling or distribution of goods, administration like salaries, etc.)

Final Accounts of a Sole Trader

Need:

The purpose of preparing the Profit and Loss Account is to ascertain the net profit or net loss from business operations. The net income of the current year can be compared with that of previous years, and deviation in incomes of different periods may be analysed to ascertain the causes of such deviations. Such an analysis will be helpful in controlling expenses that are incurred in running the business enterprise in selling the goods and in eliminating wastage.

Format of Profit and Loss Account

Profit and Loss Account

Dr.   For the year ending............   Cr.

Particulars	Amount (₹)	Particulars	Amount (₹)
To Trading a/c (Gross Loss)	....	By Trading A/c (Gross Profit)	....
To Salaries & Wages	....	By Interest Earned	....
To Rent, Rates & Taxes	....	By Commission Earned	....
To Fire Insurance Premium	....	By Rent Earned	....
To Repairs & Maintenance	....	By Profit on Sale of Fixed Assets	....
To Royalty on Sales	....	By Income from Investments	....
To Depreciation	....	By Sale of Scrap	....
To Audit Fees	....	By Miscellaneous Incomes	....
To Bank Charges	....	By Discount Received	....
To Legal Charges	....	By Dividends Received	....
To Miscellaneous Expenses	....	By Apprentice Premium	....
To Discount Allowed	....	By Bad Debts Recovered	....
To Interest/Interest on Loans	....	By Capital a/c	....
To Carriage Outward	....	(Net Loss transferred to	
To Freight Outward	....	Capital Account)	
To Commission on Sales	....		
To Trade Expenses	....		
To Travelling Expenses	....		
To Entertainment Expenses	....		
To Sales Promotion Expenses	....		
To Advertising and Publicity	....		
To Bad Debts	....		
To Packing Expenses	....		
To Loss on Sale of Fixed Asset	....		
To Loss by Theft	....		
To Loss by Fire	....		

To Loss by Embezzlement	....		
To Printing & Stationery	....		
To Postage & Telephone Expense	....		
To Office Expenses	....		
To Other Indirect Expenses	....		
To Capital A/c (Net Profit transferred to Capital A/c)	....		
	....		....

Main Items to be Shown on the Debit Side of Profit and Loss Account

1. Gross Loss:

If trading account discloses gross loss, it is shown on the debit side of profit and loss account, first of all.

2. Indirect Expenses:

All expenses other than direct expenses are known as indirect expenses. Such expenses have no relationship with purchase of goods. These include administrative expenses (such as; salary of employees, officers employed in general office, rent and taxes of office building, printing and stationery, postage, telegrams, fax and telephone expenses, etc.), selling and distribution expenses (such as; godown expenses, advertisement expenses, commission of sales representative, freight and cartage on sales, packing expenses, etc.), finance expenses (such as; interest on loan, interest on capital, interest on bank overdraft, etc.) and other miscellaneous expenses (such as; donation, subscription, etc.).

3. Losses:

Loss on sale of fixed assets and all other losses related to business are shown on the debit side of profit and loss account. Depreciation on fixed assets, bad debts, loss of goods by theft, fire or any natural calamity etc., are some examples of these losses.

Main Items to be Shown on the Credit Side of Profit and Loss Account

1. Gross Profit:

If trading account reveals gross profit, it is shown on the credit side of profit and loss account.

2. Incomes and Gains:

All incomes and gains except those which are credited to trading account, are shown on the credit side of profit and loss account. Example of such incomes and gains are; discount received, rent received, commission received, interest received on investment, interest received from debtors, recovery of bad debts, profit on sale of fixed assets, etc.

Some Specific Items Which Are Not Shown In Profit And Loss Account

1. Drawings:

Drawings from the business by the businessman whether these are in the form of cash or goods or payment of his personal expenses (such as; life insurance premium, club membership fees, etc.) are not business expenses. Therefore, these should not be debited to profit and loss account, rather, these should be debited to businessman's capital account.

2. Income Tax:
In case of single entrepreneurship, income tax is the personal expense of a businessman. Therefore, it is treated as drawings and debited to capital account and not to profit and loss account. In case of partnership firms and companies, payable income tax is a business expense. Therefore, it is debited to profit and loss account just like other expenses.

3. Sales Tax:
It is a tax which the businessman collects from the customers and then deposits in the Government treasury. Therefore, sales tax should not be shown in profit and loss account. If the amount of sales tax, though collected but has not been deposited with the Government treasury by the time of preparation of final accounts, it should be shown on the liabilities side of balance sheet.

4. Ascertaining Net Profit or Loss:
Net profit or net loss is ascertained by comparing the totals of debit and credit sides of profit and loss account. If the total of credit side is more than that of debit side, the excess will be net profit. In the reverse case, there will be net loss. This net profit or loss is transferred to capital account.

(D) Balance Sheet
The information conveyed by the Trading and Profit and Loss Account is no doubt very valuable to the owner of a business, as it enables him to determine the Gross and Net Profit and loss resulting from his dealings during a fiscal period. This, however, is not the only point on which a businessman wants to be enlightened. As his assets and liabilities change from day to day, as a result of business transactions, he also wants to find out what his true financial position is at the end of each trading period. In the first place, he would like to know whether the net profit as is disclosed by the Profit and Loss Account is correctly arrived at, if so, his capital at the end of the period must be necessarily increased by that amount. He is equally anxious to see for himself as to how such capital is locked up, *i.e.*, what the components, assets and liabilities are, of which this capital is made up. In order, to obtain this information at the end of the trading period, he has to set out his Assets and Liabilities in the shape of a statement and this statement is called the Balance Sheet.

- A Balance Sheet may, therefore, be defined as *"A statement prepared with a view to measure the exact financial position of a business on a certain fixed date."*
- *"Balance Sheet is a screen picture of the financial position of a going business at a certain moment."*
  —Francis R. Stead

It is prepared from the Trial Balance, after all the balances on nominal accounts are transferred to the Trading and Profit and Loss Account and the corresponding accounts in the Ledger are closed. The balances now left in the Trial Balance and remaining open in the Ledger represent either Personal Accounts or Real Accounts. In other words, they represent either Assets or Liabilities existing at the date of the financial close.

All such assets and liabilities are set out in the Balance Sheet in a classified form. On the right-hand side are shown the various assets or possessions of the business and on the left-hand side, the various liabilities, *i.e.*, the amounts owing by the business. The excess of assets over liabilities represents the capital of the owner. This figure of capital must tally with the closing balance of the Capital Account in the Ledger after the net profit or loss has been transferred thereto. As the balance of Profit and Loss Account is transferred to the Capital Account and as the closing balance on the Capital Account is shown in the Balance Sheet, it is clear that the Balance Sheet shows the financial position, inclusion of the profit or loss made during the trading period. It is called a Balance Sheet because it is a sheet of balances of ledger accounts which are still open after the preparation of the Trading and Profit and Loss Account.

The Balance Sheet is prepared on a particular date and, therefore, the information contained in it is valid only for that date. In a Balance Sheet, the total of all assets and all liabilities must be equal to the total of all liabilities and capital at a given date, *i.e.*,

Total Assets = Capital + Liabilities
or
Capital = Total Assets − Liabilities

In preparing the Balance Sheet, the accounting equation serves as the base. The accounting equation states that Total Assets = Capital + Liabilities or Capital = Total Assets − Liabilities. It becomes convenient and logical that there should be two sides—the Assets and the Liabilities. thus, both the sides should tally.

Preparation of Balance Sheet

As the purpose of Balance Sheet is to show the financial position of the business, it follows that it should be drawn out in some intelligible form or order.

The Assets and Liabilities should be grouped together and properly classified under appropriate heads so as to convey the information in a summarized form. The Debtors and Creditors need not be shown in the shape of individual balances, but must be set out in total. Further, the balance owing by customers must be shown separately under the heading of "Trade Debtors" or "Book Debts" and must not be mixed up with Debtors for Loans or Prepaid Expenses. Similarly, Trade Creditors must be distinguished from Creditors for Loans, or from Liabilities for Expenses. In fact, the whole of the Assets and Liabilities must be disclosed in a manner as would present a clear view of the true state of affairs to anyone reading the Balance Sheet.

No definite rules can be laid down as to the correct order in which the Assets and Liabilities shall appear in the Balance Sheet. It is usual, however, to start with the Fixed Assets, and follow it with the Floating Assets in the order of realization. Similarly, the Fixed Liabilities are stated first and are followed by Floating Liabilities. There are concerns, however, which prefer to reverse this order and in Partnership Accounts, usually the assets are shown in the natural order of their reliability and the liabilities in the order in which they are payable.

Again, banks usually prefer to state assets in order of their realisability. Thus, the most liquid assets are set out first and are followed by assets which are more difficult in realisation.

Items included on the Liability side of the Balance Sheet

1. Current Liabilities:
Current Liabilities are those liabilities which are expected to be paid within a year and which are usually to be paid out of Current Assets.

2. Bank Overdraft:
When an undertaking withdraws from the bank more than the amount deposited in its account, it is known as overdraft.

3. Outstanding Expenses:
Those expenses which have become due for payment but have not yet been paid, are known as outstanding expenses.

4. Bills Payable:
Bills of exchange accepted in favour of creditors, are known as bills payable. They represent the amount of bills which have not yet become due for payment.

5. Sundry Creditors:
This represents the sum total of credit balances appearing in the accounts of creditors.

6. Long-term Liabilities:
Those liabilities which matures for payment after a period of one year, are known as long-term liabilities.

7. Contingent Liabilities:
Those liabilities which are not liability on the date of Balance Sheet, but may or may not turn out to be a liability in future, are called contingent liabilities. Such liabilities are only 'noted' in the particulars column of the Balance Sheet and no record is made in the books of account. Guarantees in respect of loans, liability on bills discounted, disputed claims, etc., are examples of contingent liabilities.

8. Capital:
It is the excess of assets over liabilities due to outsiders. It represents the amount originally contributed by the proprietor or partner, which is increased by profits and decreased by losses and drawings.

9. Drawings:
Drawings by the proprietor has the effect of reducing the balance on his Capital Account. Therefore, the Drawings Account is closed by transferring its balance to his Capital Account. However, it is shown by way of deduction from the capital in the Balance Sheet.

Items included on the Asset side of the Balance Sheet

1. Current Assets:
These assets are those which are either in the form of cash or can be converted into cash very easily.

2. Cash at Bank:
It represents the balance of cash in the account of the enterprise with a bank.

3. Bills Receivable:
Bills of exchange received from customers are termed as 'bills receivable'. Bills receivable shown under this heading are those bills of exchange which have not

yet matured for payment and which have not been discounted or endorsed to third parties.

4. Sundry Debtors:
This represents the sum total of debit balances appearing in the customer's accounts.

5. Prepaid Expenses:
This represents the amount which have been paid in advance for services to be received in the future. It is shown as an asset in the Balance Sheet.

6. Accrued Income:
This represents the income which has been earned but has not yet been received or has become due.

7. Closing Stock:
Goods remaining unsold at the end of the accounting year.

8. Fixed Assets:
Fixed assets are those assets which are of permanent nature and which the proprietor of a business purchases because these are helpful in the operation of the business for a number of years. They are not intended for resale but are purchased for permanent use. These include plant, machinery, furniture, buildings, motor lorries, land, patent, leasehold land, etc. Fixed assets are also known as 'Capital Assets' or 'Long-term Assets'. Some accountants consider them as Block Assets.

9. Fictitious Assets:
Those assets that are not assets in reality but are shown in the Balance Sheet on the asset side are known as Fictitious Assets. These include debit balance of expenses or losses carried forward from an accounting period to the next, *e.g.*, Suspense Account. Debit balance of Profit and Loss Account is also included in the fictitious assets.

10. Intangible Assets:
Such assets have no material existence, they cannot be touched or seen, and they exist merely in form of a book entry, *e.g.*, goodwill, patent, copyright, etc. Goodwill is the value, in terms of money, attached to the good name of an established concern. It is the amount which the potential buyer would pay for a well established business over and above its net worth. Copyright refers to the exclusive right of the author of a book on its publication. The right of an inventor of a new process or machinery is called patent right.

11. Wasting Assets:
Some of the Fixed Assets may also be Wasting Assets. These are the assets which are exhausted or consumed in the course of time for example, mines, quarries, etc. The Fixed Assets depreciate in value through wear and tear and with the passage of time, whereas Wasting Assets get reduced in value through being worked.

Format of Balance Sheet

Assets and liabilities are displayed in balance sheet in a specific order. From this point of view, the orders are of two types: 1. Liquidity Order and 2. Permanence Order.

1. Liquidity Order:

This order is also known as realisation order. According to this order, in assets side, first of all cash in hand is shown. Then other assets are arranged in order of their being easily converted into cash. Similarly, in liabilities side, liabilities are shown according to their payment priorities. Format of balance sheet in liquidity order is as follows:

Specimen
Balance Sheet as on……

Liabilities	Amount (₹)	Assets	Amount (₹)
Current Liabilities:		**Current Assets:**	
Bank Overdraft	……	Cash in Hand	……
Bills Payable	……	Cash at Bank	……
Outstanding Expenses	……	Bills Receivable	……
Sundry Creditors	……	Sundry Debtors	……
Income rec. in advance	……	Accrued Income	……
Long Term Liabilities:		Stock: Finished Stock ……	
Bank Loan	……	Work-in-progress ……	
Loan on Mortgage	……	Raw Material ……	……
Capital	……	Prepaid Expenses	……
Add: Net Profit	……	**Investment**	……
or		**Fixed Assets:**	……
Less: Net Loss	……	Furniture	
Less: Drawings	……	Plant & Machinery	……
Less: Income-tax	…… ……	Building	……
		Patents	……
		Goodwill	……
	……		……

2. Permanence Order:

This order is just reverse of the liquidity order. According to this order, on assets side, first of all intangible and fixed assets, such as goodwill, patent, building etc., are shown. After fixed assets, investments are shown and at the end, current assets, such as bank balance, cash in hand, etc., are shown. In liabilities side, first of all, capital is shown and then long term liabilities, such as bank loan and at the end, current liabilities, such as bills payable, bank overdraft, etc., are shown. Format of balance sheet in permanence order is as follows:

Specimen
Balance Sheet as on......

Liabilities	Amount (₹)	Assets	Amount (₹)
Capital:		**Fixed Assets:**	
Add : Net Profit		Goodwill	......
or		Patents	......
Less :Net Loss		Building	......
Less : Drawings		Plant & Machinery	......
Less : Income Tax	......	Furniture	......
Long-term Liabilities:		**Investments**	
Loan on Mortgage	......	**Current Assets:**	
Bank Loan	......	Prepaid Expenses	......
Current Liabilities:		Stock: Raw Material	
Income received in advance	......	Work-in-progress	
Sundry Creditors	......	Finished Goods	......
Outstanding Expenses	......	Accrued Income	......
Bills Payable	......	Sundry Debtors	......
Bank Overdraft	......	Bill Receivable	......
	...	Cash at Bank	......
		Cash in Hand	......
	......		......

Sole traders and partnership firms generally prepare balance sheet in liquidity order though it is not compulsory for them to do so. According to the Companies Act, 1956, it is mandatory for companies to prepare their balance sheet in permanence order.

Illustration 1: The following is the Trial Balance of a Trading Co. as on 31st March, 2018.

Trial Balance

Particulars	L.F.	Debit (₹)	Credit (₹)
Machinery		98,000	
Land and Buildings		8,60,000	
Investments		70,000	
Bad debts		3,000	
Sundry Debtors		40,000	
Purchases		3,09,800	
Stock on 1st April, 2017		23,000	
Interest		3,500	
Bills Payable			6,750
Sundry Creditors			76,000
Travelling Expenses		700	

Trade Expenses	5,000	
Discount	1,250	2,625
Purchases Returns		9,850
Sales Returns	6,775	
Bills Receivable	2,275	
Capital		10,25,000
Sales		3,75,775
Mobile Phone Bills (Official)	6,000	
Postage	1,200	
Wages and Salaries	12,000	
Salaries and wages	51,000	
Carriage	2,500	
	14,96,000	14,96,000

The closing stock was valued at ₹ 9,000. Prepare a Trading and Profit and Loss Account and the Balance Sheet as on 31st March, 2018.

Trading Account
for the year ending 31st March, 2018

Particulars	Amount (₹)	Particulars	Amount (₹)
To Opening Stock	23,000	By Sales 3,75,775	
To Purchases 3,09,800		Less : S. Return 6,775	3,69,000
Less : P. Return 850	2,99,950	By Closing Stock	9,000
To Wages & Salaries	12,000		
To Carriage	2,500		
To Gross Profit transferred to P & L A/c	40,550		
	3,78,000		3,78,000

Profit & Loss A/c
for the year ended 31st March, 2018

Particulars	Amount (₹)	Particulars	Amount (₹)
To Bad debts	3,000	By Gross Profit transferred from Trading A/c	40,550
To Interest	3,500		
To Travelling Expenses	700	By Discount	2,625
To Trade Expenses	5,000	By Net Loss transferred to Capital A/c	28,475
To Discount	1,250		
To Mobile Phone bills	6,000		
To Postage	1,200		
To Salaries & Wages	51,000		
	71,650		71,650

Balance Sheet
as on 31st March, 2018

Liabilities	Amount (₹)	Assets	Amount (₹)
Bills Payable	6,750	Bills Receivable	2,275
Sundry Creditors	76,000	Sundry Debtors	40,000
Capital 10,25,000		Investments	70,000
Less: Net Loss 28,475	9,96,525	Closing Stock	9,000
		Land & Buildings	8,60,000
		Machinery	98,000
	10,79,275		10,79,275

Prepare a Trading, Profit & Loss Account and Balance Sheet of Krishna Enterprises for the year ended 31st March, 2019 from the following Trial Balance.

Illustration 2: The Closing Stock on 31st March was valued at ₹ 32,000.

Trial Balance

Heads of Accounts	Dr. (₹)	Cr. (₹)
Capital		29,000
Drawings	1,500	
Cash at Bank	1,450	
Purchases & Sales	22,000	39,000
Returns	2,000	1,000
Discount	200	
Carriage Outwards	600	
Salaries	6,000	
Trade Expenses	1,200	
Opening Stock	5,000	
Bad Debts	600	
Rent	1,500	
Machinery	36,000	
Furniture	8,000	
Debtors & Creditors	4,000	10,000
Stationery	2,500	
Commission		150
Bank Loan		13,400
	92,550	92,550

Trading A/c
for the year ended on 31st March, 2019

Particulars	Amount (₹)	Particulars	Amount (₹)
To Opening Stock	5,000	By Sales 39,000	37,000
To Purchases 22,000		Less: Returns 2,000	32,000
Less: Purchase Returns 1,000	21,000	By Closing Stock	
To Gross Profit transferred to Profit & Loss A/c	43,000		
	69,000		69,000

Profit & Loss A/c
for the year ended on 31st March, 2019

Particulars	Amount (₹)	Particulars	Amount (₹)
To Discount	200	By Gross Profit transferred from Trading A/c	43,000
To Carriage Outwards	600	By Commission	150
To Salaries	6,000		
To Trade Expenses	1,200		
To Bad Debts	600		
To Rent	1,500		
To Stationery	2,500		
To Net Profit transferred to Capital A/c	30,550		
	43,150		43,150

Balance Sheet
as on 31st March, 2019

Liabilities	Amount (₹)	Assets	Amount (₹)
Creditors	10,000	Cash at Bank	1,450
Bank Loan	13,400	Debtors	4,000
Capital 29,000		Closing Stock	32,000
Add: Net Profit 30,550		Furniture	8,000
59,550		Machinery	36,000
Less: Drawings 1,500	58,050		
	81,450		81,450

Difference Between Trial Balance and Balance Sheet

Basis of Difference	Trial Balance	Balance Sheet
Objectives	Trial balance is prepared with an objective to check mathematical accuracy of ledger.	Objective of balance sheet preparation is to ascertain financial position of the business.
Necessity	To prepare a trial balance is not necessary.	Preparation of balance sheet is essential to complete the accounting process.
Sides	It has debit and credit columns to show the amounts.	It has assets and liabilities sides.
Information of Profit or Loss	Trial balance does not provide any Information about profit or loss.	Information about net profit or loss can be obtained from the details of capital account shown in balance sheet.
Types of Accounts	It discloses balances of all types of accounts.	Balance of personal accounts and asset accounts are shown in it.
Display of Closing Stock	Generally, closing stock is not shown in it.	Closing stock is always shown in it.
Part of Final Accounts	Trial Balance is not a part of final accounts.	Balance sheet is a part of final accounts.
Closure of Accounts	Closure of accounts is not necessary for its preparation.	Closure of accounts is essential for its preparation.
Authenticity	Trial balance is not accepted as a proof in a court of law.	Balance sheet has got an authenticity from legal point of view.
Period	Trial balance can be prepared by trader a number of times during a year.	Balance sheet is generally prepared only at the end of the financial year.

Difference Between Trading and Profit & Loss Account and Balance Sheet

Basis of Difference	Trading and Profit & Loss Account	Balance Sheet
Objectives	Objective of preparation of trading and profit & loss account is to ascertain gross profit or loss and net profit or loss for a specific period.	Objective of preparation of balance sheet is to ascertain financial position of business on a particular date.

Sides	It has debit and credit sides.	It has assets and liabilities sides.
Nature	It is normal account.	It is a statement.
Use of 'To' and 'By'	Words 'To' and 'By' are used in it just as in other accounts.	Words 'To' and 'By' are not used in it.
Types of Accounts	Nominal accounts are shown in it.	Personal accounts and asset account are shown in it.
Order of Entry	There is no specific order to show the accounts in it.	It has two specific orders for dis-closure of assets and liabilities-liquidity order and permanence order.
Transfer of Balance	Balance of trading account is transferred to profit and loss account and that of profit & loss account is transferred to capital account.	Balance sheet does not have a balance. Totals of its both sides are equal.

LESSON AT A GLANCE

- **Final Accounts:** Every businessman wants to know whether he has earned a profit or suffered a loss during the accounting period and what is the financial position of business at the end of said accounting period. To obtain this information, final accounts are prepared which include (i) Trading account (ii) Profit and loss account (iii) Balance sheet.
- **Sole Proprietor:** Single owner of an unincorporated business.
- **Trading Account:** It is a summarised form of all transactions occurring during a trading period which have direct relation to the goods dealt in by the business. It is prepared for ascertaining the gross profit or gross loss.
- **Profit and Loss Account:** It is an account which shows the net result of the operations of an enterprise during the financial period. The main feature of a Profit and Loss Account is that it contains indirect gains and indirect expenses. It helps in ascertaining net profit or net loss from business operations, in an accounting year.
- **Balance Sheet:** It is a statement prepared with a view to measure the exact financial position of a business on a certain date. It is prepared from the Trial balance. In a Balance Sheet, the total of all assets and all liabilities must be equal.

Visit a trading organisation and record their process of accounting and preparation of final accounts.

ASSIGNMENT

You are a Chief Accountant of a company. How will you explain the importance of Trading and Profit and Loss Account and Balance Sheet to your colleagues of other departments?

QUESTIONS

A. **Short Answer Type Questions:**
1. What is trading account?
2. What is profit and loss account?
3. What is a balance sheet?
4. What are the characteristics of balance sheet?
5. Distinguish between liquidity preference and permanence preference.
6. What are fictitious assets?
7. Who is a sole trader?
8. What tax does a sole trader pay?
9. What are contingent liabilities?
10. What is current assets?
11. Distinguish between trading account and profit and loss account.
12. Distinguish between profit and loss account and a balance sheet.

B. **Essay Type Questions:**
1. Give the format of profit and loss account and trading account.
2. Give the format of a balance sheet.
3. Distinguish between profit and loss account and balance sheet.
4. Who is a sole proprietor?
5. Write a short note on trading account.
6. Explain the purpose of preparing final accounts.

C. **Numerical Problems:**
1. The following is the Trial Balance of A.B. Chandra as on 31st December 2019.

Trial Balance of A.B. Chandra
as on 31.12.2019

Particulars	Amount (Dr.)	Particulars	Amount (Cr.)
Cash in Hand	2,000	Discount Received	750
Drawings	2,800	Capital	40,000
Opening Stock (1-1-2018)	4,000	Purchases Returns	1,250
Wages	2,000	Sales	83,000
Cash at Bank	3,500	Creditors	15,000
Insurance	700	Bank Loan	10,000
Trade Expenses	1,200		

Furniture	20,000		
Buildings	61,000		
Salaries	5,000		
Discount Allowed	750		
Sales Returns	3,000		
Purchases	31,250		
Debtors	10,000		
Telephone Charges	1,000		
Bills Receivable	1,800		
Total	1,50,000		1,50,000

The closing stock was valued at ₹ 12,000.

You are required to prepare a Trading Account and a Profit and Loss Account for the year ending 31st December, 2019 and a Balance Sheet as on 31st December, 2019. [ICSE 2020]

2. The following is the Trial Balance of ABC Industries as on 31st December 2015.

Trial Balance of ABC Industries
as on 31.12.2015

Particulars	Amount (Dr.)	Particulars	Amount (Cr.)
Salaries	4,000·00	Sales	83,000·00
Cash Balance	2,000·00	Rent Received	2,000·00
Bank Balance	3,000·00	Purchases Returns	1,000·00
Wages	1,500·00	Creditors	7,000·00
Insurance	500·00	Capital Account	25,000·00
Trade Expenses	7,000·00		
Discount Allowed	750·00		
Opening Stock (1.1.2015)	5,000·00		
Buildings	40,000·00		
Furniture	15,000·00		
Sales Returns	250·00		
Drawings	1,000·00		
Debtors	5,000·00		
Purchases	30,000·00		
Legal Charges	1,000·00		
Advertisement Expenses	2,000·00		
Total	1,18,000·00		1,18,000·00

The closing stock was valued at ₹ 9,000.

You are required to prepare a Trading Account and a Profit and Loss Account for the year ending 31st December 2015 and a Balance Sheet as on 31st December, 2015. [ICSE 2019]

3. The Trial Balance given below was prepared by Pratim Pal on 31st December, 2000.

   Prepare a Trading Account and a Profit and Loss Account for the year ending 31st December, 2000 and Balance Sheet as on 31st December, 2000.

Trial Balance

	Dr. (₹)		Cr. (₹)
Drawings Account	1,000.00	Capital Account	14,400.00
Premises	7,500.00	Sales	23,120.00
Fixtures and Fittings	1,560.00	Discount Received	330.00
Opening Stock (1.1.2000)	2,730.00	Purchase Returns	730.00
Purchases	15,410.00	Sundry Creditors	1,700.00
Discount Allowed	580.00		
Sales Returns	1,020.00		
Rates	750.00		
Insurance	210.00		
Wages	1,250.00		
Trade Expenses	960.00		
Sundry Debtors	2,310.00		
Cash in Hand	650.00		
Cash at Bank	2,350.00		
Salaries	2,000.00		
	40,280.00		40,280.00

Closing stock was valued at ₹ 3,140.00 on 31st December, 2000.

4. The value of stock on 31st December, 2014 was ₹ 14,920. [ICSE 2018]

   Prepare a Trading Account and a Profit and Loss Account for the year ended 31st December, 2014 and a Balance Sheet as at that date in the books of ABC enterprises.

Trial Balance

	Dr. (₹)		Cr. (₹)
Drawings Account	7,000.00	Capital Account	90,000.00
Purchases	82,210.00	Purchase Return	4,240.00
Sales Return	1,820.00	Sales	1,49,840.00
Opening Stock	11,460.00	Discount	180.00
Salaries	6,280.00	Sundry Creditors	16,980.00
Wages	8,560.00		
Leasehold Premises	25,000.00		
Rent, Rates and Insurance	6,940.00		
Carriage Inward	2,310.00		

Office Expenses	9,520.00		
Plant and Machinery	24,000.00		
Light and Water	7,950.00		
Bills Receivable	1,240.00		
Sundry Debtors	38,970.00		
Cash at Bank	12,400.00		
Cash in Hand	2,210.00		
Office Furniture	3,500.00		
Travelling Expenses	9,870.00		
	2,61,240.00		2,61,240.00

[ICSE 2017]

5. Prepare a Trading, Profit & Loss A/c and Balance Sheet of Mr. A. Haridas for the year ended 31st March, 1980 from the following Trial Balance.
The Closing Stock on 31.03.80 was valued at ₹ 40,000.

Trial Balance

	Dr. (₹)	Cr. (₹)
Capital		1,55,000
Drawings	9,000	
Trade Expenses	12,000	
Cash in Hand	750	
Cash at Bank	22,700	
Land & Buildings	1,30,000	
Stock as on 1-4-79	35,000	
Purchases & Sales	75,000	2,50,000
Returns	2,800	2,000
Carriage Inwards	1,500	
Carriage Outwards	3,500	
Debtors & Creditors	48,000	25,000
Bills Receivables & Bills Payables	22,000	10,500
Furniture & Fixtures	15,400	
Discount Allowed	1,500	
Wages	25,000	
Salaries	19,850	
Advertisement	15,000	
Rent, Rates & Taxes	3,500	
	4,42,500	4,42,500

[ICSE 2016]

CHAPTER-11
Fundamental Concept of Costs

COST

'Cost' means the money expenditure incurred by the producer to purchase (or hire) factors of production and raw materials to produce goods and service.

Cost, in a way, is a sacrifice made by the producer, *i.e.*, sacrifice in terms of making payments such as wages to labourers, rent for use of land etc.

In broad terms, cost has been defined by AICPA as, *"Cost is the amount measured in money or cash expended or other property transferred, capital stock issued, services performed or a liability incurred in consideration of goods or services received or to be received."*

- *Meaning of Cost*
- *Elements of Cost*
- *Elements of Total Cost*
- *Classification of Costs*
- *Expenses excluded from Costs*
- *Cost Centre*
- *Cost Unit*

Thus, cost is the aggregate amount spent in producing a product or rendering a service; taking together all elements of it.

The accounting 'cost' figures are useful to meet the legal, financial and tax needs of the firm but are not directly helpful to the management in the decision making process. Normally, the management uses the concept of cost :

1. To fix the price of a product for a prospective buyer;
2. To find out whether a particular investment should or should not be made;
3. To determine the profit of the firm;
4. To estimate the amount of dividend, a firm would like to pay to the shareholders; and
5. To estimate additional cost that would be incurred if the firm accepts a large order for its products.

Elements of Cost

Cost of production consists of various expenses incurred on production of goods or services. These are the elements of cost, which can be divided into three groups (i) Material (ii) Labour and (iii) Expenses. All the three elements are further divided into two categories: (a) Direct and (b) Indirect. The direct cost is also known as Prime Cost which is a sum of Direct Material, Direct Labour and Direct Expenses. Indirect cost is known as Overheads.

The elements of cost may be depicted as:

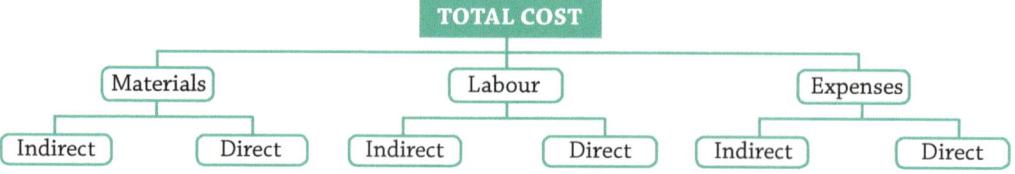

The terms given above are discussed below:

1. Material Cost:

Substances which can be identified in the product and can be conveniently measured and directly charged to the product, are called materials. In simple terms, substances from which the products are made are known as materials. The cost of commodities purchased by an organisation to manufacture or finish the product, is known as Material Cost.

Thus, materials directly enter into the process of production in a raw state or in a manufactured state and form a part of the finished product. For example, timber in furniture making, bricks in building a house are materials.

(a) **Direct Materials:** Direct materials are those materials which can be easily identified and related with specific product, job and process. The following are included in direct materials:
  (i) Any material specially purchased for manufacturing a particular item.
  (ii) Any material, semi-finished goods or components used in manufacturing a particular item.
  (iii) The primary packing materials. For example the bottle used in Pepsi or Coke is a direct material.

(b) **Indirect Materials:** Indirect materials are those materials which cannot be easily and conveniently identified and related with a particular product, job and process. For example, grease, oil, stationery, nails, small tools, brushes, etc.

2. Labour Cost:

Human efforts expended in altering the construction, composition, and condition of the product, is called labour. In simple words, it is that labour which can be conveniently identified or attributed wholly to a particular job, product or process. That is, human resources needed for conversion of raw materials into finished goods is termed as labour. Wages of such labour are known as direct wages.

The cost of remuneration paid to the workers, supervisors, factory manager of an organisation comes under this head.

(a) **Direct Labour:** Direct labour is referred to as one which can be easily identified and related to a specific product, job and process. Direct labour is easily traceable to specific products and varies directly with the volume of output. Wages paid to the carpenter in furniture industry is the example of direct labour. The following are included in direct labour:
  (i) Labour engaged in actual production of the product.
  (ii) Labour engaged in aiding manufacturing by supervision, maintenance, etc.
  (iii) Inspectors, analysts, etc. specially required for such production.

(b) **Indirect Labour:** Indirect labour refers to the one which cannot be easily identified and related with specific product, job and process. It includes all labour not directly engaged in converting raw material into finished product. It may or may not vary directly with the volume of output. The salaries paid to storekeeper, foremen, time-keeper, inspectors, etc., are the examples of indirect labour.

3. Expenses:

Expenses refer to all the cost incurred in the production of finished goods and services, other than the material cost and labour cost. It also refers to the cost of services provided to an organisation.

(a) Direct Expenses: Direct expenses are those expenses which can be identified with and allocated to cost centers or cost units. In simple terms, all direct costs, other than direct material and direct labour, are termed as direct expenses. Direct expenses are also called chargeable expenses. For example, hire charges of a special machinery or plant, experimental expenses, cost of patents, royalties, etc.

(b) Indirect Expenses: Indirect expenses are those which cannot be directly and wholly allocated to specific cost centre or cost units. In simple terms, all indirect costs, other than indirect material and indirect labour, are termed as indirect expenses. Indirect expenses are treated as part of overheads. They fall under three heads :

(i) Factory overheads: Indirect Material: For example, grease, oil, consumable stores, etc. Indirect Wages: For example, salary of storekeeper, etc., and Indirect Expenses : For example, power and fuel, carriage inwards, etc.

(ii) Office and Administrative Overheads: Indirect Material: For example, printing and stationery, postage, etc. Indirect Labour : For example, salaries of office managers, clerks, etc. Indirect Expenses: For example, office rent, legal expenses, etc.

(iii) Selling and Distribution overheads:Indirect Materials : For example, samples, catalogues, price list, etc. Indirect labour : For example, sales commission, etc. Indirect Expenses: For example, advertising, rent, bad debts, etc.

Elements of Total Cost—the alternate method

The total cost may be expressed in two terms :

(i) Total cost of production, or total cost of goods produced, and

(ii) Total cost of sales or total cost of goods sold.

The major components of total cost are as follows :

(1) Prime Cost:

It consists of three items:

(i) Direct Material, (ii) Direct Labour, and (iii) Direct Expenses.

All the three direct costs combined together make what is known as Prime Cost or Direct Cost or First Cost.

(2) Factory Cost:

It comprises the prime cost plus factory (or works) overheads or expenses. Factory expenses include indirect material, indirect labour and indirect factory expenses. This cost is also known as Works Cost or Manufacturing Cost or Production Cost.

(3) Office Cost:

It comprises factory cost plus office and administrative overheads or expenses. This is also called total cost of production or total cost of goods produced.

Fundamental Concept of Costs

(4) Selling and Distribution Cost:
It comprises office cost plus selling and distribution overheads or expenses. This is also called total cost or total cost of sales, or total cost of goods sold.

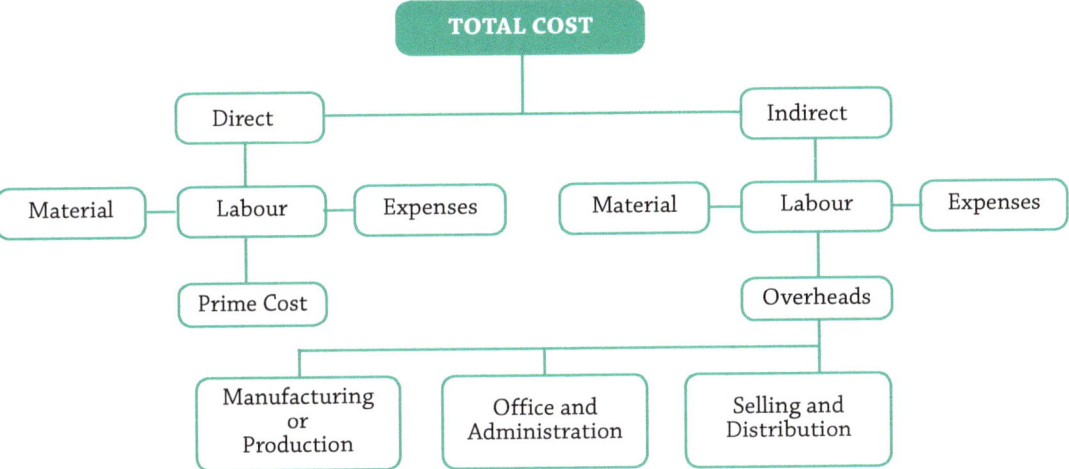

Classification of Costs

Apart from elements of cost, the costs can be classified by grouping them according to the following features :

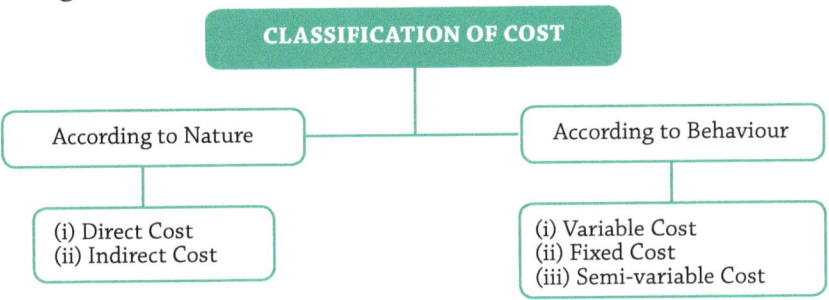

1. According to Nature

(A) Direct Costs:
Material, labour and other expenses which are directly or easily traceable to a product, service or job are known as direct cost. In the production of an article, materials are purchased, wages are paid to workers and certain other expenses are incurred directly. All these take an active and direct part in the manufacturing of a product and are, therefore, called direct cost. These costs have a direct relationship with a product, process or department of the firm and can be directly identified with a particular unit of output. For example, the cost of gravel, sand, cement and wages incured on the production of concrete.

Direct Costs include:
(i) Direct Material: All material which becomes an integral part of the finished product and which can be conveniently assigned to specific physical units of the finished product is known as direct material or process material.
(ii) Direct Labour: Labour which takes an active and direct part in the production of a particular commodity is known as direct labour. Direct labour costs are

specifically and conveniently traceable to specific products. Direct labour is also known as productive or operating labour.

(iii) Direct Productive Expenses: These are the expenses which can be directly, conveniently and wholly allocated to specific cost centers or cost units. Rent paid for hire of a special machine required for a particular contract, cost of defective work incurred in connection with a particular job, etc., are examples of direct expenses. These are also known as chargeable expenses.

(B) Indirect Costs:

Indirect costs refer to the expenses incurred on those items which are not directly chargeable to production. Salaries of timekeeper, storekeeper, foremen are examples of indirect costs. In the running of a particular train, cost of railway station and railway staff are indirect costs.

Indirect costs include:

(i) Indirect Material: All material which is used for ancillary purposes and which cannot be conveniently assigned to specific physical units is known as indirect material. Consumable stores, oil and waste, printing and stationery material, etc., are a few examples of indirect material. Such material may be used in the factory, office or selling and distribution division.

(ii) Indirect Labour: Labour employed for the purpose of carrying out tasks incidental to goods produced or services provided is indirect labour. Such labour does not alter the composition, construction or condition of the product. It cannot be easily traced to specific units of output. Wages of storekeepers, timekeepers, foremen, salesmen's salaries, directors' fees, etc., are examples of indirect labour costs.

(iii) Indirect Expenses: These are the expenses which cannot be directly, conveniently and wholly traced to a particular product. Rent, lighting, insurance charges, etc., are examples of indirect expenses.

The distinction between the direct costs and the indirect costs is important. Modern big firms are often multi product firms. Any decision to expand output or change the product mix affects the total costs in many ways. A producer will like to know the effect of his decision on costs so as to minimise costs and maximize profits. Different processes involved in production may have some common costs and changes in these processes may affect costs. Thus, traceability of costs is important to management for making decisions concerning pricing, marketing, addition and deletion of product lines, expansion of output, etc.

Distinction between Direct Costs and Indirect Costs

Basis of Distinction	Direct Costs	Indirect Costs
Meaning	Costs that are easily attributed to a cost object are called direct costs.	Costs that cannot be allocated to a particular cost object are called indirect costs.
Benefits	Specific projects.	Multiple projects.

Classification	Direct material, direct labour, direct expenses.	Indirect material, indirect labour, indirect expenses.
Aggregate	When all the direct costs are taken together, they are known as prime costs.	Total of all the indirect costs is called as overheads.
Traceable	Yes	No.
Behaviour	Direct costs tend to be variable costs.	Indirect costs are more likely to be either fixed costs or period costs.

Note : A cost object is something for which a cost is compiled, such as a product, service, customer, project, or activity.

2. According to Behaviour

(A) Variable Costs:

The costs which vary or change with change in the size of output are called variable costs. These are attributable to the use of variable inputs. Such costs increase or decrease in the same proportion in which the output changes *i.e.*, these costs increase, when output increases and decrease when output falls. That is why they are called direct cost, since they vary directly with the change in the level of output. In other words, variable costs are incurred so long as production continues but the moment production stops, variable costs also cease to exist. The costs incurred on raw material, power, fuel, wages of temporary labour, wear and tear of machines, etc., are examples of variable cost. For instance, when sugar mill is working, the mill owner has to incur costs on sugarcane, power, wages of temporary labour, etc. If production of sugar has to be increased, these costs will also increase and if production has to be decreased, these costs will also decrease. And if sugar mill closes, variable costs will also fall to zero.

Thus,   Total Cost = Total Fixed cost + Total Variable Cost

$$TC = TFC + TVC$$

(B) Fixed Costs:

Costs which are generally attributed to fixed factors of production, are called fixed costs. *These are the costs which do not change with the change in the size of output during short period.* These are primarily incurred on fixed factors like machines, building, etc. These are not related to the level or quantity of output in the short run. Production may come down to zero or be doubled, but fixed costs remain the same. These have to be borne even if no output is produced. For instance, a sugar mill usually remains closed for about 3 months during a year for want of raw material (sugarcane) but still the mill owner has to incur certain costs like rent of building, interest on past borrowings, salaries of permanent employees, municipal taxes, insurance premium etc. These costs are called fixed costs or *supplementary costs or overhead costs.* They remain the same during short period whether quantity of production is less or more or nil.

(C) Semi-variable Costs:

The costs which vary with every increase or decrease in the volume of production but do not vary proportionately are called as semi-variable costs. They also do not remain stationary at all times. Such costs contain fixed and variable elements. Because of the variable element, they fluctuate with volume and because of the fixed element they do not change in direct proportion to output. Semi- variable or semi-fixed costs change in the same direction as that of the output but not in the same proportion. Depreciation, repairs,, etc. are the examples of semi-variable costs.

EXPENSES EXCLUDED FROM COSTS

The total cost of a product should include only those items of expenses which are charge, against profit. Items of expenses, which relate to capital assets, capital losses, payments by way of distribution of profits, payments made for arranging finances, should not form a part of the costs. Examples of such expenses which are excluded from the costs are : interest paid on loans, depreciation, discounts, income tax, dividends, abnormal wastage, loss on sale of assets, discount on shares or debentures, interest on capital, expenses on raising of capital, preliminary expenses, underwriting commission, etc.

COST CENTRE

A cost centre is a location, person or item of equipment or group of these, for which costs may be ascertained and used for the purpose of cost control. A cost centre is the smallest organizational sub-unit for which separate cost allocation is sought or attempted. It is an individual activity or group of similar activities for which costs are accumulated or collected. Thus, cost centre refers to one of the convenient sub-units into which the whole company has been appropriately divided for costing purpose. Typically, cost centres are division, departments, sections, a machine, or a group of persons in a company. Thus if we identify all costs relating to marketing department and accumulate them to know its total cost, then marketing department is said to be a cost centre in this case. Similarly, the Production Manager or the Automatic Polythene Bags Machine can be cost centres.

COST UNIT

In preparing cost accounts, it becomes necessary to select a unit of measurement in terms of which expenditure may be identified. The quantity in terms of which cost can be conveniently allocated, is known as a cost unit or unit of cost. Thus, a cost unit may be defined as a unit of quantity of product or service or time in relation to which costs may be ascertained or expressed. Some examples of cost unit may be given as follows:

(a) Textile companies   –   Per metre of cloth manufactured or yarn spun
(b) Steel companies   –   Per tonne of steel manufactured
(c) Transport companies   –   Per passenger kilometer, or per tonne kilometer
(d) Electricity companies –   Per unit of electricity generated
(e) Coal mines   –   Per tonne of coal extracted
(f) Brick fields   –   Per 1,000 bricks made

(g) Machines   –   Per hour of use
(h) Labour   –   Per hour of employment.

Lesson at a Glance

- **Cost:** Cost, in common terminology, means the 'price paid for something'. According to AICPA, "Cost is the amount measured in money or cash expended or other property transferred, capital stock issued, services performed or a liability incurred, in consideration of goods or services received or to be received." Thus, cost is the aggregate amount spent in producing a product or rendering a service taking together all elements of it.
- **Elements of Cost:** There are basically three elements of cost: (i) Material (ii) Labour (iii) Expenses. All these three elements are further divided into two categories : (a) Direct (b) Indirect.
- **Material Cost:** (i) Direct Materials; (ii) Indirect Materials.
- **Labour Cost:** The cost of human efforts expended in altering the construction, composition, confirmation or condition of the product, is called labour cost. The cost of remuneration paid to the workers, supervisors and factory manager of an organisation, comes under this head. It includes : (i) Direct Labour; (ii) Indirect Labour.
- **Expenses:** All costs incurred other than the material and labour costs for a particular product or process, are called expenses. This includes: (i) Direct Expenses; (ii) Indirect Expenses.
- **Elements of Total cost:** (i) Prime cost; (ii) Factory Cost; (iii) Office cost; (iv) Selling and distribution cost.
- **Classification of Costs:**
  - *According to Nature:* (i) Direct Costs; (ii) Indirect Costs.
  - *According to Behaviour:* (i) Variable Costs; (ii) Fixed Costs; (iii) Semi-Variable Costs.

Visit an organisation which is into manufacturing business and find out the components of the total cost of one of its products. For this you will require the details about raw materials being used, the method and cost of procurement, consumption pattern and labour employed, besides cost of fuel, electricity, rent of building, etc. Please take necessary guidance from your subject teacher and prepare cost sheet for that product. Compare with its selling price and find out margin of profit.

Explain to your friend who does not have Commercial Studies as his subject, the various types of costs.

QUESTIONS

A. Short Answer Type Questions:
1. Define the term 'Cost'.
2. Define fixed costs of a firm. Give examples.
3. What are overheads?
4. Name the elements of cost.
5. Define variable costs of a firm. Give examples.
6. What is direct cost?
7. What do you understand by indirect cost?
8. What is meant by cost centre?
9. Name the expenses which are excluded from costs.
10. What is meant by labour costs?
11. Distinguish between Direct costs and Indirect costs. [ICSE 2017]
12. Distinguish between variable cost and semi-variable costs.
13. What do you mean by 'Indirect Material'? Give two examples. [ICSE 2018]
14. What is fixed cost? [ICSE 2020]
15. What do you mean understand by 'semi variable cost'? [ICSE 2019]
    OR
    What is semi-variable cost? Give one example. [ICSE 2017]

B. Essay Type Questions:
1. Discuss the various elements of cost.
2. "The term 'cost' must be qualified according to its context." Discuss this statement referring to important concepts of cost.
3. Explain different components of direct costs and indirect costs.
4. Write notes on:
   (i) Variable costs
   (ii) Fixed costs
   (iii) Semi-variable costs
5. What is cost? Discuss the components of total cost.
6. Differentiate between direct cost and indirect cost.
7. Explain with an example for each, the meaning of fixed costs and variable costs.

CHAPTER-12
Budgeting

BUDGET

Budget is a forecast of the financial activities of the business to achieve certain specific purpose, over a specified time period. In short, budget is an estimate of the future receipts and payments. It is compiled and re-evaluated on a periodic basis. Budgets can be prepared for a person, a family, a group of people, a business, a government, a country, a multinational organisation etc.

- Budget
- Forecast
- Comparison between Budgeting and Forecasting
- Types of Budget
- Utility of Budget
- Limitations of Budget

Kotler defines budget as:

(i) Any financial plan serving as an estimate of and a control over future operations.

(ii) Hence, any estimate of future costs.

(iii) Any systematic plan for the utilisation of manpower, material or other resources.

According to Chartered Institute of Management Accountants, London, Budget can be defined as:

- "A financial and/or quantitative statement, prepared prior to a defined period of time, of the policy to be pursued during that period for the purpose of attaining a given objective."

A budget, thus, is an estimate of expenditure, revenue and resources, over a specified time period, providing a reading of future financial conditions and goals.

The essential features of a budget are as follows:

1. It is a statement expressed in monetary and/or physical units prepared for the implementation of policy formulated by the management.
2. It is laid down prior to the budget period during which it is followed.
3. It is prepared for the definite future period.
4. The policy to be followed to attain the given objective must be laid before the budget is prepared.

FORECAST

A forecast is an assessment of probable future events. That is, it is an act of predicting business activity for a future period of time, based upon specific assumptions. At planning stage, it is necessary to prepare forecasts of probable course of action for the business in future. Budget is a sort of commitment or a target which the management seeks to attain on the basis of the forecasts made. Forecasts are made regarding sales, production cost and financial requirements of the business. A forecast denotes some degree of flexibility while a budget denotes a definite target.

Difference Between Budgeting and Forecasting

Basis of Comparison	Budget	Forecast
Meaning	It shows the policy and program to be followed in future period under planned conditions.	It is a mere estimate of what is likely to happen. It is a statement of probable events which are likely to happen under anticipated conditions during a specified period of time.
Time Period	It is usually planned separately for each accounting period.	It may cover a long period or years.
Functional Area Covered	It comprises the whole business unit. Sectional budgets are coordinated into a logical whole.	It may cover a limited function or activity of business as sales forecast.
Target	Budget sets target.	There are no targets.
Control	It acts as an instrument of control by providing standards for evaluating performance.	Forecasting, being statements of future events, do not connote any sense of control.
Updation	Annual basis	At regular intervals.
Estimates	What business wants to achieve.	What business will achieve.
Order	It begins when forecasting ends. Forecasts are converted into budgets.	Forecasting is a preliminary step for budgeting. It ends with the forecast of likely events.
Scope	It has limited scope. It can only be made of phenomenon capable of being expressed quantitatively.	It has a wider scope, since it can be made in those spheres also where budgets cannot interfere.
Variance Analysis	The budget is compared to actual results to determine variances from expected performance.	There is no variance analysis that compares the forecast to actual results.

TYPES OF BUDGET

1. Sales Budget

The sales budget is the most important budget and forms the base of all other budgets. The sales budget is a forecast of total sales, expressed in terms of money and quantity. The first step in the preparation of the sales budget is to forecast as accurately as possible the sales anticipated during the budget period. The sales budget is based on sales forecasting which is the responsibility of the sales manager and market research staff. The sales budget is regarded as the pivotal point of budgeting.

Sales forecasts are influenced by a variety of factors, external as well as internal. They are:

(a) Past Sales Figures and Trends:
As the past performance is based on actual business conditions, the record of previous year's sales and their trend is the most reliable basis of the future sales.

(b) Salesmen's Estimates:
The estimates of the sales received from salesmen should be considered while preparing sales budget because being in direct contact with customers, their estimates are more accurate.

(c) Availability of Raw Materials and Other Supplies:
Adequate supply of raw materials and other supplies should be ensured before preparing the sales estimates. Sales estimates should be adjusted according to the availability of raw material, if the raw materials are in short supply.

(d) General Trade Prospects:
General prospects of trade or industry affects the sales probability of the firm. Trade journals, papers or magazines can provide valuable information in this regard.

(e) Orders in Hand:
Value of orders in hand and booked, have considerable influence on the amount of sales to be budgeted.

(f) Seasonal Fluctuations:
Special concessions and off-season discounts should be used as measures to minimise the effects of seasonal fluctuations on sales.

(g) Competition:
To have a realistic sales budget the nature and degree of competition prevailing in the industry should be taken into consideration while preparing sales budget.

(h) Miscellaneous Considerations:
Other considerations, such as advertising, production, government intervention, import possibility, product profitability etc., should also be kept in view.

2. Production Cost Budget

The production cost budget is a forecast of the production for the budget period. It is prepared in two parts, viz., production volume budget for the physical units of the products to be manufactured and the cost of manufacturing budget detailing the budgeted costs. The main steps involved in the preparation of a production budget are production planning; consideration of capacity; integration with sales forecasts; inventory-policies; management's overall policies. The operation of a production budget results in various advantages, major being optimum utilisation of productive resources of the enterprise, production of goods according to schedule enabling the firm to adhere to delivery dates, proper scheduling of factors of production. The Works Manager is responsible for the total production budget and the Departmental

Managers are responsible for the departmental production budget. While preparing the production budget, the following five questions are to be answered:

(i) What is to be produced?
(ii) When is to be produced?
(iii) How is to be produced?
(iv) Where is to be produced?
(v) How much is to be produced?

The material, labour and plant requirements should be ascertained to have the desired production to meet the sales programme.

Production cost budget is prepared to answer the above questions, to plan and organise production programme and to prepare a cash forecast.

Production forecasts are influenced by a variety of factors, which are as follows:

(a) Sales Requirements:
The quantity of goods to be produced will depend mainly on the quantity of goods to be sold in the market. Therefore, sales requirements will mainly decide the production budget.

(b) Inventory Policy:
Inventory levels influence the output. Therefore, inventory levels should be decided in advance so that neither there is shortage of goods nor overstocking of goods.

(c) Plant Capacity:
The maximum quantity of goods that can be produced depends upon the available plant capacity. Production should be evenly distributed throughout the year so as to ensure better utilisation of plant facilities and to reduce costs.

(d) Time Taken in Production Process:
Production process should be started well in time, keeping in view the time taken in the factory to convert the raw materials into finished goods.

3. Cash Budget

Cash budget is an estimate of cash receipts and payments. Working capital is required to meet the day-to-day requirements of the business. These cash requirements are met out of cash sales, amount collected from debtors and from other receipts. Cash is also received from non-trading receipts, such as sales of fixed assets, issue of shares and debentures, increase in loans and from other non-regular sources. These cash proceeds are used to meet various trading expenses which include cash purchases of goods, payment to creditors and payment of manufacturing, selling and distribution expenses. Non-trading expenses include purchase of fixed assets, redemption of debentures, payment of loans and payment of taxes and dividend. Cash budget may be both short-term and long-term. Cash budget in this way anticipates future cash requirements and makes arrangement of the requisite cash. It is a recorded plan of the financial operations of the business expressed in quantitative terms.

Objectives of Cash Budget: The main objectives of preparing cash budget are as follows:

(a) The probable cash position as a result of planned operation is indicated and thus, the excess or shortage of cash is known. This helps in arranging short-term borrowings in advance to meet the situations of shortage of cash or making investments in times of cash in excess.

(b) Cash can be coordinated in relation to total working capital, sales investment and debt.

(c) The effect of sudden and seasonal requirements, large stocks, delay in collection of receipts etc., on the cash position of the organisation is revealed.

4. Purchase Budget

A purchase budget is an estimate of the amount of inventory that a company must purchase during each budget period. The amount stated in the budget is the amount needed to ensure that there is sufficient inventory on hand to meet customer orders for products. Therefore, the amount stated in the budget should match the exact number of units expected to be sold in the budget period.

The budget outlines the cost of inventory in terms of current and future inventory levels. Determining the value of the company inventory enables the business owners to allocate the cash required to purchase materials. It also enables the company to prepare for increase or change in product lines or for new product launches.

Purchase forecasts are influenced by a variety of factors, which are as follows:

(a) Inventory Levels:

If there are considerable number of units on hand at the beginning of the budget period, the number of units to be purchased will have to be reduced. Therefore, inventory levels should be known in advance so that neither there is shortage of goods nor overstocking of goods.

(b) Service Levels:

If management wants to keep more units on hand to meet short-term customer needs, it may be necessary to increase the number of units purchased. A purchase budget should take this into account.

(c) Product Termination:

If a product line has to be terminated, a purchase budget should reflect the number of units needed through the termination date.

5. Master Budget

Master budget is a consolidated summary of the various functional budgets. According to C.I.M.A. London, a master budget is "the summary budget incorporating its component functional budgets and which is finally approved, adopted and employed". It is the culmination of the preparation of all other budgets, like the sales budget, production budget, purchase budget etc. It consists in reality the budgeted profit and loss account, the balance sheet and the budgeted funds flow statement.

The master budget is prepared by the budget committee on the basis of coordinated functional budgets and becomes the target of the company during the budget period when it is finally approved. This budget acts as the company's individualised key to successful financial planning and control. It provides the basis of computing the effect of any changes in any phase of operations, such as sales volume, product mix, prices, labour costs, material costs or change in facilities. It segregates income, costs and profits by areas of responsibility. Master budget presents all this information to the depth appropriate for the top management action.

In the master budget, costs are classified and summarised by types of expenses as well as by departments. This information extends the range of usefulness of the master budget. It is considered as the best mode of understanding the company's micro-economic position relating to the forthcoming budget period. The figures, that it contains, are the reflection of the actual intentions of the company relating to different areas for the forthcoming budget period.

UTILITY OF BUDGET

Budget expresses plans in terms of physical units or monetary units, and provides target to be achieved. It is not only essential for large business undertakings or Government of the country but also for a very small business unit or a family, to ensure long term financial security, Planning and foresight. Thus, budget is the integral part of planning strategy.

The following points enumerate the utility of a budget:

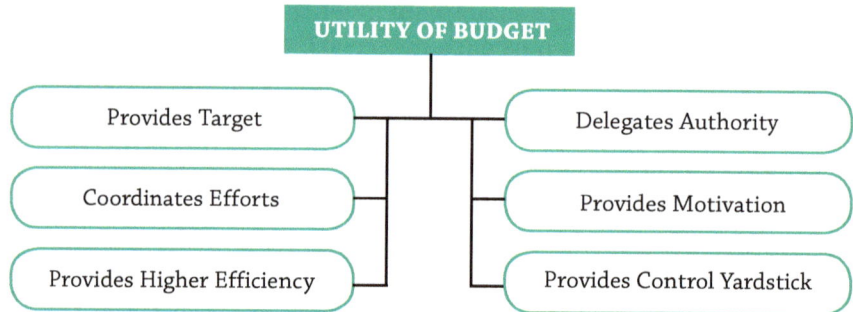

1. Provides Target:
A budget fixes the target in physical and financial terms. This helps the managers to understand their responsibilities precisely, by which they can take decisions to attain the set targets. This prevents the use of discretionary power by which the managers would have wasted resources and time.

2. Coordinates Efforts:
A budget helps to coordinate the efforts of various divisions and departments. It is possible to fix the divisional or departmental targets so that all divisions or departments may work harmoniously.

3. Provides Higher Efficiency:
A budget brings efficiency and economy in the working of an enterprise. It helps the management to achieve the most profitable combination of different factors of production. Budget also establishes divisional and departmental responsibility.

4. Delegates Authority:
A budget allows delegation of authority without loss of control. It permits participation of employees at all levels. According to KOONTZ and O' DONNELL, "reduction of plans to definite numbers, forces a kind of orderliness that permits the managers to see clearly what capital will be spent by whom, and where, and what expense, revenue or units of physical input or output his plans will involve. Having ascertained this, the manager can more freely delegate authority to effect the plan within the limits of the budget. Budget is somewhat a democratic way of managing."

5. Provides Motivation:
A budget represents the goals to be achieved. It tells the management what efforts and results are expected out of them. It motivates them to work hard in order to achieve the target represented by the budget. Budget works as a source of motivation to people.

6. Provides Control Yardstick:
A budget fixes control yardsticks. Performance of various managers, divisions and departments is evaluated, against the budget. This is done by finding out the difference between the budgets and actuals and analysing the results thereof.

LIMITATIONS OF BUDGET
Although Budget offers multiple advantages, it has few limitations, which are listed below:

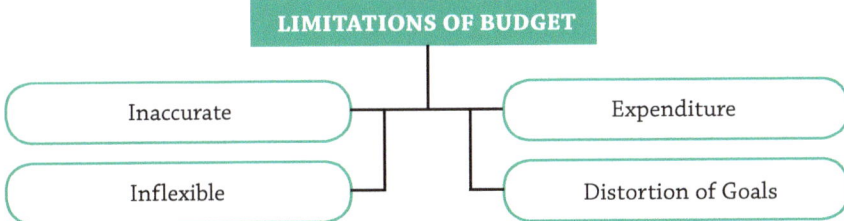

1. Inaccurate:
Forecasts, projections and historical trends form the base of budget making. But as forecasts may not be absolutely correct and trends may not repeat, budgets may prove to be inaccurate. The budgets estimates may become meaningless in the state of inflation or depression in the market.

2. Inflexible:
Many-a-times budgets are prepared in such a detailed way that their flexibility ends and they become cumbersome. Rigidity is caused by over-budgeting and managers are deprived of the freedom and flexibility in dealing and managing their departments.

3. Expenditure:
Budget-making process involves a lot of expenditure in terms of time, money and efforts. Preparation of various kinds of budgets is a difficult task for the management.

4. Distortion of Goals:
Sometimes, the limits in budgets are treated as hard marked lines by the management. People become extra cautious to function within the boundaries of budget figures. As such goals of the organisation may be overlooked.

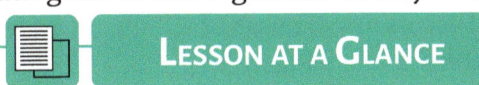

LESSON AT A GLANCE

- **Meaning of Budget:** Budget is a forecast of the financial activities of the business to achieve certain specific purpose. It is an estimate of the future receipts and payments.
- **Classification or Types of Budget:** (i) Sales Budget; (ii) Production Cost Budget; (iii) Cash Budget; (iv) Purchase Budget, (v) Master Budget.

- **Utility of Budgets:** (i) Provides Target; (ii) Co-ordinates Efforts; (iii) Provides Higher Efficiency; (iv) Delegates Authority; (v) Provides Motivation; (vi) Provides Control Yardstick.
- **Limitations of Budgets:** (i) Inaccurate; (ii) Inflexible; (iii) Expenditure; (iv) Distortion of goals.

Project Work

1. Prepare a Budget for expenditure on your studies in the coming year.
2. Prepare a Budget for the month, in respect of your family. Based on the monthly salary of your parent, find out likely expenditures of various items—quantity and cost of each.

Assignment

Explain to your family members (other than father) about the relevance of Budgets and their utility in planning.

Questions

A. Short Answer Type Questions:

1. Define the term 'Budget'.
2. What is a master budget?
3. Give any three benefits of budgets.
4. State two limitations of budgets.
5. Give a list of any four functional budgets.
6. Distinguish between production budget and master budget.
7. Distinguish between Budget and Forecast.
8. What is a Budget? [ICSE 2020]
9. Explain 'Sales Budget'. [ICSE 2019]
10. Why is 'Master Budget' also known as summary budget? [ICSE 2019]
11. Mention any two utilities of a budget. [ICSE 2018]

B. Essay Type Questions:

1. Explain the main types of budgets used in business enterprises.
2. Discuss the advantages and limitations of budget.
3. What do you understand by master budget?
4. What is a Budget? Discuss any six uses of a Budget to a business enterprise.
5. Describe any five utilities of a budget.
6. Briefly explain any five types of budget.
7. "Budgets are useful for management". Justify.

CHAPTER-13
Sources of Finance

Economic development of any country depends upon the existence of a well organized financial market. It is the financial market which supplies necessary financial inputs for the production of goods and services in a country, which in turn, promotes the well being and standard of living of the people.

- Financial Market
- Capital Market
- Functions of Capital Market
- Sources of Raising Capital
- Difference between Shares & Debentures

FINANCIAL MARKET

A financial market is a market where financial assets and financial liabilities are bought and sold. Financial markets perform the essential economic function of channelising funds from savers, who have an excess of funds to business firms and governments, who have shortage of funds.

Financial markets may be classified into two types: Capital Market and Money Market.

(i) Capital Market:
Capital market deals in the lending and borrowing of long term finance. Thus, capital market is a market for financial assets which have a maturity period of more than one year. Capital Market caters to the long-term credit needs of the industrialists and provides fixed capital to buy land, machinery, etc. The main instruments used in capital market are Stocks, Shares, Debentures, Bonds etc and the important institutions operating in a capital market are stock exchanges, commercial banks and non-banking institutions, such as insurance companies, mortgage banks, etc.

(ii) Money Market:
Money market deals in the lending and borrowing of short-term finance. Thus, money market is a market for financial assets of short term nature, that is, which have a maturity period of upto one year. Money market meets the short-term credit needs of businesses by providing working capital to the industrialists. Main credit instruments used in Money Market are commercial bills, commercial papers and bills of exchange. Money Market instruments have the characteristics of liquidity (quick conversion into money), minimum transaction cost and no loss in value. Important institutions operating in the Money Market are central banks, commercial banks, acceptance houses, non-banking financial institutions etc.

CAPITAL MARKET

Capital market is a financial market where buyers and sellers engage in trade of financial securities of long term nature like shares, debentures etc. A capital market comprises of a number of institutions and mechanisms through which medium term funds and long term funds are pooled and are made available to individuals, businesses, and governments for use in productive ventures. An efficient and well organised capital market is essential for raising capital by the corporate sector of the economy and for the protection of the interest of investors in financial securities.

The capital market has two interdependent and inseparable segments, namely, the primary market and the secondary market.

1. Primary Market:
It refers to a market where new securities are bought and sold for the first time. In other words, the market wherein resources are mobilised by companies through issue of new securities is called the primary market. These resources are required for new projects as well as for existing projects for expansion, modernisation, diversification and upgradation. Thus, primary market is the market where companies issue their Initial Public Offerings (IPOs). First public offering of equity shares and other securities by a company followed by the listing of the company's shares on a stock exchange is known as initial public offering (IPO).

It is through the primary market that funds flow for productive purposes from savers (lenders) to entrepreneurs and business firms (borrowers). The latter use the funds for creating new products and rendering services to the customers.

2. Secondary Market:
Secondary Market refers to a market where securities are traded after being initially offered to the public in the primary market and/or listed on the stock exchange. Majority of the trading is done in the Secondary Market. It can be stated that secondary markets consist of stock exchanges and over the counter markets. In the secondary markets, securities are traded, cleared and settled within the regulatory framework prescribed by the Securities and Exchange Board of India (SEBI).

Functions of Capital Market

1. Acts as a link between Savers and Investors:
Capital Market is composed of those who demand funds (borrowers) and those who supply funds (savers and lenders). Transfer of resources from those with surplus funds (that is, households and individuals) to others with deficiency of funds (that is, investors and entrpreneurs) and in productive need for them, is perhaps the most crucial function of capital market. Thus, capital markets acts as a linking pin between savers and investors. Healthy, efficient and transparent functioning of the capital market is therefore imperative for industrialisation and economic development of a country.

2. Encouragement to Saving:
Efficient and well functioning capital markets provide good returns and enhance profitability of the investments. This encourages people to save and invest more. In the absence of a capital market, there are very little savings and those who save often invest their savings in unproductive activities, for example, in buying gold, land, luxury items etc.

3. Encouragement to Investment:
Capital markets facilitate lending to the business firms and the Government and thus encourage investment. They provide an investment avenue to people who wish to invest resources for a long period of time. Instruments such as bond, equities, mutual funds, insurance policies, etc. provide diverse investment avenues and suitable interest rate returns to the public. With the development of capital markets, funds become more accessible and therefore, investment increases.

4. Promotes Economic Growth:
Capital Market not only reflects the general condition of the economy, but also smoothens and accelerates the process of economic growth. Various institutions of the capital market allocate resources rationally in accordance with the development needs of the country. Proper allocation of resources results in the expansion of trade and industry in both public and private sectors, thus promoting balanced economic growth in the country.

5. Stability in Security Prices:
Capital Market tends to stabilise the values of stocks and securities and reduce the fluctuations in the prices to the minimum. The process of stabilisation is facilitated by providing capital to the borrowers at a lower interest rate and reducing the speculative and unproductive activities.

6. Benefits the Investors:
Capital markets bring together buyers and sellers of securities and thus ensure the marketability of investments. By advertising security prices, they enable the investors to keep track of their investments and channelise them into most profitable lines. It is also responsible for safeguarding the interests of the investors by compensating them from the Stock Exchange Compensating Fund in the event of fraud and default.

SOURCES OF RAISING CAPITAL
Sources of raising capital refer to the mediums through which an organization raises funds for its long-term capital requirements and for meeting working capital needs. Capital can be raised in two ways, namely, through long-term sources of finance and through short- term sources of finance.

1. Long-term Sources of Finance:
Long-term financing means capital requirements for a period of more than 5 years. Capital expenditures of a business in fixed assets like plant and machinery, land and building etc. are generally funded using long-term sources of finance. Part of working capital which permanently stays with the business is also financed through long-term sources of finance. Long-term financing sources can be in the form of Shares, Debentures, Term Loans from Financial Institutions and Commercial Banks ,Venture Funding , etc.

(a) Shares:
The total capital of a company is divided into convenient units of equal value and each unit is called a share. Shares represent the interest of a shareholder in the company and attach various rights and liabilities to the shareholder. It is an

invisible unit of capital which expresses the relationship of ownership between each shareholder and the company. The shareholders are also part owners of the company. There are two types of shares–Equity Shares and Preference Shares.

(i) Equity Shares:

Equity shares, commonly referred to as ordinary shares, represents the form of fractional ownership in which a shareholder, as a fractional owner, undertakes the maximum entrepreneurial risk associated with a business venture. Equity shareholders get dividend only after the holders of preference shares receive their share of profit because of which the rate of dividend received by the equity shareholders is not fixed. The holders of such shares are the members of the company and have voting rights.

(ii) Preference Shares:

Preference shares are those shares which carry a preferential right over equity shares in the case of distribution of dividend and repayment of capital in the event of winding up of a company. They generally carry a fixed rate of dividend and are redeemable after specific period of time. However, preference shareholders do not have voting rights in a company.

(b) Debentures:

Debentures are medium to long term debt instruments, used to borrow money at a fixed rate of interest. They are issued by a company as a certificate of its indebtedness and they establish the fact that the company has to pay a specified amount with interest to the debentureholder. Debentures usually indicate the date of redemption and also provides for the repayment of principal and payment of interest at specified dates. They, however, create a charge on the assets of the company. If the company does not pay interest or if it does not repay the principal amount, the lenders may take action against the company to realise their dues by sale of the assets earmarked as security for the debt.

Difference Between Shares and Debentures

Basis of Difference	Shares	Debentures
Meaning	Shares are the owned funds of the company and represent the capital of the company.	Debentures are the borrowed funds of the company and rep-resent the debt of the company.
Holder	The holder of shares is known as shareholder.	The holder of debentures is known as debentureholder.
Status of Holders	Owners	Creditors
Form of Return	Shareholders get dividend	Debentureholders get interest.
Payment of Return	Dividend can be paid to shareholders only out of profits	Interest has to be paid to debentureholders even if there is no profit.

Voting Rights	The holders of shares have voting rights.	The holders of debentures do not have any voting rights.
Repayment of Capital in the Event of Winding up.	Shareholders are repaid after the payment of all the liabilities and debt.	Debentureholders get priority over shares, so they are repaid before shareholders.
Conversion	Shares can never be converted into debentures.	Debentures can be converted into shares.

2. Short-term Sources of Finance:

Short-term financing means financing for a period of less than one year. Short-term finance may be needed to finance the working capital requirements of a business like for buying inventory of raw material and finished goods, for paying debtors, to maintain minimum cash and bank balance etc. Thus, short term financing is also termed as working capital financing. Short term finances are available in the form of cash credit, overdraft facilities from commercial banks, discounting of bills etc., Fixed Deposits for a period of 1 year or less, Advances received from customers etc.

(a) Cash Credit:

Cash Credit is an arrangement by which a bank advances cash loans of a specified limit to the customers against a bond or other securities. When the cash loan is granted, the borrower opens a current account with that amount in the bank. The borrower has the right to withdraw the full amount of loan. Interest is charged on the amount actually utilised by the borrower and not on the whole amount granted to him.

(b) Credit Draft or Overdraft:

A Commercial Bank allows the facility of overdraft only to its depositors who have current accounts in the bank. Under this arrangement, a depositor is allowed to withdraw more than what he has deposited. But, this extra withdrawal has to be repaid by the customer within a short period, along with the interest charged by the bank on the extra amount withdrawn. The rate of this interest may be somewhat more than the interest rate charged on loans. Banks, however, give overdraft facility only on the security of some assets or on the personal security of the customer.

(c) Discounting of Bills:

Banks provide financial help to their customers (the business-men, the merchants, the exporters etc.) by way of discounting their bills of exchange.

A bill of exchange is an instrument in writing containing an unconditional order, signed by the maker, directing a certain person to pay a certain sum of money only to the bearer of the instrument.

When a customer (say, an exporter) comes to the bank with a bill of exchange, the bank pays him the amount of the bill after deducting the usual discount (interest) charges. The bank, thus assists its merchant customers considerably by accepting their bills of exchange and by providing them cash in return to meet their short term capital requirements. After a few months or weeks, when the bill matures (a bill generally matures in 90 days), the bank presents it to the Acceptor (say, an importer) and gets back its full amount. In this case, a bill of exchange is of great benefit, both to the importer and the exporter. By using bill of exchange, the exporter gets the amount from the bank and the importer does not have to pay anything to the exporter immediately. Importer pays the amount only when he has funds in his hands. In case the payment is not received on due date, the bank recovers this amount from the customers (that is, the exporter in this case).

LESSON AT A GLANCE

- **Capital Market:** Capital market is a financial market where buyers and sellers engage in trade of financial securities of long term nature like shares, debentures etc.
- **Functions of Capital Market:** (i) Acts as a link between Savers and Investors; (ii) Encouragement to Savings; (iii) Encouragement to Investment; (iv) Promotes Economic Growth; (v) Stability in Security Prices; (vi) Benefits the Investors.
- **Sources of Raising Capital:**
  - **Long-term Sources of Finance:** (i) Shares-Equity Shares, Preference Shares (ii) Debentures
  - **Short-term Sources of Finance:** (i) Cash Credit (ii) Credit Draft or Overdraft (iii) Discounting of Bills.

PROJECT WORK

Find out and list the different financial regulators functioning in India.

ASSIGNMENT

With the help of proper examples show how the absence or the presence of a proper capital market has an impact on an economy.

QUESTIONS

A. **Short Answer Type Questions:**
   1. Define Capital Market.
   2. List the six functions of a Capital Market.
   3. State two sources of raising capital.
   4. What is Long-term source of financing?
   5. What is Short-term source of financing?
   6. Define Shares.
   7. What are equity shares?
   8. What are preference shares?
   9. Define Debentures.

10. Give examples of two different short-term sources of financing.

B. **Essay Type Questions:**
   1. Describe the functions of Capital Market in detail.
   2. Explain the various sources of raising capital.
   3. State the differences between Shares and Debentures.
   4. Write short notes on:
      (i) Equity shares
      (ii) Preference shares
      (iii) Overdraft
      (iv) Cash credit
      (v) Discounting of bills

CHAPTER-14
Recruitment and Selection

Human element is undoubtedly an essential, active and sensitive factor of production. Without human factor, all other physical factors are useless. working force does not only initiate and sustain work but it also activates other factors of production. It is rightly said that, an organisation without workers is an unproductive shell. It clearly stresses on the fact that recruitment and selection of employees should be done very carefully.

- Meaning of Recruitment
- Sources of Recruitment
- Internal Sources of Recruitment and their Evaluation
- External Sources of Recruitment and their Evaluation
- Meaning of Selection
- Steps in Selection of Employees
- Importance of Selection
- Difference between Recruitment and Selection

RECRUITMENT

Without employees the enterprise would have been a collection of materials and equipments. While efficient employees are assets of the enterprise, inefficient employees prove to be a liability. Therefore, every organisation should recruit the most suitable and competent employees on the basis of the needs and nature of the job. The process of identification of different sources of personnel is known as recruitment. It is the process of attracting potential candidates to the business concern. In other words, recruitment implies locating, maintaining and contacting the sources of manpower. A logical sequence of events would be: Identifying the different sources of labour supply–Assessing their validity–Choosing the most suitable source–Inviting applications from the prospective candidates.

In this way, recruitment is an activity of establishing a contact between an employer an applicant. The most important objective of any recruitment policy is to keep the labour turnover ratio as low as possible. It is the positive activity in the sense that it aims at reaching as many job seekers as possible for jobs in the enterprise. Recruitment process is the first step towards creating the competitive strength and the strategic advantage for the organisation. The process begins when new recruits are sought and ends when their applications are submitted. The result is a pool of applications from which new employees are selected.

- *"Recruitment as process of searching for prospective employees and stimulating them to apply for jobs in the organisation."* —Edwin B. Flippo
- *"Recruitment is the development and maintenance of adequate manpower resources. It involves the creation of a pool of available labour force upon whom the organisation can draw when it needs additional employees."* —Dale S. Beach

Thus, recruitment is a continuous process by which an organisation seeks to develop a pool of qualified applicants for the future human resource needs, even though specific vacancies do not exist at present.

The main objective of the recruitment process is to expedite the selection process.

Sources of recruitment

The sources of recruitment of personnel may be classified into two broad categories:
1. Internal sources (recruitment from within the enterprise); and
2. External sources (recruitment from outside).

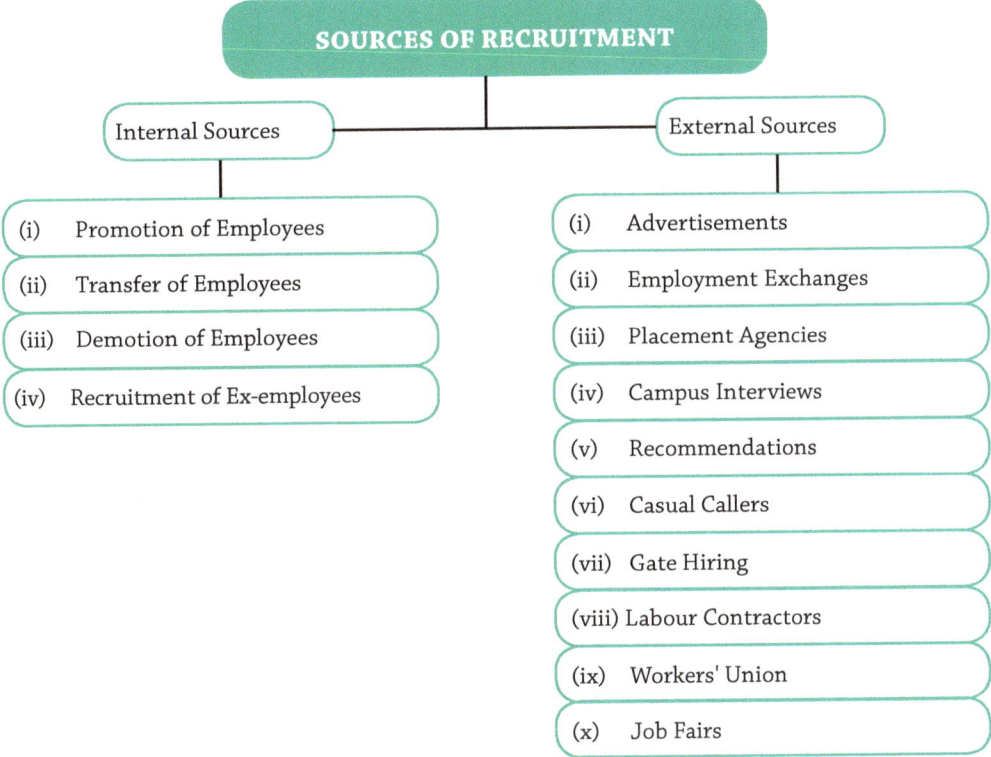

1. Internal Sources

Internal sources of recruitment means shifting of the existing employees of the organisation from one department to another department and from one post to another post. The sources of internal recruitment are as under:

(i) Promotion of Employees:

Promotion implies vertical movement or advancement of an employee from a lower position to a higher one. Positions falling vacant in higher ranks may conveniently be filled up by promoting suitable employees from below. This promotion may be based upon both, the seniority and merit. In a good promotion policy, employees should know what will be the contribution of their seniority in merit for their promotion. The employee has the privilege of working in the real situations of the business, so he does not feel any difficulty in case of promotion. Thus, promotion leads to shifting an employee to a higher position carrying higher responsibilities, facilities, status and pay.

(ii) Transfer of Employees:

Transfer involves the shifting of an employee from one job to another without special reference to change in responsibility, rank or compensation. Transfer is the change in a job equal to the old one in terms of pay, status and responsibilities. If the management finds that a person is misfit or he will be more useful at some other place, he is shifted. However, it may significantly affect the efficiency and morale of the employee, depending on the type of environment where he has been transferred.

(iii) Demotion of Employees:
Employees may be demoted back to their original jobs. Demotion shakes the morale and self-respect of employees, so it should be avoided. Demotions are generally made, when the promotion is conditional or the court has dis-approved or vacancy was temporarily caused by the leave of a senior employee.

(iv) Recruitment of Ex-employees:
This source of internal recruitment is adopted to re-employ the ex-employees of the organisation. It may happen when employees who have left the organisation are willing to rejoin it. In such a case, the organisation accords them priority and enterprise too gets trusted, competent and experienced employees.

Advantages:

(i) Upgradation of Several Employees:
The existing employees of the organisation get an opportunity for promotion. When a certain person is promoted, several other persons below his rank are automatically promoted. In this way, one vacancy filled from within, results in upgradation of several employees.

(ii) Familiarity with Policies:
The Existing employees are aware of policies, plans and the actual working conditions of the enterprise, so they are not required to waste time and energy in learning it.

(iii) Economical:
Internal source is economical because the enterprise is not required to incur expenses on recruitment from outside the organisation. There are lesser number of candidates and the most suitable candidate is selected according to merit or seniority or both.

(iv) Availability of Experienced Employees:
Promoted employees have already been performing the job in the organisation before their promotion, so they do not have any difficulty. The organisation is also benefitted because employees are efficient and experienced and they start working without any formal training.

(v) Increase in employees' Morale:
Promotion from within the organisation increases employees' morale. The policy of internal promotions makes them enthusiastic and optimistic and they contribute their best efforts and energies.

(vi) References not Required:
The service records of employees are available in the organisation. It knows the abilities and loyalties of its employees. Therefore, any outside reference about their ability, integrity and moral character is not required.

Disadvantages:

(i) No Opportunity for Fresh Talent:
The major drawback of this source is that the enterprise may deprive competent, talented and deserving candidates from outside to get an opportunity to take up challenging jobs.

(ii) Promotion of Inefficient Employees:
Sometimes, unsuitable persons use their influence to get promotions. They are promoted from within the organisation without giving any importance to their merit simply because they are working in that organisation.

(iii) Not a Complete solution:
Internal source of recruitment is not capable to meet entire requirement of the organisation. The management has to knock at the doors of external sources also.

Evaluation of Internal Sources of Recruitment

Advantages	Disadvantages
(i) Upgrading of several employees	(i) No opportunity for fresh talent
(ii) Familiarity with policies	(ii) Promotion of inefficient employees
(iii) Economical	(iii) Not a complete solution
(iv) Availability of experienced employees	
(v) Increase in Employees, Morale	
(vi) References not required	

2. External Sources

All the vacancies at all the levels, cannot be filled up through internal sources of recruitment only. Therefore, use of external sources is also necessary for all organisations. External recruitment means the sources through which the suitable candidates are sourced from outside the concern. The recruitment at lower levels is made from external sources only. Main external sources of recruitment are as under:

(i) Advertisements:
Recruitment through advertising in local or national newspapers or trade or professional journals is one of the most common methods of attracting personnel of all types — skilled workers, clerical staff and higher staff. It is very convenient and economical also. The vacancies are advertised in newspapers and the interested candidates submit their applications, on the basis of such advertisements. Sometimes, an enterprise may not disclose its name in the advertisement and ask candidates to reply to a Post Box Number, or to a consulting firm. This may be because the enterprise does not want to reveal its identity for some reasons, or because the advertisement relates to a vacancy that is to be filled internally.

(ii) Employment Exchanges:
The Government has set up employment exchanges throughout the country. Anyone seeking employment can get himself registered at the employment exchange. Employees notify the vacancies and the various exchanges refer suitable candidates for recruitment. Employment exchanges are a useful source of semi-skilled and unskilled personnel. But skilled personnel may not be available. Persons with specialised skills and experience do not prefer registration at the employment exchange because they consider it below their dignity. Employers too have a feeling that employment exchanges cannot provide personnel having specialised skills and experience.

(iii) Placement Agencies:
Several recruitment agencies, like ABC consultants, A. F. Ferguson Associates, etc., provide recruitment and selection services. The employer can hire such an agency to payon the complete task of recruitment. The agency will advertise the job, receive and screen applications and shortlist suitable persons them. The employer saves his time and effort and gets the benefit of the agency's expertise. His identity is also kept secret. But the agency charges a substantial fee for this task. This source of recruitment is employed for recruitment of senior positions (technical as well as managerial).

(iv) Campus Interviews:
Managers, officers, technicians; like engineers, electricians, mechanics and skilled workmen are often recruited from institutions, like Indian Institute of Management (IIM), Indian Institute of Technology (IIT), Engineering Colleges, Industrial Training Institutes, Polytechnics, etc. Companies send their managers to such institutions where there are suitable candidates recommended by the institutes. These candidates are interviewed for selection by the managers.

(v) Recommendations:
Many organisations have a structured system where the current employees of the organisation can refer their friends and relatives for some position in the organisation. when a present employee recommends a person, a type of preliminary screening takes place. Indeed, many employers prefer to take such persons because something about their background is known.

(vi) Casual Callers:
These are the persons who either gather at the factory gate to serve as casual workers or reach the employer by letter, telephone or in person, with request for appointment against a real or presumed vacancy. Applicants apply on their own initiative assuming that certain vacancies are likely to be filled up. Managers keep record of such applications and contact suitable ones when they need them.

(vii) Gate Hiring:
This type of recruitment is made by labour officers. Generally, workers gather at factory gate or they are called through a notice. The suitable candidates are recruited. This method is applied to meet the casual needs of the employees. These casual workers having once served in the factory for sometime, are considered for regular employment.

(viii) Labour Contractors:
It is quite common to engage jobbers and contractors to supply workers for vacancies which are of casual nature, or which may be filled at the factory gate itself. In fact,

where the workers have to be hired on a short notice and without going through the usual selection procedure, jobbers and contractors serve as an ideal and economical source. Jobbers and contractors maintain close links with small towns and villages which offer a ready and plentiful supply of unskilled workers. They, also, sometimes at their own expense, bring workers to the place of work.

(ix) Workers' Union:
In order to keep workers and their union satisfied, employers can recruit through workers' union also. The unions have agreement with the managements, whereby managers are required to consider their recommendations on a priority basis.

(x) Job Fairs:
Job fairs are conducted by different companies to attract candidates for entry level jobs.

Advantages:

(i) Wider Choice:
Selection from external sources facilitates the choice of personnel from among a large number of applicants. The enterprise can carefully weigh the plus and minus points of all the candidates and then select the best.

(ii) Fresh Outlook:
The enterprise greatly benefits from the freshness of outlook and approach of personnel chosen from external sources. This is because they are without any in-built preferences and prejudices, so common in the case of personnel promoted or transferred to fill the vacancies internally.

Disadvantages:

(i) Heart-Burning Among Old Employees:
Personnel chosen from external sources may cause heart-burning and demoralisation among old employees, for whom any outsider is unwanted, especially so if he deprives them of a coveted job.

(ii) Expensive:
Recruitment of staff from outside sources may sometimes, be quite expensive. Beginning with advertisements in the press, which itself is a costly affair, then the holding of written tests and personal interviews may involve substantial expenditure. A new employee learns after a considerable expense and waste in terms of time and material.

(iii) Chances of Maladjustment:
If a person chosen from an external source fails to adjust himself to working in the enterprise, or is an idler or otherwise undesirable, he may have to be shunted out. This means there will be yet more expenditure on finding his replacement.

Evaluation of External Sources of Recruitment

Advantages	Disadvantages
(i) Wider Choice	(i) Heart-Burning among Old employees
(ii) Fresh Outlook	(ii) Expensive
	(iii) Chances of Maladjustment

SELECTION

Selection means going through the qualifications and experience of the candidates to decide whether the candidates fulfill the requirements of the job or not. It involves evaluation of the applicants. It is the process of dividing the applicants into two categories: (i) those who are to be employed; and (ii) those who are to be rejected. Selection is a very important activity because it helps to minimize labour turnover and absenteeism. The process of selection starts with comparing the requirements of a job with the qualifications of the applicants. The purpose of selecting the right person for the right job also helps to improve the quantity and quality of performance. Selection is said to be a negative process, because the number of candidates rejected is much more than that of selected persons. There are some stages of selection. At every stage, the qualities of candidates are tested. Number of candidates goes on reducing at each subsequent stage. it eliminates the unsuitable candidates at every step. It is the process of picking up the most competent and suitable candidates.

- "Selection is the process in which candidates for employment are divided in two classes, those who are to be offered employment and those who are not." —Dale Yoder
- "Selection means making a choice by preference. This choice by preference is based on comparison between two factors: (i) What the job requires for successful execution, and (ii) What the applicant has to offer. For the most part, the better the balance between these two factors, the better the selection work and more likely the attainment of a satisfactory working force." —George Terry

Steps in the Process of Selection of Employees

The basic principle for the recruitment and selection is, the "right man for the right job." Presuming that all the requirements that are necessary for inviting applications have been fulfilled and the applications have been received in the office, the following steps are generally performed for the selection of employees:

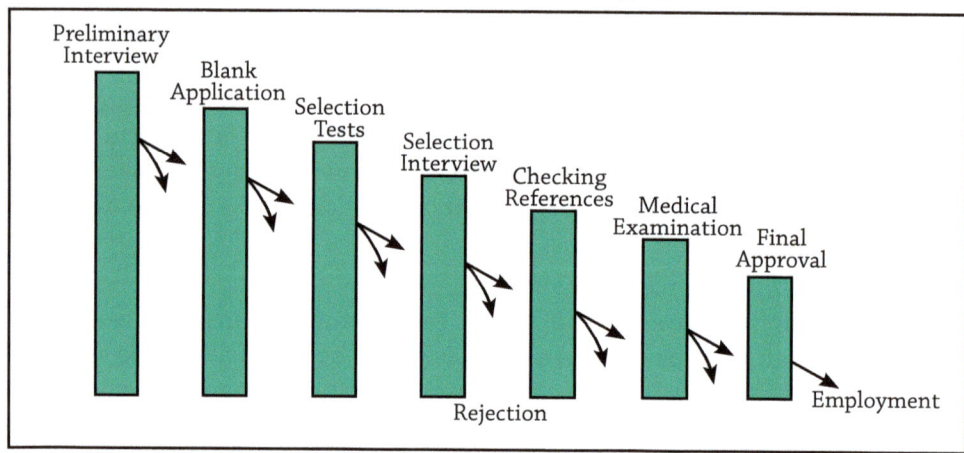

1. Preliminary Interview

The Executive of the organisation conduct a brief interview of the candidates to determine whether it is worthwhile for the candidate to fill up the blank application. Minimum qualifications and experience of the candidate, his age, etc., are ascertained. Preliminary interview helps to eliminate those candidates who are obviously unfit for the job.

2. Blank Application

The candidates who succeed in preliminary interviews are required to fill in a specially drafted blank application form. It provides a written record of the qualifications, experience age, etc., of candidates. It can be used as a good test device for the expression, handwriting and other abilities of the candidates. Therefore, it should be designed carefully so as to secure all relevant information about the candidate. There is no standard form of blank application for all firms. As far as possible, it should be simple and brief.

3. Selection Tests

Candidates may have to undertake selection tests to establish their claim for the job. These tests are based on the assumption that, human behaviour in an actual work situation can be predicted by sampling it.

Selection tests are classified into six types. They are as follow :

(i) Aptitude Tests.

(ii) Achievement Tests.

(iii) Situational Tests.

(iv) Proficiency Tests.

(v) Interest Tests.

(vi) Personality Tests.

(i) Aptitude Tests:

Aptitude means the potential which an individual has for learning the skills required to do a job efficiently. Aptitude tests measures an applicant's capacity and his ability to learn a given job if given adequate training. These tests are the most promising indices for predicting employee's success. Aptitude tests can be divided into general and mental ability or intelligence tests and specific aptitude tests such as mechanical aptitude tests, clerical aptitude tests, etc.

(A) Intelligence Tests: These tests are used to measure a person's capacity for reasoning and comprehension in terms of his memory, mental alertness, vocabulary, and grasping capacity. A candidate's IQ or mental alertness can be estimated through intelligence tests. The tests consists of logical reasoning ability, data interpretation, comprehension skills and basic language skills. Though these tests are accepted as useful ones, they are criticized to be against deprived sections of the community.

(B) Mechanical Aptitude Tests: These tests deal with the ability of the candidate to do mechanical work. They are used to judge and measure the specialised knowledge, perceptual speed and problem solving ability. These tests are useful for selecting apprentices, skilled mechanical employees, technicians, etc.

(C) Psychomotor Tests: These tests judge abilities like manual dexterity, motor ability and eye-hand coordination of candidates. These tests are useful to select semi-skilled workers and workers for repetitive operations like packing, watch assembly, quality inspection, etc.

(D) Clerical Aptitude Tests: These tests measure specific capacities involved in office work, like spelling, computation, comprehension, copying, word measuring, etc.

(ii) Achievement Tests:

The candidate's achievement in his career is tested regarding his knowledge about the job and actual work experience. These tests are more useful to measure the value of specific achievement when an organization wishes to employ experienced candidates. These test are classified into:

(A) Job Knowledge Tests: Under this test, a candidate's knowledge is tested for a particular job. For example, if a junior lecturer applies for the job of a senior lecturer in Economics, he may be tested in job knowledge where he is asked questions about microeconomics, macroeconomics, central bank, etc.

(B) Work Sample Test: Under this test a portion of the actual work is given to the candidate as a test and the candidate is asked to do it. If a candidate applies for a post of a lecturer in Management, he may be asked to deliver a lecture on Management Information System as work sample test.

(iii) Situational Tests:

These tests evaluate a candidate in a similar real life situation. In these tests, the candidate is asked either to cope with the situation or to solve critical situations of the job. Situational tests are classified into:

(A) Group Discussion: Under this test, candidates are observed in the areas of leadership, proposing valuable ideas, conciliating skills, oral communicating skills, coordinating and concluding skills.

(B) In Basket: Situational test is also administered through 'in basket'. The candidate, in this test, is supplied with actual letters, telephone and telegraphic message, reports and requirements by various officers of the organization. The candidate is asked to take decisions on various items based on the in basket information. The candidate is then evaluated by the decisions he took, during the test.

(iv) Proficiency Tests:

Proficiency tests seek to measure the skill and abilities which the candidate already possesses at the time of testing. Trade tests or skill tests are examples of proficiency tests. They determine whether the claims made by the candidate about his skills and abilities are proved by his actual test performance.

(v) Interest Tests:

Interest tests identify patterns of interest, that is, areas in which the individual shows special concern, fascination and involvement. These tests will suggest what types of jobs may be satisfying to the employees.

(vi) Personality Tests:

Personality tests are aimed at finding out emotional balance, maturity, temperament, etc., of the candidate. It is very difficult to design and use these tests as they are concerned with discovering clues to an individual's emotional reactions, maturity, etc. Personality tests have disadvantage in the sense that they can be faked by sophisticated candidates and most candidates give socially acceptable answers. Further, personality tests may not successfully predict job success.

4. Selection Interview

Interview serves as a means of checking the information given in the application forms and the tests results. It also provides an opportunity to the candidates to enquire about the job during interview. Managers get an opportunity to take a decision about their suitability for employment. Selection interview should be conducted in an atmosphere which is free from disturbance, noise and interruption. Interview should be conducted in great depth to judge the suitability of the candidates.

There are no hard and fast rules of interviewing candidates. Interviews, in general, can be conducted in the following ways:

(A) Structured or Patterned Interview:

In such an interview different sets of questions, having the same pattern and with the same difficulty level, are framed in advance. Different candidates are asked different series of questions. Each series, having the same pattern and the same difficulty level, bring about objectivity in the interview.

(B) Unstructured or Non-directive Interview:

In this interview, questions to be asked are not planned in advance. Questions pertaining to the job are asked and candidates are asked to respond freely to show their ability for the job.

(C) Stress Interview:

This interview is held to note how thick-skinned the candidate is. The candidates are asked awkward questions and it is seen how they react to such questions. If they do not lose their balance of mind, they prove their worth as suitable candidates.

(D) Group Interview:

In this interview, a number of candidates face the interview committee together. The candidates are asked to give their opinion on an issue or they are asked to discuss on a topic. When the candidates respond and give reasons and counter-reasons, their ability to communicate, presence of mind, expression, etc., are judged by the inter-viewers.

5. Checking References

References are generally required to enquire about the conduct of those candidates who have been found suitable in the interviews and tests. References can be collected from the previous employers, colleges last attended or from any other reliable source. Before forming a balanced opinion, it is necessary to enquire from three to five persons about the conduct of the prospective candidate. However, this exercise may not always produce the desired results because (i) no candidate will cite the name of a referee who might speak unfavourably about him; (ii) the referee may not always respond; and (iii) due to a prejudice the referee may deliberately speak against the candidate.

6. Medical Examination

A physical examination of the potential employee is necessary for the company, to protect itself against the risk of claims for compensation from individuals who are afflicted with disabilities. The medical examination should be both general and thorough. The findings, should be carefully recorded so as to give a complete medical history, the scope of current physical capacities, and the nature of disabilities, if any. But, it need to be remembered that the medical examination is an aid to selecting employees who, besides fulfilling the requirements as to abilities and skills, also possess necessary physical characteristics. In other words, medical examination should not be used unfairly to reject an otherwise suitable candidate.

7. Final Approval
After a candidate has cleared all the hurdles in the selection procedure, he is formally appointed by issuing him an appointment letter or by making a service agreement with him. No selection procedure is foolproof and the best way to judge a person, is by observing him working on the job.

8. Employment
Candidates who give satisfactory performance during the probationary period are made permanent.

Importance of Selection

It is an accepted fact, that the efficient, competent and devoted employees are the most valuable asset of the business enterprise, whereas the incompetent workers are liability of the firm. It is, therefore, necessary that the selection of employees should be made very carefully, because any lapse or errors committed in the selection may prove fatal to the enterprise. Defective selection will lead to:

1. Absenteeism resulting in loss of work and reduction in labour turnover.
2. Decline in the efficiency of the organisation.
3. Shirking responsibility of the employees.
4. Suspension, retrenchment and termination of employees. Such practice will pollute the atmosphere.
5. Wastage of time, energy and money in hiring, training and developing unsuitable employees.

Effective selection of employees will result in:

1. Building up a suitable work force.
2. Low absenteeism and high labour turnover.
3. Boosting the morale of employees.
4. Higher efficiency and maximum production at minimum cost.

DIFFERENCE BETWEEN RECRUITMENT AND SELECTION

Recruitment and selection are closely inter-connected. Recruitment is inviting and procuring applications from various sources. Whereas selection starts after applications have been received, *i.e.*, where recruitment ends.

In the recruitment process, there is matching of the applicants with the requirements of the job and selection tasks place after that thus, recruitment facilitates the work of selection. Recruitment is a positive process as it seeks to persuade people to apply for vacant posts. Selection is a negative process in the sense that it eliminates the unsuitable candidates while retaining the suitable ones.

Both recruitment and selection are the two phases of the same process. Recruitment being the first phase envisages taking decisions on the choice of tapping the sources of labour supply. Selection is the second phase which involves giving various types of tests to the candidates and interviewing them in order to select the suitable candidates.

Basis of Comparison	Recruitment	Selection
Meaning	Searching prospective candidates and stimulating them to apply for jobs.	Choosing the candidates having necessary qualifications.
Nature	Positive process.	Negative process.
Aim	To create a large pool of candidates.	To eliminate all unsuitable candidates.
Process	Simple, as candidates are not required to cross many hurdles.	Complex, as the candidates are required to cross several hurdles.
Number	No restriction upon the number of candidates.	Only a limited number of candidates are selected.
Order	It is done prior to selection.	It is made only after recruitment.

Lesson at a Glance

- **Recruitment:** It is the process of searching for prospective employees and stimulating and encouraging them to apply for jobs in an organisation. The process of identification of different sources of personnel is known as recruitment. According to DALE S. BEACH, "Recruitment is the development and maintenance of adequate manpower resources. It involves the creation of a pool of available labour force upon whom the organisation can draw when it needs additional employees."

Sources of Recruitment
- **Internal Sources:** (i) Promotion of employees; (ii) Transfer of employees; (iii) Demotion of employees; (iv) Recruitment of ex-employees.
- **Merits:** (i) Upgradation of several employees; (ii) Familiarity with policies; (iii) Economical; (iv) Availability of experienced employees; (v) Increase in employee's morale; (vi) References not required.
- **Demerits:** (i) No opportunity for fresh talent; (ii) Promotion of inefficient employees; (iii) Not a complete solution.
- **External Sources:** (i) Advertisements; (ii) Employment exchanges; (iii) Placement agencies; (iv) Campus interviews; (v) Recommendations; (vi) Casual callers; (vii) Gate hiring; (viii) Labour contractors; (ix) Worker's union; (x) Job fairs.
- **Merits:** (i) Wider choice; (ii) Fresh outlook.

- **Demerits:** (i) Heart-Burning among old employees; (ii) Expensive; (iii) Danger of maladjustment.
- **Selection:** Selection means going through the qualifications and experience of the candidates to decide whether the candidates fulfill the requirements of the job. It is the process of dividing the applicants into two categories : (i) those who are to be employed; (ii) those who are to be rejected.
- **Steps in Selection of Employees:** (i) Preliminary interview; (ii) Blank application; (iii) Selection tests : (a) Aptitude tests; (b) Achievement tests; (c) Situational tests; (d) Proficiency test; (e) Interest tests; (f) Personality tests; (iv) Selection interview : (a) Structured or patterned interview, (b) Unstructured or non-directive interview, (c) Stress interview, (d) Group interview; (v) Checking references; (vi) Medical examination; (vii) Final approval; (viii) Employment.
- **Difference between Recruitment and Selection:** (i) Meaning; (ii) Nature; (iii) Aim; (iv) Process; (v) Number; (vi) Order.

Project Work

Visit any four big organisations and record their methods of recruitment and selection of the staff. Compare the methods and procedure adopted by different organisations.

Assignment

You are the principal of a school. Which methods would you adopt for recruitment of teaching and non-teaching staff for school ? What procedure would you follow to make the final selection of the staff ?

Questions

A. **Short Answer Type Questions:**
1. Define recruitment.
2. Name any three methods of recruitment.
3. State in brief the internal sources of recruitment.
4. State the external sources of recruitment.
5. Define selection.
6. What is the significance of selection?
7. Name any three methods of selection.
8. What are the types of interviews?
9. Distinguish between recruitment and selection. [ICSE 2017]
10. Distinguish between internal recruitment and external recruitment.
11. What is meant by Gate Hiring in recruitment?
12. State two advantages of internal recruitment. [ICSE 2020]

13. State two advantages of campus recruitment as an external source of recruitment. [ICSE 2020]
14. Breifly explain any two types of selection tests. [ICSE 2020]
15. "Selection is a negative process'. Explain. [ICSE 2018]
16. State two disadvantage of internal recruitment. [ICSE 2017]

B. Essay Type Questions:
 1. What do you mean by recruitment of employees?
 2. Explain briefly merits and demerits of internal and external sources of recruitment.
 3. Explain in the external sources of recruitment.
 4. What is meant by selection? Explain the steps involved in the selection process.
 5. Discuss the various types of tests and interviews as a part of the selection process.
 6. An organisation has decided to follow a three tier selection process of appointing Executive Trainees: Aptitude Test (A.T.), Group Discussion (G.D.) and Final Interview (F.I.). Outline the details of this process stating clearly the tasks involved at each stage.
 7. Briefly discuss the various methods of recruitment.
 8. How would you recruit and select new sales representatives to persuade the dealers?

CHAPTER-15
Training of Employees

The most valuable asset of any business enterprise is its work force, gifted with understanding, competence and skill to accomplish their work faultlessly. In order to develop such proficiency in the work, proper training of employees is must. Training acquaints the workers with the intricacies of work and ensures greater efficiency and productivity.

- Meaning of Training
- Training and Development
- Training and Education
- Objectives of Training
- Importance of Training
- Levels of Training
- Types of Training
- Methods of Training

TRAINING

Training means imparting the knowledge, skills and aptitudes necessary to undertake the required jobs efficiently with a view to developing the worker to his fullest potential. As an organised activity, training is designed to create a change in the thinking and behaviour of people. Training is a two-way and continuous process because there is no end to learning and secondly, a person gets to learn new technology, new patterns etc. continuously. The training acquaints the employee with the requisite skill, real life situations at the work place and helps him in the faultless accomplishment of the work. Training, thus, involves the development of the manual and mental skills that are necessary for performing a specific work, through instruction, drill and discipline.

- *"Training is the act of increasing the knowledge and skill of an employee for doing a particular job."*
  —Edwin B. Flippo
- *"Training is a process by which the attitudes, skills and abilities of employees to perform specific jobs are increased."*
  —Michael J. Jucious
- *"Training is the organised procedure by which people learn knowledge and/or skill for a definite purpose."*
  —E. F. L. BReach

TRAINING AND DEVELOPMENT

Though no clear cut distinction can be made between the terms 'training' and 'development'; yet it is apparent that training always leads to the development and growth of workers. Further, the word 'training' is mostly used in relation to first level managers or non-managerial personnel, *i.e.*, the operative employees, while the term 'development' is applied to the growth of managerial personnel, *i.e.*, the second and third level managers. 'Training' is used to add to the skills and abilities of the workers, while 'development' involves improving the capacity and capability of the managerial personnel to take up more difficult and risky ventures with greater success besides increasing their skill and competency in their present jobs.

TRAINING AND EDUCATION

According to *Michael Jucious*, "training is any process by which the aptitudes, skills and abilities of employees to perform specific jobs are increased". On the other hand, "education is the process of increasing the general knowledge and understanding of employees." Education involves the general knowledge and developing overall understanding of the total environment. For example, a mechanic who is trained can bind an electric motor better than an engineer but, can not design a next generation advanced electrical device because he is uneducated and is not exposed to the basic principles and fundamentals of engineering. The scope of education is much wider than that of training. Secondly, the purpose of education is general development whereas, training has a specific and immediate purpose of making a person proficient in a particular job. Thirdly, education involves formal instruction in a school or college whereas, training can be given on the job itself. Fourthly, education is generally theoretical whereas, training is practical in nature. Finally, the cost of education is generally paid by the government and the student. On the other hand, the cost of training is generally borne by the employer.

OBJECTIVES OF TRAINING

The training objectives are laid down keeping in view the company's goals and objectives. The general objectives of a training programme are as follows:

(1) To Increase Productivity of Employees:
Training helps in developing the capacities and capabilities of the employees–both new and old, by upgrading their skills and knowledge so that the organization could gainfully avail their services for higher grade professional, technical, sales or production positions from within the organization. In case of new employees, training aims to provide them with basic knowledge and skill they need for an intelligent performance of their specific tasks.

(2) To Remain Competitive in the Market:
To tackle the immensely growing competition in the target market, it is important for an employer to increase the productivity of its workers while reducing the cost of production of the products. Training, therefore, aims to bring about efficiency and effectiveness in an organization to enable it to remain competitive in a highly competitive market situation and for the achievement of organizational goals.

(3) To Change Attitude of the Workers:
Training not only provides new knowledge and job skills to employees, but also brings about a change in their attitude towards fellow workers, supervisor and the organization. It increases job satisfaction among employees and keeps them motivated. It gives them security at the workplace and as a result, labour turnover and absenteeism rates are reduced. It also develops in them self consciousness and a greater awareness to recognize their responsibilities and contribute their very best to the organization.

(4) To Enable Workers to Adapt Quickly to Changes:
Technology is changing at a fast pace. Technological changes like automation and development of highly mechanized and computer oriented systems, threaten the survival of dynamic companies by creating new problems, new methods, new procedures, new equipments, new jobs, new skills and knowledge, new product and services etc. In such a situation, the employees may find themselves helpless to adapt to the changes and may feel frustrated and compelled to leave their jobs.

Thus, training acts as a continuous process to update the employees in the new methods and procedures and make them efficient in handling advanced technology.

(5) To Mitigate the Risk of Accidents:
Trained workers can handle the machines safely. They also know the use of various safety devices in the factory. Thus, they are less prone to industrial accidents.

(6) To Reduce Wastage of Time and Resources:
Training aims at making employees efficient in handling materials, machines and equipment and thus to avoid wastage of time and resources. It also helps in imparting new skills among the workers systematically so that they may learn quickly. If the workers learn through trial and error, they will take a longer time and even then, may not be able to learn right methods of doing work.

(7) To Provide Growth Opportunities to Existing Employees:
Sometimes, it may not be possible for the management to fill in higher work positions from outside. Under such conditions, the apprenticeship programmes aiming at improving the skills of the present employees come to the aid of the company by make available their requirements of the personnel from within the organization. This reduces the need for recruiting people from outside and also improves the morale of the existing employees.

(8) To Make the Management Effective:
One of the primary objectives of training and development process is to give rise to a new and improved management which is capable of handling the planning and control without any serious problem. Knowledge and experience gathered through training enables them to handle the tough situations and confusing realities, thus opening the way for bigger and better opportunities for business. It can also be used for strengthening values, building teams, improving inter-groups relations and quality of work life.

IMPORTANCE OF TRAINING

Training is useful for both employers and employees. A well-trained employee is an asset to the enterprise. Training enables the employee to get job security, higher earnings and promotion. It increases the productivity of the workers and the output for the organisation. The main advantages of training are as follows:

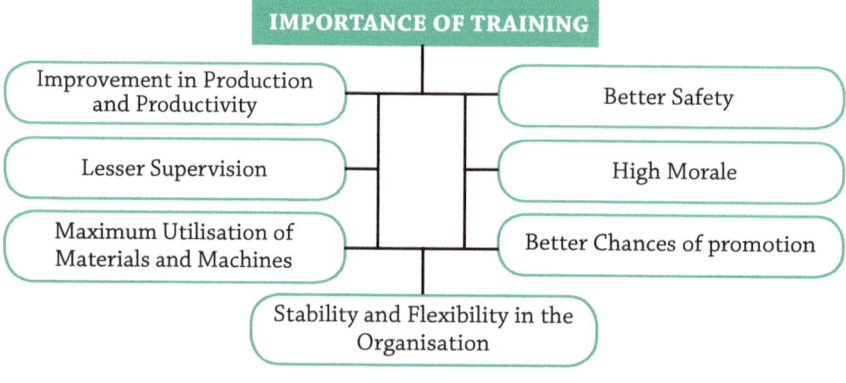

1. Improvement in Production and Productivity:
Training helps to improve the efficiency and productivity of employees. Well-trained employees make better use of materials and machinery. Wastage is reduced and as a result quality and quantity of production becomes higher.

2. Lesser Supervision:
Well-trained employees, have the knowledge about their jobs and equipments and can do their work efficiently. Thus, the training reduces the need of supervision to bare minimum.

3. Maximum Utilisation of Materials and Machines:
Training teaches the employees the method of doing their job in the best possible manner. They have knowledge of operating machines and equipments and handle them properly and methodically. As a result of it, they make the best possible utilisation of materials and machines.

4. Better Safety:
Human error or negligence is the major cause of accidents in the industry. Due to the operational efficiency of the trained workers and the complete knowledge about the working of the plants and machines, chances of accidents are reduced.

5. High Morale:
Effective training improves the self-confidence and job satisfaction of employees. Well-trained employees take greater interest in their job and derive a sense of security. By boosting the morale of employees, training helps to reduce absenteeism and improve labour turnover.

6. Better Chances of Promotion:
As the trained employees have the requisite qualification and training, they can be promoted to higher grades and position more easily than untrained workers.

7. Stability and Flexibility in the Organisation:
An enterprise, where trained personnel's are available, can expand and grow easily. Its survival is not threatened when a few key personnel's are lost because proper replacements are available. Well-trained employees can be transferred from one job to another in order to meet the requirements of other departments. Thus, training also lends flexibility to the organisation.

LEVELS OF TRAINING

Just as the distribution of administration at different levels is essential for the efficient management, similarly the training program may have its own levels for effective results. The following are some of the important levels of training of the employees:

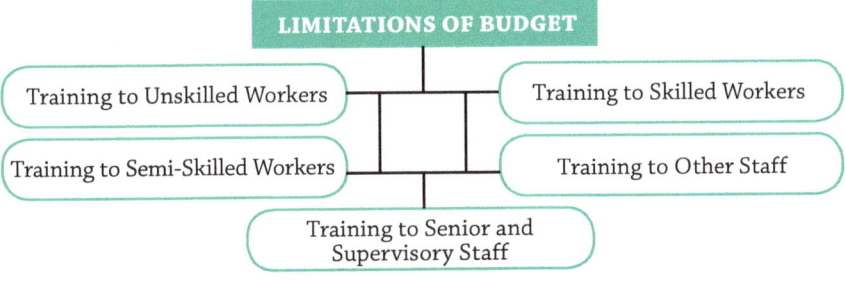

1. Training to Unskilled Workers:

Unskilled workers require training to acquaint themselves with improved methods of handling their work to reduce the cost of production and do the job in the most economical and efficient way. Such employees are given training on the job itself and the training is imparted either by their immediate superior officers, or foremen.

2. Training to Semi-Skilled Workers:

This category of employees requires training to cope with the requirements of the industry arising out of the adoption of mechanisation and rationalisation. These employees are given training either in the section or department itself, or in segregated training shops, where machines and other facilities are easily available. The training is usually imparted by more proficient workers and it lasts for a few hours or weeks, depending upon the number of operations and speed and accuracy required.

3. Training to Skilled Workers:

Skilled workers are given training through the system of apprenticeship, varying in length upto a period of 5 years. Crafts training is imparted through training centres and the industry itself.

4. Training to Other Staff:

Besides the above categories of unskilled, semi-skilled and skilled workers, other employees are also required to be trained, they are computer operators, typists, stenographers, accounts clerks, etc. They need training in their field but such training is usually not provided. Salesmen are also given training about the nature of the products; routine involved in putting through the deal and art of salesmanship, alongwith the latest knowledge of the products being developed in the organisation.

5. Training to Senior and Supervisory Staff:

Since the supervisors form a very important link in the chain of administration, therefore, they need advanced up-to-date training at frequent intervals. The training programmes for the supervisory staff must be specific and tailor-made to fit the need of the undertaking. They are generally given training in :

(a) Organisation and control of production, maintenance and materials handling at the departmental levels.

(b) Planning, allocation and control of work and personnel.

(c) Planning their own work and allocation of time to their various responsibilities.

(d) Effect of industrial legislation at the departmental level.

(e) Cost factors and costs control.

(f) Accident prevention.

(g) Training of subordinates.

(h) Communication, effective instructing, report-writing.

(i) Handling and settling human/labour problems.

(j) Leadership for effective working of the undertaking.

TYPES OF TRAINING

Following are the main types of training:

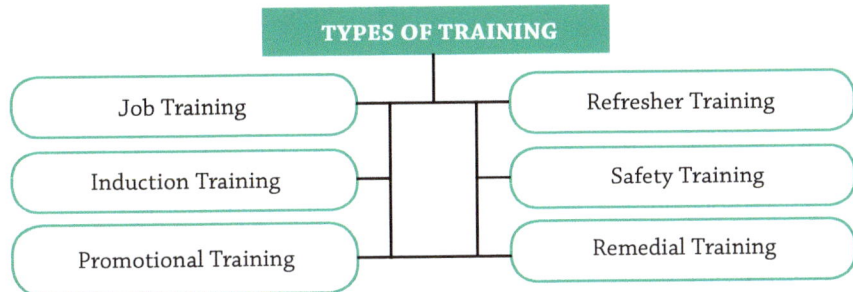

1. Job Training:
Such training is given to make the employees proficient in performing the operations of the job. The new entrants are trained to handle the equipments and raw-materials correctly and perform the job operations efficiently. Old employees are acquainted with the latest methods of executing the jobs.

2. Induction Training:
Induction or orientation training refers to the training given to the new employees. The training is imparted by a competent and experienced executive, who provides knowledge about the work, tools, equipments, techniques and situational problems. The object is to make the employee aware and believe in the ideologies of the working.

3. Promotional Training:
Promotions provide encouragement to employees, and in many organisations, senior posts are filled by promotions. Promotion carries with it new responsibilities for which the incumbent must be prepared. The purpose of this type of training is to meet this demand.

4. Refresher Training:
Such training is designed to revive the earlier learning and to train employees in the use of new tools and work equipments. Short-term refresher courses are organised for this purpose. Such training helps to avoid personnel obsolescence.

5. Safety Training:
Under this type of training, employees are familiarised with safety devices, so that accidents may be prevented. The purpose of this training is to create safety consciousness among employees.

6. Remedial Training:
This type of training is designed to correct the mistakes and shortcomings in the work behaviour and job performance of employees.

METHODS OF TRAINING

Training is concerned with the development of the employees and impart the skills, knowledge and attitudes that are required for specific jobs. The nature of training method will depend on the nature of the job, the type of trainees and the purpose of training. Different methods are followed for providing training to its employees by different organisations. The main methods of training for workers are explained below:

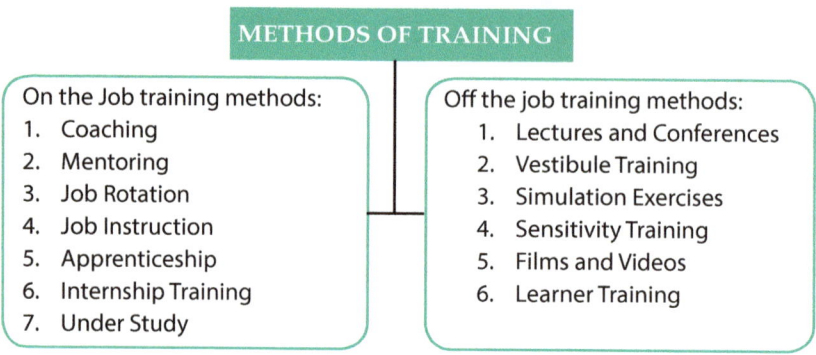

A. On the Job Training

On the job training involves assignment of the new employee to a specific job at a machine or work place in the shop, office or laboratory. The worker is trained while he is engaged in the work by utilising the actual work situation for the purpose. He is given the work straight away under the supervision of some senior employee and he learns the job at the hands of this experienced worker. He carries out his orders and instructions and follows the technique of operations advised to him. In this way, he is able to learn the work practically. Problems faced by him are immediately tackled; doubts if any removed and effective leadership offered. In this way, he goes on learning step by step by practically doing his job and reach mastery level. Thus, even during the course of his training, such worker contributes towards total production. There is no problem of adjustment to the actual job after the training. With competent instructor, this type of training may be most effective for rapid training of large number of unskilled and semi-skilled workers. But sometime, employees may cause damage to expensive equipment and the rate of accidents may be high. It is not a suitable method where the job is of complex nature. The success depends entirely on the trainee's own initiative and capabilities.

On the job training methods include the following:

1. Coaching:
Coaching is a one-to-one training. It helps in quickly identifying the weak areas and focus on them. It also offers the benefit of transferring theory learning to practice. The biggest problem is that it perpetrates the existing practices and styles.

2. Mentoring:
The focus of this training is the development of attitude. It is used for managerial employees. Mentoring is always done by a senior person. It involves one-to-one interaction, like coaching.

3. Job Rotation:
It is the process of training employees by rotating them through a series of related jobs. Rotation not only makes a person well acquainted with different jobs, but it also alleviates boredom and allows to develop rapport with a number of people. However, rotation must be logical.

4. Job Instruction:

It is a step by step (structured) on the job training method in which a suitable trainer (a) prepares a trainee with an overview of the job, its purpose, and the results desired, (b) demonstrates the task or the skill to the trainee, (c) allows the trainee to show the demonstration on his or her own, and (d) follows up to provide feedback and help. The trainees are presented the learning material in written or by learning machines through a series called 'frames'.

5. Apprenticeship Training:

This method of training is in vogue in those trades, crafts and technical fields in which a long period is required for gaining proficiency. Apprenticeship training aims at providing necessary background practical knowledge and necessary experience to the worker. Its purpose is to prepare employees for skilled occupations, like carpentry, plumbing, etc. It combines classroom instructions, demonstrations and on the job training. This method familiarises the trainee with the complications and intricacies of the job. A trainee, serving as an apprentice, has to work in direct association and under the direct supervision of his masters. Sometimes, workers are also placed as assistants to experienced workers to learn the process of work by imitation and experience. The apprentice works under his master. During the period of apprenticeship, the trainee may be given a stipend.

In India, apprenticeship training is governed by 'Apprenticeship Act, 1961'. According to this Act, a contract must be signed between the enterprise and the trainee regarding apprenticeship. A copy of the contract must be registered with Apprenticeship authorities. The maximum period of the contract is five years.

6. Internship Training:

This method of training refers to a joint programme of training in which the technical institutions and business houses cooperate. The objects of such cooperation is to provide such training which will bring about a balance between theory and practice. The trainees are given theoretical instructions in technical or professional institutions. After theoretical instructions, they get practical training in factories or offices. In medical, auditing, management and lawyer's profession, internship training is essential. The candidates while in institutions or sometimes, even after their theoretical education receive internship training in hospitals, courts, management institutions and auditing firms. Internship training is useful in the case of technical and professional employees who require advanced theoretical knowledge and practical experience on the job. The method makes them familiar with the complications and intricacies of the work. However, this method is time consuming.

7. Under Study:

In this method, a superior gives training to a subordinate as his understudy like an assistant to a manager or director (in a film). The subordinate learns through experience and observation by participating in handling day to day problems. Basic purpose is to prepare subordinate for assuming the full responsibilities and duties.

B. Off the Job Training

Off the job training is conducted separately from the job environment. Study material is supplied and there is full concentration on learning rather than performing. Importance of the off the job training method include:

1. Lectures and Conferences:

Lectures and conferences are the traditional and direct method of instruction. Every training programme starts with lecture and conference. It's a verbal presentation for a large audience. However, the lectures have to be motivating and interesting to the trainees. The speaker must have considerable knowledge in the subject. In the colleges and universities, lectures and seminars are the most common methods used for training.

2. Vestibule Training:

Under this method, new workers are trained with special machines or equipment in a separate location near the actual place of work under practical work situation. This place is called a vestibule and the actual work situation is duplicated here. An enterprise will arrange vestibule training when the number of workers to be trained is very large, and the line managers are not in a position to spare time for providing training. This type of training emphasis on teaching the best method of doing a task. Furthermore, trainees have an opportunity to get accustomed to the work routine and recover from their initial nervousness before going on the actual jobs. Workers are, thus, trained, without hampering the actual work of production, by qualified instructors. But vestibule training is comparatively expensive and trainees are not able to experience the actual work situations on the shop floor. It may be used as a supplement to 'on the job training.'.

3. Simulation Exercises:

Simulation is any artificial environment exactly similar to the actual situation. These are four basic simulation techniques used for imparting training : management games, case study, role playing, and in basket training.

(a) Management Games:

Properly designed games help to ingrain thinking habits, analytical, logical, and reasoning capabilities, importance of team work, time management, communication and leadership capabilities etc. Use of management games can encourage novel and innovative mechanisms for coping with stress. Management games orient a candidate with practical applicability of the subjects. Different games are used for training general managers and the middle management and functional heads.

Example: In a trucking business, managers could create games that teach truckers the impact of late deliveries, poor customer service or unsafe driving.

(b) Case Study:

Case studies are complex examples which give an insight into the context of a problem as well as illustrate the main point. Case studies are trainee centered activities based on topics that demonstrate theoretical concepts in an applied setting.

A case study allows the application of theoretical concepts to a situation, thus bridging the gap between theory and practice, encourage active learning, provides an opportunity for the development of key skills such as communication, group working and problem solving, and increases the trainees' confidence hence their desire to learn.

(c) Role Playing:
Each trainee takes the role of a person affected by an issue and studies the impact of the issues on human life and/or the effects of human activities from the perspective of that person.

In particular, role-playing presents the student a valuable opportunity to learn not just the course content, but other perspectives on it. The steps involved in role playing include defining objectives, choose context and roles, introducing the exercise, trainee preparation/research, the role-play, concluding discussion, and assessment. Types of role play may be multiple role play, single role play, role rotation, and spontaneous role play.

Role playing can be effective in connecting theory and practice, but may not be popular with people who don't feel comfortable performing in front of a group of people.

(d) In-basket Training:
In-basket exercise, also known as in-tray training, consists of a set of business papers which include e-mail, SMS, reports, memos, and other items. Now the trainer is asked to prioritise the decisions to be made immediately and the ones that can be delayed.

4. Sensitivity Training:
Sensitivity training is also know as laboratory or T-group training. This training is to make people understand about themselves and others reasonably, which is done by developing in them social sensitivity and behavioral flexibility. It is the ability of an individual to sense what others feel and think from their own point of view.

Sensitivity training program comprises of three steps–unfreezing the old values, development of new values and refreezing of new values. It reveals information about his or her own personal qualities, concerns, emotional issues and things that he or she has in common with other members of the group.

5. Films and Videos:
Films and videos can be used on their own or in conjunction with other training methods. To be truly effective, training films and videos should be geared towards a specific objective. They are also effective in stimulating discussion on specific issues after the film or video is finished.

Films and videos are good training tools, but have some of the same disadvantages as a lecture *i.e.*, there is no interaction with the trainees.

6. Learner Training:
This method is also known as vocational school training. This method combines training with education. Learners are those who join industry for semi-skilled jobs without any prior knowledge about the elements of industrial engineering. They have, therefore need to undergo a programme of educational training. For this purpose, it may become necessary to send them to vocational schools for some time for the study of workshop mathematics and learning operation of machines. After this, they may be assigned a regular production jobs.

LESSON AT A GLANCE

- **Training:** Training means imparting the knowledge, skills and aptitudes necessary to undertake the required jobs efficiently with a view to develop the worker to his fullest potential.
- **Training and Development:** Training always leads to the development and growth of workers. Training adds to the skills and abilities of workers.
- **Training and Education:** Training is any process by which the aptitudes, skills and abilities of employees to perform specific jobs are increased. On the other hand, education is the process of increasing the general knowledge and understanding of the employees.
- **Objectives of Training:** The basic objective of training is to help develop capacities and capabilities of employees and improve their level of performance : (i) To increase productivity of empolyees; (ii) To remain competitive in the market; (iii) To change attitude of the workers; (iv) To enable workers to adopt quickly to changes; (v) To mitigate the risk of accidents; (vi) To reduce wastage of time and resources; (vii) To provide growth opportunities to existing employees; (viii) To make the management effective.
- **Importance of Training:** (i) Improvement in production and productivity; (ii) Lesser supervision; (iii) Maximum utilisation of materials and machines; (iv) Better safety; (v) High morale; (vi) Better chances of promotion; (vii) Stability and flexibility in the organisation.
- Levels of Training: (i) Training to unskilled workers; (ii) Training to semi-skilled workers; (iii) Training to skilled workers; (iv) Training to other staff; (v) Training to senior and supervisory staff.
- **Types of Training:** (i) Job training; (ii) Induction training, (iii) Promotional training; (iv) Refresher training; (v) Safety training; (vi) Remedial Training.
- **Methods of Training:** (i) On the Job Training method; (a) Coaching; (b) Mentoring; (c) Job Rotation; (d) Job instruction; (e) Apprenticeship Training; (f) Internship training; (g) Under study. (ii) Off the job training method : (a) Lectures and Conferences; (b) Vestibule Training; (c) Simulation exercise; (d) Sensitivity Training; (e) Films and Videos; (f) Learner Training.

PROJECT WORK

Visit any four big organisations. Find out the methods of training used by each organisation to train their workers. How have training programmes helped the workers in increasing their working capacity? Compare the results of training programme of each organisation.

ASSIGNMENT

You are the Human Resource Manager in an organisation. How would you train the workers of your organisation ?

QUESTIONS

A. Short Answer Type Questions:
1. Define training.
2. What is the difference between training and development?
3. List two importance of training.
4. Name the different levels of training.
5. What are the different types of training?
6. State different methods of training.
7. What is on the job training?
8. What is meant by vestibule training?
9. Distinguish between training and education.
10. Explain the benefits of training.
11. List two main objectives of orientation training.
12. What do you mean by on-the-job training and off-the-job training? [ICSE 2019]
13. Name and explain the type of training designed to correct mistakes. [ICSE 2018]

B. Essay Type Questions:
1. What is training? Differentiate between training and development.
2. Explain the different levels of training.
3. Enumerate the various types of training.
4. What do you mean by: (i) On the job training; (ii) Vestibule training; (iii) Apprenticeship training; and (iv) Internship training.
5. What is training? How does it differ from education and development?
6. Suppose in a large modern organisation, you have been recruited as a staff training officer. Name and explain briefly different types of training programmes you would like to organise. Also indicate what should be your pre-training and post-training activities?
7. What is 'induction training'? Is it the same as on the job training?
8. Describe the importance of training.
9. Suggest on the job training by explaining its major techniques that would increase the level of productivity of employees.
10. Explain the two methods of 'off-the-job training'. [ICSE 2017]

CHAPTER-16
Industrial Relations and Trade Unions

Maintaining cordial industrial relations has been one of the several challenges faced by the modern industrial society. With growing prosperity and rising wages, workers have attained a higher standard of living; they have acquired education, sophistication and greater mobility. In such a scenario, to achieve the objectives of industrial development and of social justice simultaneously, the relations between labour and management must be cordial and harmonious. Such relations can be established and maintained in an industry only when both the workers and employers realise their duties and responsibilities towards each other. Factors such as poor working environment, automation and mechanization, computerization, nepotism, disproportionate wages, lay off, militancy of the trade unions etc. have become a cause of friction between the interests of workers and employers. As a result of such frictions, many industrial problems like—strikes, agitations, lock-outs etc., have become frequent. These have vitiated the industrial atmosphere, decreased the production and productivity of the enterprise, increased the costs of production, decreased the real income of the workers and hampered the industrial development of the country. Therefore, to avoid these consequences, it has become necessary that there must be harmonious relations between labour and management.

- Meaning of Industrial Relations
- Causes for Poor Industrial Relations
- Objectives of Industrial Relations
- Meaning of Trade Unions
- Functions of Trade Unions
- Advantages of Trade Union

INDUSTRIAL RELATIONS

The term 'industrial relations' refers to the complex set of human relationships which emerge in work situations. In other words, the relationships between employers and employees or trade unions are called Industrial Relation. Thus, Industrial Relations deals with the workers and employers relation in any industry. Industrial relations are also known as labour-management relations or employee-employers relations. Industrial relations involve attempts to arrive at workable solutions between the conflicting objectives of profit motive and social gains, of discipline and freedom, of authority and industrial democracy and of bargaining and cooperation.

Industrial Disputes Act, 1947 defines industrial relation as "a relation between employer and employees, employees and employees and employees and trade unions".

- *the term industrial relations "include recruitment, selection, and training of workers, personnel management as well as collective bargaining policies and practices".*

—Dale Yoder

- *"It is the complex of inter-relations among workers, managers and government."*

—Prof. Dunlop

On the basis of analytical study of above definitions, it may be concluded that industrial relations are the results of those mutual feelings and views of employers and employees which they adopted to get better results of planning, organising, supervision, direction, co-ordination and control of their industrial enterprise. It includes their efforts to minimise mutual frictions and to develop mutual co-operation and co-ordination. It also includes the laws passed by the Government for the settlement of industrial disputes and for the establishment of harmonious industrial relations. Thus, Industrial Relations are the inter-relations between employees, employers and Government. In other words, there are three parties to industrial relations:

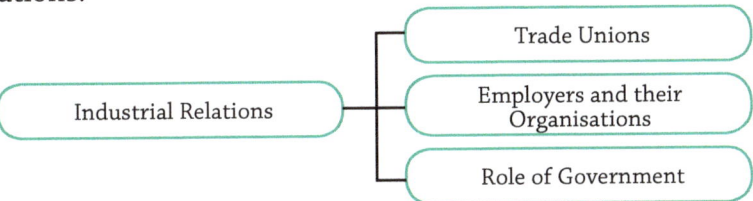

1. Trade Unions:
Trade Unions try to protect the interests of workers. These unions stress upon the development of cultural and educational qualities of their members.

2. Employers and their Organisations:
Employers and their organisations try to protect the interests of employers to create a healthy industrial atmosphere so that the organisational objectives may be achieved. They try to get full co-operation of workers in achieving this objective.

3. Role of Government:
Government also plays an important role in establishing better industrial relations. Government tries to protect the interests of both the employees and employers. For this purpose, the Government enforces various acts and laws.

Therefore, it can be said that industrial relations are the joint liability of labour unions, employers and the Government.

Causes For Poor Industrial Relations

Industrial Relations are characterised by both conflict and co-operations. This is the basis of adverse relationship. So the objective of Industrial Relations is to focus on the attitudes, relationships, practices and procedures developed by the contending parties (that is, by the workers and the employers) to resolve or at least minimize conflicts.

Major causes of rapid decline in the industrial relations and rising industrial disputes are:

1. Economic Causes:
Poor wages and poor working conditions are the main reason for unhealthy relations among management and labour. When employers deny equitable and fair remuneration and good working and living conditions to the working class, trade unions agitate and industrial peace is disturbed. Narrow mindedness of the employers and the employees is also the cause of straining industrial relations. Employers want to extract maximum work with minimum remuneration, while the workers try to avoid work and get more hike in wages.

2. Organisational Causes:
Among organisational causes responsible for poor industrial relations are : Faulty communication system, dilution of supervision and command, non-recognition of trade unions, rapid changes in the methods and techniques of production, nepotism, unequal work loads, disproportionate wage, and responsibilities, etc.

3. Social Causes:
Tensions and conflicts in society, break-up of joint family system, growing intolerance, cultural, religious and linguistic differences among workers have also led to poor industrial relations. Dissatisfaction with job and in personal life culminates in industrial conflicts.

4. Psychological Causes:
Psychological reasons for unsatisfactory employer-employee relations are : Lack of job security, poor organisational culture, non-recognition of merit and performance etc.

5. Political Causes:
Political nature of trade unions, multiple unions and inter-union rivalry weakens trade union movement. Attitude of the government and political parties who may indirectly control some the unions for their own gains or to get a hold on the industry may also strain industrial relations.

Objectives of Industrial Relations
Important objectives of industrial relations are as under:

1. To Create Mutual Faith and Trust between Workers and Management:
Most important objective of industrial relations is to create an atmosphere in the enterprise in which both the workers and management may have faith and trust upon each other. To achieve this object, it is necessary that both the parties should get proper opportunities to express their feelings and emotions.

2. To Settle Industrial Disputes:
Another important objective of industrial relations is to settle industrial disputes peacefully and, at the earliest, so that the harmonious atmosphere may be created and the production and productivity of the enterprise may be increased.

3. To Create Full Employment:
Industrial relations have to be maintained to enhance productivity of the workers and to ensure full employment by reducing the rate of labour turnover and absenteeism.

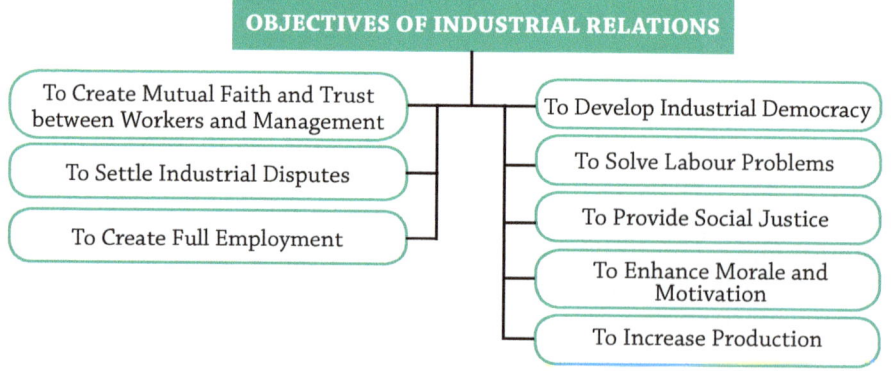

4. To Develop Industrial Democracy:
Industrial relations aims to establish good and harmonious labour-management relations which promote mutual understanding, mutual confidence and resolve the mutual differences. Workers get an opportunity of participation in management. It develops the feelings of responsibility among them and they direct their efforts for the achievement of organisational objectives.

5. To Solve Labour Problems:
Good industrial relations aim at minimising labour problems, such as strikes, lock-outs, gheraos etc. They strive to eliminate labour problems by providing reasonable wages, fringe benefits, improved living and working conditions, etc. Industrial relations also strive to change the traditional and contrary views of labour and management towards each other so that they may develop mutual understanding and co-operation and both may work in the best interests of the concern.

6. To Provide Social Justice:
Industrial relations help in providing social justice to the workers by ensuring fair and equitable wages and thus improving their standard of living.

7. To Enhance Morale and Motivation:
Good industrial relations increase the morale of the workers and motivate the workers to put in more efforts. Every problem is solved by mutual consent which increases worker's participation in management and profits of the firm and also provides job satisfaction to the workers.

8. To Increase Production:
Good industrial relations boost the production and improve both the quality and the quantity of the goods produced. It also increases labour efficiency. An increase in the morale of workers reduces per unit cost of production. Thus, industrial relations have far reaching impact on the production.

TRADE UNION

In every industrial community there are two distinct classes, the employees and the employers, without whom production at a large scale is not possible. Both these parties usually have contradictory motives, which create many problems. Individually, the labourers can do little to resolve their grievances against their employers and to prevent their exploitation. They are effective only when they act in union. This idea of joint action laid down the foundation of the instrument of struggle for security and advancement called "Trade Union".

Trade union is the association of the workers for maintaining and improving the conditions of their working lives and for securing them a better status in the industry and the society. Workers form unions in order to resist employers' exploitation and protect and safeguard their interests.

According to V.V Giri, *"Trade unions are voluntary organisations of workers founded to promote and protect their interests by collective action."*

Edwin B. Flippo defines trade union as *"an organisation of workers to promote, protect and improve, through collective action the social, economic and political interests of its members."*

It is apparent from the above definitions that trade unions are voluntary organisations of workers. The workers form an association in order to protect and safeguard their economic interests and to put up a united resistance against exploitation by the industrialists. The most outstanding feature of the trade unions is their own accord. Generally, all workers in a particular occupation are the members of the trade union representing their occupation. But there is no element of compulsion in membership. If a worker so desires he can stay away from the trade union.

Functions of Trade Union

All functions concerning the well being of workers are mostly regulated by trade unions. These functions may broadly be divided into three headings:

1. Intra-mural Activities:

Intra-mural activities refer to those efforts of trade unions which are mainly performed for the betterment of workers in relation to their employment. Through these activities, trade unions ensure adequate wages, better working conditions, better treatment and a reasonable share and control in the profits and management of industry.

2. Extra-mural Activities:

Extra-mural activities refer to those activities of the trade unions which are performed for providing help to workers in times of need. Therefore, trade unions help the workers in case of sickness and accident and give them financial support during the period of unemployment, strikes and lock-out. They also foster a spirit of co-operation and diffuse education among labourers.

3. Political Activities:

Trade unions, at present are not only confined to their intra-mural and extra-mural activities. They also contest elections and try to send their representatives in Parliament and State Legislatures. In India, such development is not yet significant and trade unions are politically unorganised.

Advantages of Trade Union

(A) Advantages to Workers

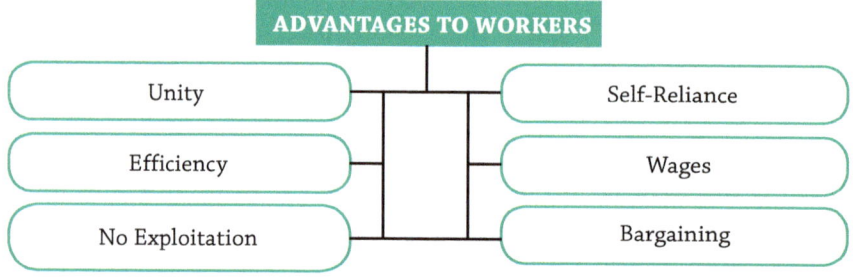

1. Unity:

It promotes unity among workers.

2. Efficiency:

Worker's efficiency is increased by improving their working conditions and by providing them with better welfare facilities.

3. No Exploitation:
Employer's attitude of exploiting workers changes.

4. Self-Reliance:
Trade unions induce self-reliance and self-respect among the workers. They are paid fair share of the profits based on the actual work done.

5. Wages:
Trade unions help to maintain the wages at a uniform level in terms of the actual economic value.

6. Bargaining:
Trade unions negotiate better with the employers through collective bargaining. Being an organised body, they may avoid strike and disputes by putting pressure on the employers to solve the problems amicably and mutually.

(B) Advantages to Employers/Producers

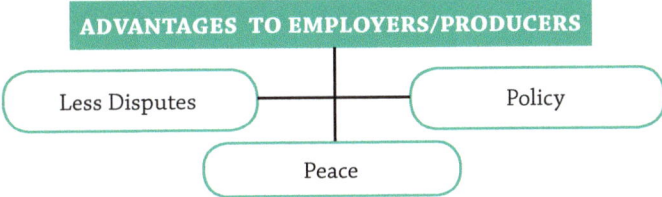

1. Less Disputes:
Industrial disputes can be avoided or may be solved amicably by developing mutual interests and thus, employers can maintain work flow.

2. Peace:
Trade unions may develop a sense of responsibility and loyalty among workers through counselling and collective bargaining. In this way, they help in maintaining industrial peace.

3. Policy:
Trade unions may associate with the employers in framing healthy labour policies which may weaken the chances of disputes in future.

In this way labour unions play an important role in developing labour-force, promoting industrial peace, increasing production and improving working conditions.

 LESSON AT A GLANCE

- **Industrial Relations:** Industrial Relations means the relations between employees and employers. According to Prof. Dunlop, "Industrial Relations may be defined as the complex of inter-relations among workers, managers and government." Thus, there are three parties to industrial relations: (i) Trade unions; (ii) Employers and their organisations; (iii) Government.
- **Causes for Poor Industrial Relations:** (i) Economic causes; (ii) Organisational causes; (iii) Social causes; (iv) Psychological causes; (v) Political causes.
- **Objectives of Industrial Relations:** (i) To create mutual faith and trust between workers and management; (ii) To settle industrial disputes; (iii) To create full-

employment; (iv) To develop industrial democracy; (v) To solve labour problems; (vi) To provide social justice, (vii) To enhance morose a motivation; (viii) To increase production.
- **Trade Union:** Trade union is the association of the workers for maintaining and improving the conditions of their working lives and securing them a better status in the industry and society.
- **Role/Functions of Trade Unions:** (i) Intra-mural activities; (ii) Extra-mural activities; (iii) Political activities.

Advantages of Trade Unions
- **Advantages to Workers:** (i) Unity; (ii) Efficiency; (iii) No exploitation; (iv) Self-reliance; (v) Wages; (vi) Bargaining.
- **Advantages to Employers/Producers:** (i) Less disputes; (ii) Peace; (iii) Policy.

Visit a big organisation and talk to the President/Secretary of its trade union about the reasons of its formation, benefits which workers are getting etc. Thereafter, make a brief report on the working of the trade union in that organisation.

Explain to your friend the importance of trade unions in an organisation.

A. Short Answer Type Questions:
1. What do you mean by industrial relations? [ICSE 2020]
2. What are objectives of industrial relations?
3. What is a trade union?
4. What is the role of trade unions in relation to its members?
5. What is the role of a trade union in relation to the industrial organisation in which it has been established?
6. What are the advantages of trade union to workers?
7. Explain the extra-mural function of trade unions.
8. Mention two objectives of industrial relations.

B. Essay Type Questions:
1. What do you mean by industrial relations? Explain the objectives of industrial relations.
2. Discuss the causes of poor industrial relations in India.
3. Define trade union. Discuss the objectives of trade unions.
4. Point out the advantages of trade unions.
5. Discuss the functions of trade unions.
6. Discuss the role of trade unions in a business concern. [ICSE 2018]
7. Explain any five objectives of Industrial Relations. [ICSE 2019]

CHAPTER-17
Social Security

Social security is a dynamic concept which is considered as an indispensable chapter of the national programme in all advanced countries of the world. With the development of the idea of the welfare state, it has been considered to be most essential for the industrial workers, though it includes all sections of the society. Social security refers to the protection provided by the society to its members against providential mishaps over which a person has no control. As the name stands for the general well being of the people, it is the duty of the state to promote social security which may provide the citizens with benefits designed to prevent or cure disease, to support him when he is not able to earn and to restore him to gainful activity. To enjoy security one must be confident that benefits will be available as and when required.

- Evolution of Social Security
- Characteristics of Social Security
- Scope of Social Security
- Social Security in India
- New Pension Scheme

EVOLUTION OF SOCIAL SECURITY

The term 'Social Security' originated in U.S.A. in 1935. The Social Security Act was passed there and the Social Security Board was established to govern and administer the scheme of unemployment, sickness and old age insurance. In 1938, social security was adopted by New Zealand, when it created for the first time, a comprehensive social security system—a measure of income security for all citizens. Later on, the term was adopted in various countries in various forms conveying different meanings.

- *According to the International Labour Organisation, "Social security is the security that society furnishes through appropriate organisation against certain risks to which its members are exposed. These risks are essentially contingencies against which the individual of small means and meager resources cannot effectively provide by his own ability or foresight alone or even in private combination with his fellows. These risks being sickness, maternity, invalidity, old age and death. It is the characteristic of these contingencies that they impair the ability of the working man to support himself and his dependents in health and decency."*
- *According to WIlliam Beveridge, "Social security means the security of an income to take the place of earnings when they are interrupted by unemployment, sickness or accident, to provide for the retirement through old age, to provide against loss of support by death of another person and to meet exceptional expenditure connected with birth, death or marriage. The purpose of social security is to provide an income upto a minimum and also medical treatment to bring the interruption of earnings to an end as soon as possible."*
- *Encyclopedia of social work defines social security as the endeavour of community as a whole, to afford itself to the utmost extent possible to any individual during periods of*

physical distress consequent on illness or injury and from the economic distress consequent on reduction or loss of earnings due to illness, disablement, maternity, unemployment, old age or death of the working members."

The concept of social security is primarily an instrument of social and economic justice. It is essentially related to the high ideals of human dignity. The social security system of a country consists of its social insurance and social assistance schemes and a clear cut demarcation cannot be made between these two.

CHARACTERISTICS OF SOCIAL SECURITY

On the basis of the above mentioned definitions, the following characteristics of social security can be listed:

(a) Social security is an instrument of ensuring social and economic justice.
(b) In a welfare state, social security is an essential part of public policy.
(c) Social security is not static; it is a dynamic concept which changes with the change in social and economic conditions prevailing in a country at a particular point of time.
(d) The basic aim of social security is to provide protection to people of small means against risks or contingencies.
(e) The contingencies which may impair a person's ability to support himself and his family may include sickness, old age, invalidity, unemployment, death etc.
(f) Social security measures are generally guided by social legislation.
(g) Social security measures provide for cash payment to affected persons to partly compensate them for the loss of income due to any of the contingencies mentioned above.
(h) Social security is a must for the protection and stability of the labour force Social security is a wise investment made by the state which yields good social dividends in the long run.

SCOPE OF SOCIAL SECURITY

The scope of social security is very wide. Even though the social security measures differ from country to country, they have some basic features in common. Generally, the social security schemes are of the following types:

(1) Social Insurance:
Under social insurance, workers and employers make periodical contribution to a fund, with or without a subsidy from the Government. Out of these contributions, benefits are provided to the contributors necessary for satisfying wants during old age, sickness, unemployment and other contingencies of life.

(2) Social Assistance:
Social assistance includes non-contributory benefits towards the maintenance of children, mothers, invalids, the aged, the disabled and others like the unemployed. Under this scheme, the Government provides benefits to persons of small means in sufficient quantity so that their minimum standards of needs could be satisfied.

The social security (Minimum standards) convention of the International Labour Organisation prescribes the following components of social security:

(a) Medical care
(b) Sickness benefit
(c) Old age or retirement benefits
(d) Employment injury benefit
(e) Family benefit
(f) Maternity benefit
(g) Invalidity benefit
(h) Survivor's benefit

(3) Public Service:
Public service programmes are usually financed directly by the Government from its general revenue in the form of cash payments or services to every member of the community falling within a defined category.

SOCIAL SECURITY IN INDIA

Although social security measures had been introduced in many countries decades ago, in India, they were introduced only after the independence of the country. It was partly due to lack of official sympathy and the comparative weakness of the trade unions in pressing their demands for such measures. After independence, India declared itself a welfare state under the constitution and as such, several social security measures were introduced.

According to Article 41 of the Constitution of India, *"The state shall within the limits of its economic capacity and development make effective provision securing the right to work, to education and to public assistance in case of unemployment, old age, sickness and disablement and other cases of unserved wants."*

Social security is an important step towards the goal of welfare state. Many State Governments have introduced old age assistance schemes and other types of social assistance benefits. Several laws have been enacted since independence in the country to provide for social security to the workers. Some of the important social security laws are given below:

(1) The Workmen's Compensation Act, 1923

In 1923, the Government of India passed the Workmen's Compensation Act. This Act, marked the beginning of social security system in India. The main objective of this Act is to impose upon the employers an obligation to pay compensation to workers for accidents arising out of and in the course of employment. It also helps to reduce the number of accidents, to give workers greater freedom from anxiety and to make industry more attractive to workers. The Act has been amended several times. The last amendment was made in April 2017 by which the government specified that this Act may now be called as 'Employees' Compensation (Amendment) Act 2017. The government by this amendment has made it mandatory for employees to inform the employee of his rights to compensation under this Act, at the time of his employment. The Act applies to all permanent employees employed in railways, factories, mines, plantations, mechanically propelled vehicles, construction work and certain other hazardous operations. It does not apply to members of armed forces, casual workers and workers covered under the Employee's State Insurance Act, 1948. The State Governments administer this Act and are empowered to extend the application of this Act to other classes of persons or diseases not covered by the Act. The State Governments have appointed labour compensation commissioners for the settlement of disputed cases.

Under this Act, the employer is liable to pay, the compensation in case of personal injury caused by accident arising out of and in the course of employment. No compensation is, however, payable if the incapacity does not last for more than 3 days or if it is caused by the default of the worker, not resulting in death. Besides, body injuries, compensation is also payable in the case of certain occupational diseases.

The amount of compensation payable depends upon the nature of injury and the average monthly wages of the worker concerned. For this purpose injury has been divided under three categories: (i) causing death; (ii) total or partial permanent disablement; and (iii) temporary disablement.

In order to protect the interest of dependents in case of fatal accidents, it is provided in the Act that all cases of fatal accidents are to be brought into the notice of commissioner of labour. In case of admission of liabilities by the employer, the amount of compensation is to be deposited with the commissioner. If the employer denies his liability, the commissioner must decide whether or not there is a ground for claim. The commissioner may inform the dependents and it is open to them for accepting a claim, if they feel so.

(2) The Employee's State Insurance Act, 1948

The Employee's State Insurance Act was passed in 1948 to provide medical facilities and unemployment insurance to industrial workers during their illness. This Act provides medical benefits in the form of medical attendance, treatment, drugs and injections to insured persons and to members of their families, where the facility has been extended to the families also. The ESI Act is applicable to all non-seasonal factories run with power and employing 20 or more persons. It covers all types of employees—manual, clerical, supervisory and technical. This Act is a land mark in the history of social security in India and its object is to introduce social insurance for workers.

The Employees State Insurance Scheme introduced under this Act is compulsory and contributory. Compulsory in the sense that all workers covered under this Act must be insured and contributory in the sense that it is financed by the contributions from both the employees and the employers.

The administration of the Act has been entrusted to an autonomous body called the Employees State Insurance Corporation. The corporation is managed by a governing body representing the Union and the State Governments, Parliament, employers and employees organisations and the medical professionals. This body elects a Standing Committee. A third body called the Medical Benefit Council, advises the corporation on matters relating to medical benefits. State-wise regional boards have also been constituted.

The scheme is financed by the Employees State Insurance Fund which consists of contributions from employers and employees, grants, donations and gifts from Central and State Governments, local authorities or any individual or body. The rate of contribution of employees depends upon the daily wages.

The Scheme provides for five types of benefits to the injured workers and their dependents. These benefits are:

(i) Sickness Benefit:

Sickness benefit consists of cash payment for a maximum period of 91 days per year to the sick worker. The daily rate of sickness benefit is calculated at half of average daily wages. The Insured worker who is getting this benefit must be under the medical treatment at a dispensary or hospital maintained by the Corporation. The benefit is useful to a worker who is unable to attend his work due to sickness.

Workers suffering from long term diseases like T.B., leprosy etc. are entitled for extended sickness benefit at 62·5% of average wage for a period of 309 days.

(ii) Maternity Benefit:

An insured women is entitled to receive cash benefit for confinement, miscarriage or sickness arising out of pregnancy. The benefit is paid at double the sickness benefit rate for a period of 12 weeks of which not more than 6 weeks shall precede the expected date of confinement. If the insured woman dies during the period of confinement, her nominee will receive the benefit for the entire period.

(iii) Disablement Benefit:

Disablement benefit is given in case of temporary as well as permanent disablement. An insured person is entitled to receive disablement benefit for any injury arising out of and in the course of employment which lasts for not less than 3 days excluding the date of accident. In case of temporary disablement, full pay is paid in addition to free medical treatment. In case of permanent partial disablement, the insured worker is entitled for cash benefit for life to be paid at a percentage of the full rate on the basis of percentage of disability. In case of permanent total disablement, the cash benefit will be paid at full rate for the whole life.

(iv) Dependent Benefit:

This benefit is given to the dependents of an insured deceased person. If a person dies as a result of employment accidents, his widow and children are entitled to pension. The widow get it throughout her life or till remarriage. The sons get it upto the age of 18 years while the daughters get it upto the age of 18 years or marriage whichever is earlier.

(v) Medical Benefit:

This benefit is given to a worker claiming sickness benefit, maternity benefit or disablement benefit. This benefit is also available to the family members of the worker. It consists of free medical treatment at dispensary or hospital run by the corporation or at home of the sick.

The ESI Act has provided much needed protection to workers. However, the ESI scheme is criticised on the grounds that the medical treatment given is not satisfactory and there is delay in providing benefits to insured workers. The Act needs to be enforced more effectively. However, in general, the scheme is working in a satisfactory manner.

(3) The Maternity Benefits act, 1961

The Maternity Benefits Act, 1961 was enacted to provide uniform standards for maternity protection. It applied in the first instance to all factories, mines and plantations except those to which the Employee's State Insurance Act applied. This

Act was amended in 1976 to extend the benefit to all women workers covered by the ESI Act. The main purposes of this Act are :

(i) To regulate the employment of women in certain establishments for certain specified periods before and after child birth.

(ii) To provide for the payment of maternity benefits to women workers.

(iii) To provide for certain benefits in case of miscarriage, premature birth or illness arising out of pregnancy.

Under this Act, a women worker can get paid maternity leave upto 26 weeks. Out of this 8 weeks could be availed prior to the delivery of the child and remaining 18 weeks can be availed post childbirth. However, for woman expecting their third child, the duration of paid maternity leave shall be 12 weeks. During the period of leave, the employee is entitled to full wage/salary. In addition, a medical bonus of ₹25 per day is payable if the employer provides no free medical care. In order to avail of these benefits, the employee must have worked for at least 100 days in the 12 months immediately preceding the date of expected delivery. The maternity claim will be forfeited if the employees works in any other establishment during the period of leave.

(4) The Employee's Provident Fund Act, 1952

Retirement benefits in the form of provident fund, family pension and deposit linked insurance are available to the employees under the Employees' Provident Fund (and Miscellaneous Provisions) Act, 1952. The Act is applicable to a factory in any industry in which 20 or more persons are employed or which the Central Government notifies in the official Gazette. The Act does not apply to cooperative societies employing less than 50 persons and working without the aid of power. It also does not apply to new establishments for 3 years from the date of establishment. The Government is empowered to grant exemption from the operation of this Act to any class of establishments under certain conditions.

The schemes under this Act are administered by a Tripartite Central Board of Trustees, consisting of representatives of employers, employees and the Government. The Act provides the following benefits:

(i) Provident Fund Scheme:

Under the contributory provident fund scheme, monthly deductions from the employee's salary are made. The employer contributes an equivalent amount. The total contributions are deposited with the provident fund commissioner or invested in the prescribed manner. An employee can obtain advances, and permanent withdrawals (after 15 years of service) for construction of house, higher education/ marriage of children, purchase of car etc. On retirement, death, migration, leaving service etc. the full balance at his credit with interest is payable.

(ii) Employee's Family Pension Scheme, 1971:

Under the Employee's Family Pension Scheme, pension is paid to the widow/ children of the employee who dies while in service. Under the new pension scheme, pension is payable to the employee after his retirement in place of provident fund. According to the new regulations all new employee will have to opt for pension scheme. Persons already employed can switch over from provident fund to pension scheme.

(iii) Employee's Deposit Linked Insurance Scheme, 1976:

The Employee's Deposit linked Insurance Scheme, 1976 was introduced for the members of the Employee Provident Fund with effect from August 1976. On the death of the member, the person entitled to receive the provident fund accumulations would be paid an additional amount equal to average balance in the provident fund account of the deceased during the preceding three years, if such average balance was not below ₹ 10,000 during the said period. The maximum amount of benefit payable under this scheme is ₹ 35,000 and the employees do not have to make any contribution for it.

(5) The Payment of Gratuity Act, 1972

This Act is applicable to all factories, mines, oil fields, plantations, ports, railways, ships or establishments in which 10 or more workers are employed. All persons employed in these establishments are entitled to receive gratuity irrespective of the amount of their wages. The Central Government is empowered under the Act to extend this Act to any establishment.

Gratuity is payable on retirement, death, disablement or termination, subject to the condition that the employee has rendered five years of continuous service with the same employer. Gratuity is payable at the rate of 15 days wages for each year of completed service or part there of subject to a maximum of 20 months wages or ₹ 3,50,000 whichever is lower.

(6) Group Life Insurance

Group life insurance may be defined as a plan which provides coverage for the risks on the lives of a number of persons under one contract. The basic feature of this scheme is the coverage of a number of persons under one contract. Group insurance facility is provided to the employees working with one employer. The important features of this scheme are as follows:

(a) Insurance is provided to all employees working under one employer without any evidence of insurability.
(b) This scheme provides risk coverage to the employees so long as they remain in the service of the employer.
(c) Group life insurance is a contract between the employer and the insurance company. The policy issued to the employer is called Master contract.
(d) The premium is paid jointly by the employer and the employees.
(e) The amount of premium is payable at a flat rate without any regard of the age and the salary of the employees.
(f) In case of injury or death of an employee, the claim received by the employer is paid to the employee or his nominee.

Group insurance proves to be very cheap because of economy in mass administration. It is a welcome relief for the employees as they get insurance cover by paying a very small amount of premium. High salaried people can use group insurance as a supplement to the individual life insurance. For the insurance company, the cost of administration is low as only one policy is issued for several persons. The employer can provide security cover for the employees at very low cost. Because of these reasons, Group life insurance is becoming very popular nowadays.

PENSION

Today, major retirement schemes in India include provident fund, gratuity, and pension plus. The first two plans provide lump sum retirement benefit while the last one makes payment in the form of a monthly annuity. A pension is a type of retirement plan that provides monthly income in retirement. It has the following objectives :

(a) To provide old age income.

(b) To provide reasonable market based return over long run.

(c) To extend old age security coverage to all citizens.

National Pension Scheme:

Government of India establishment Pension Fund Regulatory and Development Authority (PFRDA) on 10th October, 2003 to develop and regulate pension sector in the country. The National Pension System (NPS) was launched on 1st January, 2004 with the objective of providing retirement income to all the citizens. It is a voluntary defined contribution pension system, launched in 2004 by the Government of India. It is administered and regulated by Pension Fund Regulatory and Development Authority of India. NPS aims to institute pension reforms and to inculcate the habit of saving for retirement amongst the citizens. It can be regarded as the most economical pension scheme in India. It is a market linked retirement plan and it is till date the cheapest. The minimum yearly contribution is INR 6000. This can be paid either in one go or in monthly installments of INR 500. The age of the applicant should be between 18 to 60 years. NPS offers following important features to help subscriber save for retirement:

- The subscriber will be allotted a unique Permanent Retirement Account Number (PRAN). This unique account number will remain the same for the rest of subscriber's life. This unique PRAN can be used from any location in India.

Types of account under National Pension Scheme:

- **Tier I Account:** This is a non-withdrawable account meant for savings for retirement. The applicant can claim tax benefits against the contribution made to this account, subject to income tax rules applicable.
- **Tier II Account:** This is simply a voluntary savings facility. The subscriber is free to withdraw savings from this account whenever subscriber wishes. No tax benefit is available on this account. PRAN provides the subscriber an access to Tier I account and Tier II Account.

New Pension Scheme:

The New Pension Scheme was initiated by the government in 2009, to enable people to receive a pension after they retire. Government employees already receive pension as per the National Pension Scheme (NPS) and this new schemes was introduced under NPS to provide pension for all citizens of the country including the unorganised sector workers on a voluntary basis.

A contribution of a certain amount is made every month during the years when an individual is actively working. This amount is invested as per the individual's preference. There are a couple of options for investment to choose from based on the individual's preference of asset allocation and withdrawal. The money can then be withdrawn at a minimum age of 60 years.

Eligibility creteria and contribution requirements for New Pension Scheme is as follows:

- The applicant for the scheme should be an Indian citizen.
- The applicant should be of atleast 18 years of age.
- The applicant should be a maximum of 60 years of age.
- The minimum contribution to be paid is INR 500.
- The contribution has to be made at least once a year.
- The minimum annual contribution should be INR 6,000.
- The maximum contribution to the scheme should not exceed INR 12,000 per annum.

Benefits of the New Pension Scheme:

The following are the major benefits of the New Pension Scheme:

1. Tax Benefits:
There is no direct tax exemption mentioned except that during the time of withdrawal, the amount is free from tax as per the Income Tax Act, 1961.

2. Options of Investment:
There are two options for investments under this scheme, Tier I account restricts withdrawal before the individual reaches the age of withdrawal *i.e.*, 60 years, while Tier 2 account allows the facility of withdrawal before the maturity age which is 60 years.

3. Low Investment Charges:
NPS has a low investment charge, which is 0·0001% of the total amount of investment and hence is a relief in the savings effort for senior citizens.

4. Minimum Requirements:
The investor can deposit a minimum of ₹ 500 per month and the minimum amount to be deposited per year is only ₹ 6,000, making it extremely convenient for common Indian citizens.

5. Government Initiative:
Since this is an initiative of the Indian Government, there is a guarantee of receiving the pension on retirement, without any potential risk of default.

Lesson at a Glance

- **Concept of Social Security:** Social security is that security which the society furnishes through appropriate organisation against certain risks or contingencies to which its members are exposed.
- **Evolution of Social Security:** The term 'Social Security' originated in U.S.A. in 1935. Later on the term was adopted in various countries in different forms conveying different meanings.

- **Scope of Social Security:** (i) Social insurance, (ii) Social assistance; (iii) Public service.
- **Social Security in India:** India became a welfare state after independence under the constitution, and as such, several social security measures were introduced.
  - *(a) The Workmen's Compensation Act, 1923:* Under the Act, the employer is liable to pay the compensation, in case of personal injury caused by accident arising out of and in the course of employment.
  - *(b) The Employee's State Insurance Act, 1948:* The object of the Act is to introduce social insurance for workers in the form of (i) Sickness benefit; (ii) Maternity benefit; (iii) Disablement benefit; (iv) Dependent benefit; (v) Medical benefits.
  - *(c) The Maternity Benefits Act, 1961:* The Act was enacted to provide uniform standards for maternity protection.
  - *(d) The Employees Provident Fund Act, 1952:* The Act provides retirement benefits in the form of (i) provident fund; (ii) family pension; (iii) deposit linked insurance.
  - *(e) The Payment of Gratuity Act, 1972:* Gratuity is payable on retirement, death, disablement or termination subject to the condition that the employee has rendered five years of continuous service with the same employer.
  - *(f) Group Life Insurance:* It provides coverage for the risks on the lives of a number of persons under one contract.
- **National Pension Scheme:** National Pension Scheme is a voluntary defined contribution pension system administered and regulated by the Pension Fund Regulatory and Development Authority (PFRDA).

Visit a big organisation and talk to Labour Welfare Officer about the social security facilities available in the organisation. Make a brief report of each facility available and the persons benefitted from it.

Explain to your friend the social security measures available in India.

A. **Short Answer Type Questions:**
   1. What do you mean by social security?
   2. Give one definition of social security.
   3. Give two characteristics of social security.
   4. List the scope of social security.
   5. What is Workmen's Compensation Act?
   6. List two benefits which are available under Employee's State Insurance Act.

7. Mention purpose of maternity benefit Act.
8. What do you understand by provident fund scheme?
9. List two benefits of group insurance to employees and employers.
10. Briefly explain provident fund. [ICSE 2020]
11. Distinguish between Gratuity and Provident Fund. [ICSE 2017]

B. Essay Type Questions:
1. Explain the concept and scope of social security.
2. What social security measures have been initiated by the Government of India?
3. Discuss in brief the social security measures available to the workers under the workmen's compensation Act.
4. Discuss the role of Employee's State Insurance Scheme.
5. Explain the retirement benefits available to employees in India.
6. Write a note on Group Life Insurance.
7. What is National Pension Scheme? What are the types of accounts under it?

CHAPTER-18
Logistics : An Overview

LOGISTICS

- Meaning of Logistics
- Features of Logistics
- Classifications of Logistics

In ancient times, logistics management was mostly confined to military science. In today's industrial and commercial age, this term has attained a broader significance. It covers a variety of business activities for the material flow from the various sources to the processing facilities and the consecutive distribution of finished products to the ultimate users.

Logistics refers to that part of supply chain management that plans, implements and controls the flow and storage of goods, services and related information between the point of origin and the point of consumption in order to meet customers' requirements.

In other words, logistics refers to designing, developing, producing and operating an integrated system, which responds to customer expectations by making available the essential quantity and quality of products as and when required in order to provide best customer service at the least possible costs.

Logistics is an internal combination of inter-related managerial functions that ensures a smooth flow of raw materials, semi-finished goods and finished goods from the first point of production to the point of consumption. Thus, the range of logistics includes a set of activities like procurement, material handling, transportation, warehousing, insurance etc.

Logistics create value for customers, suppliers and stakeholders of an organisation. Here, value is expressed in terms of time and place. Products and services have no value unless they are in possession of the customers at the right place and at the right time. An efficient logistics system creates both time utility and place utility for both, the customers and the producers. Thus, good logistics management looks at the overall activity of the supply chain as contributing to the process of adding value to the products and services. If an activity adds very less value to the product, the need for its existence should be scrutinised. In case customers are ready to pay more than the actual cost for a product or a service as a result of pursuing a particular activity, then it means that the concerned activity has added value to the product.

Features of Logistics

A close scrutiny of the definitions of logistics can help us to enlist the following salient features of Logistics:

1. Logistics ensures an uninterrupted and uniform flow of goods such as raw materials, semi-finished and finished goods.

2. It possesses the ability of meeting customers' expectations and customers' requirements of goods and services.
3. It ensures delivery of quality products on time.
4. It provides the best possible customer service at the lowest possible cost.
5. It is an integration of various managerial functions for the optimum utilisation of resources.
6. It deals with the movement and storage of goods in appropriate quantity.
7. Logistics enhances productivity and profitability of business enterprises.

Classification of Logistics

Logistics can be classified into the following categories:

(i) Transportation:
Transportation means the movement of goods from the point of production to the place where they are required for consumption. It is an important part of commerce as it creates time utility and place utility. Geographical and climate factors force certain industries to be located in particular places. These places are far away from the markets and places where production takes place may not have any demand for their products. As such transport bridges the gap between production and consumption centres.

(ii) Warehousing:
Warehousing is the practice of storing goods in properly constructed buildings with the main objective of protecting them from fire, dust, theft, weather, heat, cold and moisture etc. and thus preventing deterioration in quality of materials. In other words, warehousing involves the making of proper arrangements for retaining the goods in perfect state till they are needed by the consumers and are to be taken to market.

(iii) Insurance:
Insurance is a contract by which a person or an organisation, in consideration of a sum of money, undertakes to make good the loss of another person or organisation against a specified risk, *e.g.*, fire, or to compensate him or his estate on the happening of a specified event such as accident or death.

LESSON AT A GLANCE

- **Definition of Logistics:** Logistics refers to that part of supply chain management that plans, implements, and controls the flow and storage of goods, services and related information between the point of origin and the point of consumption in order to meet customers' requirements.
- **Features of Logistics:** (i) Ensures uniform flow of goods; (ii) Meet customer expectations; (iii) ensures delivery of quality products on time; (iv) provides the best possible customer service at the lowest possible cost; (v) Integrate various managerial functions; (vi) Deals with the movement and storage of goods; (vii) Enhances productivity and profitability.
- **Classification of Logistics:** (i) transportation, (ii) warehousing, (iii) insurance.

Project Work

Study the logistics operations of swiggy and write a report on their delivery network.

Assignment

Explain to your Class the concept third party logistics and how it affects the retailer market.

Questions

A. **Short Answer Type Questions:**
   1. Define the term 'Logistics'. [ICSE 2019]
   2. What do you mean by warehousing?
   3. What is insurance?
   4. What are the classifications of logistics?

B. **Essay Type Questions:**
   1. Explain the meaning of logistics.
   2. List the features of logistics.
   3. Explain the various classifications of logistics.

CHAPTER-19
Transportation

If agriculture and industry are regarded as the body and the bones of the Indian economy, transportation and communication constitute its nerves, which help in the circulation of men and materials. The transportation system helps to broaden the market for goods and by doing so, it makes possible large-scale production through division of labour. Regions may have abundant agricultural, forest and mineral resources but they cannot be developed if they continue to be remote and inaccessible. By linking the backward regions with the relatively more advanced, transportation development helps in the better and fuller utilisation of resources. Finally, expansion of transport facilities, in turn, helps industrialisation directly. Expansion of transportation is thus of fundamental importance for a developing country like India.

- Meaning of Transportation
- Functions of Transportation
- Advantages and Importance of Transportation
- Modes of Transportation: Land; Water; and Air
- Merits and Demerits of Road Transportation
- Merits and Demerits of Rail Transportation
- Types of Water Transportation : Inland and Ocean
- Merits and Demerits of Water Transportation
- Merits and Demerits of Air Transportation
- Suitability of Different means of Transportation

Transportation means the movement of goods and persons from one place to another. Transportation is the physical means whereby goods are moved from the point of production to the place where they are required for consumption. Assembling and dispersion of goods are done with the help of one or the other mode of transportation. It is an important part of commerce as it helps in removing the hindrance of distance. The road, rail, river, canal, ocean and air transport, all contribute to commerce by enabling goods to be sent where and when they are required.

No country can progress without efficient and sufficient facilities of the transport. It has been rightly said that, *"If agriculture and industry are the body and bones of national organism, transport and communications are its nerves."*

- *"The transport industries, which undertake nothing more than movement of persons and things from one place to another, have constituted one of the most important activities of men in every stage of advanced civilization."* —Professor Marshall

FUNCTIONS OF TRANSPORTATION

1. It helps in the growth of industries whose products require quick marketing. Articles like fish, green vegetables are carried to various consumers quickly, even in distant markets.

2. It increases the demand for goods. Newer customers in newer places can be easily contacted and products can be introduced to them. Today, markets have acquired national and international dimensions only because of transport.
3. It creates place utility. Geographical and climate factors force certain industries to be located at particular place. These places are far away from the markets and places where production takes place and there, they may not have any demand for their products. As such transport bridges the gap between production and consumption centres.
4. Of late it has started creating the time utility also. This has been made possible mainly by virtue of the improvements in the speed of transport. It now helps the product to be distributed in the minimum possible time.
5. Transportation exerts considerable influence upon the stabilisation of the prices of several commodities. This is achieved by moving commodities from surplus to deficit areas. This maintains the balance of supply and demand factors and keeps the price of commodities stable as well as equal.
6. It ensures even flow of commodities into the hands of the consumers throughout the period of consumption.
7. It enables the consumers to enjoy the benefits of many goods not produced locally. This increases the standard of living, an essential factor for further development of the economy.
8. Transportation intensifies competition which, in turn, reduces prices. Prices are also reduced because of the facilities offered by it for large-scale production. Thus, advantages of large scale production are possible only due to transportation.
9. Transportation increases the mobility of labour and capital. It makes people of one place to migrate to other places in search of jobs. Import of capital machinery and equipment from foreign countries is only possible due to availability of proper means of transportation.

ADVANTAGES AND IMPORTANCE OF TRANSPORTATION

The advantages provided by transportation are as follows:
1. Transportation helps in the distribution of goods in wider market and thus creates greater demand for the goods.
2. It helps in bringing the stability in the price level by transporting the goods from the surplus areas to the deficit areas.
3. It helps those industries which produce perishable goods like meat, fishing, dairy farming, etc.
4. Transportation helps in reducing the cost and increases the purchasing power of the consumers.
5. Improved means of transport benefit the consumers in many ways. The consumers can enjoy the benefits of many goods (which are not produced locally by transporting such goods from other distant places.
6. It has also helped the growth of cities and urban areas by facilitating mobility of labour and capital.

7. It helps in increasing the production and thereby raising the standard of living of the people.
8. Transportation helps the people of different regions to come in contact with each other. It encourages exchange of ideas and promotes cooperation, cordial relations and understanding amongst the people of the world.
9. It helps in increasing the wealth and income of a nation. It is also a source of revenue to the government.
10. It provides employment to millions of people throughout the world.

MODES OF TRANSPORTATION

Broadly, the various modes of transportation fall into three categories—Land, water and Air. These can further be classified on the basis of vehicle used. A detailed classification of various modes of transportation is given below:

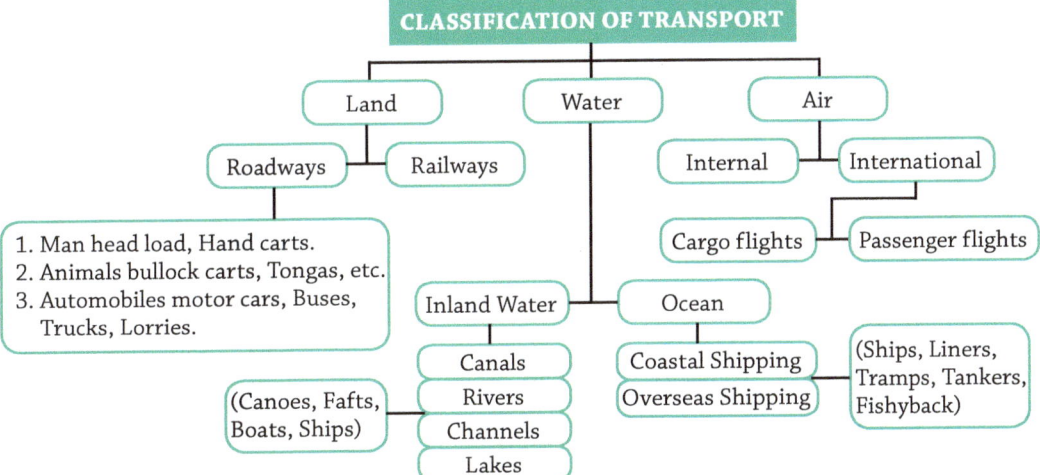

(A) Land Transportation

In land transportation, we include, Road transportation, Rail transportation, Tram-ways and Pipe lines.

(a) Road Transportation:

Road transportation is the most ancient and one of the most widely used means of transportation. Originally, man and animals used roads to carry goods and people. In remote areas or villages, animal transportation (cart, bullock cart) is used even today. The animals used in transportation are Camels, Donkey, Oxen, Mules, Buffalo, Horse etc. These are known as beasts of burden.

Motor cars and other kind of modern vehicles are the result of Industrial Revolution. They needed some regular paths and thus came modern roads—surfaced or unsurfaced, metalled or unmetalled. This is a mechanised form of transportation and has overtaken earlier modes of transportation.

Merits of Road Transportation

1. Cheapest Mode of Transportation:
All forms of road transportation—man driven, animal driven and motor driven are the cheapest form of transportation as the laying and maintenance cost of roads is the responsibility of the State and not of the owners of the vehicles.

2. Flexibility:
This is the one advantage available only to the user of road transportation. It collects goods from the point of production and delivers the goods at the place of user. Door to door service is the most attractive feature of road transportation.

3. Safety:
Damage due to handling of goods is lesser in this form of transportation, because, it unloads the goods directly at the door of the user.

4. Quick:
It is a very quick means of transportation over short distances.

5. Less Time Consuming:
It takes less time for carrying goods from one place to another and thus it helps the businessmen in increasing their turnover.

6. Frequent Service:
Bus and truck services can be as frequent as one may like. This is not possible in other means of transportation. It provides complete service to the businessmen.

Demerits of Road Transportation

1. Irregularities:
The road transportation is most irregular and uncoordinated. It plies according to its own convenience. It reduces regularity and affects the regular and continuous flow of goods.

2. Limited Carrying Capacity:
The load carrying capacity of the road transportation is limited. In case, bulky goods are to be transported, road transportation cannot be effective and also costlier. Moreover, its capacity of undertaking continuous long journey is also limited.

3. Slow Speed:
Speed of road transportation is very slow.

4. Rates:
The rate structure often is oscillating in character. Hence, it creates problems to companies that consider permanency of physical distribution a prestige.

(b) Rail Transportation:
The development and expansion of railways has revolutionised the transportation system the world over. It is a convenient mode of transportation for long distances and is most suitable for carrying heavy and bulky goods like iron ore, iron and steel, heavy machinery, minerals, etc. Railways carry raw materials from the mines and the quarries and other interior areas of the country to the industrial centres. They link up the various regions of the economy and increase the occupational mobility of people. In short, they play a crucial role in economic development.

Railways occupies a dominant role in the transportation system of a country. Rapid industrialisation took place only after the development of rail transportation system. In India also, rail transportation has played a commendable role in the development of trade. It is considered as the life line of the nation.

Merits of Rail transportation

1. Most Suitable for Heavy and Bulky Commodities:
Railways can carry the heavy and bulky goods like engineering and other industrial raw materials etc. Since, they could carry the heavy quantities, the rates are cheaper.

2. Long Distance Travel:
Railways can carry goods and people for long distance. It has now become easier to carry goods to a longer distance with the introduction of diesel and electric power. Speed has also increased considerably.

3. Cheap Rates:
Railways are cheaper than road transportation. It is because, it handles large volume of goods in a single go.

4. No Effect of Weather:
Changes in weather do not affect railways. This advantage is not found in other means of transportation.

5. Safe:
This means of transportation is safer as compared to other means of transportation. Also this means of transportation is more regular.

Demerits of Rail transportation

1. Lesser Accessibility:
It cannot serve rural areas. They can serve only those places which are connected by rails.

2. Inflexibility:
Railways cannot offer door to door service. Goods are carried to terminals (railway stations) resulting in unavoidable additional transportation cost and loading and unloading charges.

3. Not Suitable for Local Transportation:
Local or short distance transportation cannot be imagined through railways. They are profitable only for long distance transportation.

4. Huge Maintenance Expenditure:
Railways involve huge capital and maintenance cost. The low cost of transportation in most cases is, therefore only theoretically valid.

(B) Water Transportation

Water transportation is the primitive mode of transportation. In past it was the only means of transportation available for moving bulky goods. It is the cheapest mode of transportation.

Types of Water Transportation

Water transportation may be classified into two types : (a) Inland, and (b) Ocean transportation.

(a) Inland Water Transportation:

When rivers, canals, channels or even lakes within the national boundaries of a country are used for transporting goods, it is known as inland water transportation. Early civilisation and trade and commerce developed only through this mode of transportation. The primitive societies used rafts, canoes, and boats made of wood for transporting goods. Later, mechanised boats, and even steamships appeared on the scene. Now, its popularity has diminished because of the development of rail and road transports and its own inherent limitations.

(b) Ocean Transportation:

This is further classified as coastal and overseas shipping:

(i) Coastal Shipping:

Countries having long sea-coasts, use this type of water transportation. It is a dignified form of inland water transportation and serves only the coastal areas within a country with the means of modern and well equipped ships.

(ii) Overseas Shipping:

This is mainly used in international trade. In international trade, its importance grew because the road and rail transportation are purely national in character and cannot move beyond national boundaries. Quantitatively, even today shipping predominates the international transportation scene.

Shipping on the basis of purpose may be divided into Merchant ship and Navy. The former is used for commercial purposes while the latter one is meant for national defence.

According to regularity of service, the Ships are classified into Liners, tankers, tramps, and industrial carriers. Liners provide a regular service from one port to another on specified routes and move only on the basis of pre-determined schedule. Tankers are exclusively meant for transporting crude petroleum or petroleum products. Tramps are handy sized vessels and are not restricted by routes and schedules. They go wherever they find trade. Industrial Carriers are private ships owned and operated for the exclusive use of manufacturers. They transport own finished products and bring back raw materials for their own use.

Merits of Water Transportation

1. It is the cheapest mode of transportation.
2. Water ways are the gift of nature and investment required in maintenance is practically nil.
3. Its operating cost is very low when compared to others means of transportation.
4. Its load carrying capacity is much more and it can carry the heaviest load of goods.
5. It helps all nations in engaging effectively in international trade.
6. In areas, where other modes of transportation cannot be operated, water transportation is best suited.

Demerits of Water transportation

1. Its speed is very slow and so it cannot create time utilities.
2. This form of transportation is seasonal. Some rivers or seas freeze during winter and some are not navigable due to falls or shallowness.
3. Zigzag and circuitous movements required due to meandering of rivers, create inordinate delays in transportation.

4. It is fully dependent on climatic conditions. Storms, high tides and undercurrents are the usual enemies of ocean going ships.
5. It can move only where there is a route. The route cannot be constructed artificially except for a very short distance like Suez canals or Panama canals.

(C) Air Transportation

With the advent of airways, the distance is now measured not in miles but in hours. Air transportation has contributed a lot to commercial activities in international field. It has created time utility even in international markets.

Air transportation has a significant role to play. It offers saving in time that cannot be matched by surface transportation over long distances. Air transportation helps optimise technological, managerial and administrative skills in a resource scarce economy. Transportation of high value light goods and perishable goods is increasingly being done by air transportation.

Merits of Air Transport
1. It is most suitable for carrying goods of perishable nature which require quick delivery.
2. It is also suitable for light goods of high value such as gold, diamonds, jewellery, etc.
3. It provides a regular, convenient, efficient and quick service.
4. It helps in transporting goods to areas inaccessible by any other means of transportation.
5. In the event of stoppage of other means of transportation due to flood, earthquake or other natural calamities, air transportation is the only means of transportation which provides articles of necessities.

Demerits of Air Transportation
1. It is uncertain and unreliable means of transportation as it is controlled to a great extent by weather conditions.
2. The cost of operation of air transportation is higher as compared to other means of transportation.
3. Due to greater degree of possibility of accident, this means of transportation is considered to be dangerous.
4. The fares of air transportation are the highest and it is beyond the reach of a common man.
5. This means of transportation is unsuitable to carry cheap and bulky goods.
6. The construction and maintenance of aerodromes require a large amount of capital investment.

SUITABILITY OF DIFFERENT MEANS OF TRANSPORTATION

The following factors should be taken into consideration while choosing a particular means of transportation:

1. Cost:
Water transportation is comparatively a cheaper means of transportation for carrying heavy and bulky goods over long distances, particularly when time is not

an essential element. Rail transportation ranks second in terms of cost of service. It is cheaper than road transportation for carrying bulky goods over long distances. Road transportation is the cheapest means of transportation for small goods which are to be carried over short distance. Air transportation is the most costly means of transportation and its capacity is limited. It is suitable only for carrying perishable, light and valuable goods.

2. Speed:
Air transportation is the quickest means of transportation while water transportation is the slowest means of transportation. Road transportation is quicker than the rail transportation over short distances. Goods can be loaded directly into a road vehicle and transported straight to their destination. Rail transportation is faster than road transportation over long distances.

3. Flexibility:
Road transportation has the great advantage over all other means of transportation for its flexible service. Road transportation is capable of providing door-to-door services. Its routes and timing can be adjusted to individual requirements. Other means of transportation like water, rail and air transportation are not flexible and cannot provide door-to-door service. Road transportation also acts as a complementary service to other means of transportation.

4. Regularity:
Rail transportation is most certain, regular and uniform as compared to other means of transportation. It is not influenced by weather conditions. Other means of transportation like water, road and air transportation are influenced by weather conditions and are not dependable means of transportation. The effect of weather on road transportation is comparatively less as compared to water transportation and air transportation. Air transportation is most uncertain and unreliable means of transportation. Unfavourable weather may cause cancellation of scheduled flights.

5. Safety:
- Road transportation is the safest means of transportation. Rail transportation also provide sufficient safety to goods. Water transportation and air transportation are the most risky means of transportation.

From the above discussion, it can be concluded that:

(a) Road transportation is particularly suited for carrying goods which are not very cheap or bulky and over short distances. It is also suited for carrying perishable goods such as vegetables, fruits, eggs, milk, etc.

(b) Rail transportation is suited for carrying heavy and bulky goods over long distances.

(c) Water transportation is the best means of transportation for carrying heavy and bulky goods of low price which do not require quick delivery.

(d) Air transportation is suited for carrying perishable, valuable and light articles of high value such as gold, jewellery, etc., which require quicker delivery.

Lesson at a Glance

- **Transportation:** Transportation means the movement of goods and persons from one place to another.
- **Functions of Transportation:** (i) It helps in the growth of industries whose products require quick marketing; (ii) It increases the demand for goods; (iii) it creates place utility; (iv) it creates time utility; (v) helps stabilisation of prices; (vi) Regularity in consumption; (vii) Enjoyment of goods not produced locally; (viii) Intensifies competition; (ix) Increases mobility of labour and capital.
- **Modes of Transportation:** (A) Land; (B) Water; (C) Air.
- **Land Transportation:** (a) Road Transportation; (b) Rail Transportation
- **Merits of Road Transportation:** (i) Cheapest mode of transport; (ii) flexibility; (iii) Safety; (iv) Quick; (v) Less time consuming; (vi) frequent service.
- Demerits of Road Transportation: (i) Irregularities; (ii) Limited Carrying capacity; (iii) Slow speed; (iv) Rates.
- **Merits of Rail Transportation:** (i) Most suitable for heavy and bulky commodities; (ii) Long Distance Travel; (iii) Cheap Rates; (iv) No effect of weather; (v) Safe.
- **Demerits of Rail Transportation:** (i) Lesser Accessibility; (ii) Inflexibility; (iii) Not suitable for local transportation; (iv) Huge maintenance expenditure.
- **Water Transportation:** (a) Inland Water Transportation; (b) Ocean Transportation: (i) Coastal Shipping; (ii) Overseas Shipping.
- **Merits of Water Transportation:** (i) Cheap; (ii) Low maintenance; (iii) Low operating cost; (iv) High carrying capacity; (v) Helps international trade; (vi) Best suited.
- **Demerits of Water Transportation:** (i) Slow speed ; (ii) Seasonal ; (iii) Zigzag; (iv) Dependent on climatic conditions; (v) Requires route.

Air Transportation:
- **Merits of Air Transportation:** (i) Suitable for Perishable goods; (ii) Suitable for light goods of high value; (iii) Quick service; (iv) Transportation of goods to inaccessible areas; (v) Regular supply in case of natural calamities.
- **Demerits of Air Transportation:** (i) Unreliable; (ii) Cost of operation is high; (iii) Dangerous; (iv) High fare; (v) Unsuitable to carry cheap and bulky goods; (vi) High maintenance cost.
- **Suitability of Different Means of Transportation:** (i) Cost; (ii) Speed; (iii) Flexibility; (iv) Regularity; (v) Safety.

Visit a nearby store and collect the information about the different modes of transportation through which they collect the majority of goods available for sale. Ask the logistics manager about the problems and advantage of each mode they use.

Explain to your class the different modes of water transportation.

A. **Short Answer Type Questions:**
 1. Explain the meaning of transportation.
 2. Write three functions of transportation.
 3. Write two benefits of transportation.
 4. List the modes of transportation.
 5. Give three merits of road transportation.
 6. Give three demerits of road transportation.
 7. Write two advantages of rail transportation. [ICSE 2018]
 8. List three demerits of rail transportation.
 9. List two kinds of water transportation.
 10. Write two merits of water transportation.
 11. Write two demerits of water transportation.
 12. List two merits of air transportation.
 13. List two demerits of air transportation.

B. **Essay Type Questions:**
 1. "Transportation is the life blood of commerce." Discuss and explain the importance of transportation.
 2. Discuss the merits and demerits of road transportation
    OR
    Explain any five merits of road transport.
 3. Discuss the merits and demerits of rail transportation.
 4. Discuss the merits and demerits of air transportation.
    OR
    Explain any five disadvantages of Air Transport. [ICSE 2019]
    OR
    Explain any five advantages of Air transport over water transport. [ICSE 2018]
 5. Discuss the merits and demerits of water transportation.
 6. What factors should be taken into consideration in selecting a means of transportation?

CHAPTER-20
Warehousing

All the goods produced or manufactured are not consumed at the time of their production. This means that the goods are first produced and then consumed. Most of the products are produced seasonally, i.e., their supply is seasonal in nature. But the demand for these products is year-round. This means that the goods are to be stored to ensure their year round supply. The goods may therefore, be stored by the producers, the middleman or by the consumers themselves. Generally, it is the middleman, who stocks the produce because they possess facilities of warehousing.

- Meaning of Warehouse
- Characteristics of a Warehouse
- Objectives of Warehousing
- Functions of Warehouses
- Importance of Warehouse
- Types of Warehouses

Warehousing is the practice of storing goods in properly constructed buildings with the main objects of protecting them from fire, rust and corrosion, dust, theft, weather, heat, cold and moisture etc. and to prevent deterioration in quality of materials. In modern business, a warehouse is as essential as the bank. At present, warehouse is an essential function of the marketing process. In other words, warehousing involves the making of proper arrangements for retaining the goods in perfect state till they are needed by the consumers and are to be taken to the market.

WAREHOUSE

A warehouse is a properly constructed place where surplus goods can be kept safely for future use. Modern warehouse are equipped with latest equipments and facilities for safety of goods as per the requirements of different kinds of goods. Rubber goods, leather goods, textiles, metals, etc., require their own kind of care. Cold storage further enables many perishables such as butter, eggs and fruits, to be stored for regular supplies.

Warehousing is an important function of commerce. It creates time utility and removes the hindrance of time. Warehousing may be defined as the assumption of responsibility for the storage of goods. A warehouse is a place used for the storage or accumulation of goods in proper condition from the time they are produced until they are needed by consumers.

- *The importance of warehousing can be gauged from the statement of S.S. Chatterjee, who remarked that "If transporting and advertising are designed to widen the market, then storage must be taken for deepening the market."* —S.S. Chatterjee
- *"A warehouse is an establishment for the storage or accumulation of goods. It is one of the most important auxiliaries in the service of trader, since by its means the necessity for delay in availing the arrivals of goods from the producers is avoided."*
  —James Stephenson

From the above meaning and definitions of warehousing we may conclude that "Warehousing refers to the arrangement by which goods are stored when they are not immediately needed and are kept in such a manner that they are protected from deterioration." Storage of goods is necessary throughout the marketing processes. By preserving goods from the time of production to the time of consumption, it ensures the continuous flow of goods to the market.

Characteristics of A Warehouse

1. Sufficient Space:
Warehouse is a place used for the storage or accumulation of goods. Thus it requires a sufficient space to store maximum goods. Insufficient space is a hindrance in the future development of trade.

2. Safety:
Warehouse should be established at that place where there is no possibility of deterioration of goods. In other words, they should be built strong enough to be safe from pilferage's, theft, dacoities, rain, dust, sun and natural calamities.

3. Proper Supervision:
Warehouse should be properly supervised to avoid the possibility of deterioration of the goods.

4. Near to the Means of Transport:
Warehouses should be established at that place where there is a facility of means of transport.

5. Easy Approach:
Warehouses should be established at that place where buyers and sellers and other related persons (such as a middlemen) may reach conveniently.

6. Economy:
Warehouses should be properly managed so that goods may be stored economically. This is possible only if there is a full utilisation of space.

Objectives of Warehousing

There are four main objectives of warehousing:
1. To protect all goods in warehouse against losses.
2. To provide maximum warehousing service at a minimum cost.
3. To provide prompt delivery of goods.
4. To provide variety of goods of different grades, throughout the year.

Functions of Warehouses

Warehouses thus aid in making an adjustment between production, on the one hand, and demand, on the other. The following are the main functions of the warehouses:

1. Storage of Goods:
The primary function of a warehouse is the storage of surplus goods.

2. Sharing the Risk:
When a storekeeper receives goods for storage he accepts the responsibility for returning them in as good a condition as he receives them. He thus takes over from

the owner the risks attached with the goods and becomes responsible if the goods while in storage, are lost or damaged.

3. Sorting, Packing and Labelling:
Modern warehouses provide the services of sorting the commodities, packing and placing labels on them.

4. Incidental Services for Marketing:
Modern warehouses clean, dry and prepare goods for the market.

5. Exhibiting and Selling of Goods:
Some warehouses provide the facilities of exhibiting and even selling of goods on behalf of the depositor.

6. Economy in Time:
Goods produced by the producers are stored in warehouses which are situated in the central place of the towns, thus the time which ordinarily is to be spent for collecting the goods from the producers scattered far away in the industrial units is saved.

7. Provision of Market:
It performs the most important function of facilitating the retailers to examine the variety of goods at different grades.

8. Regulation of Supply:
By storing goods during periods of excess supply and releasing them during the time of excess demand, warehouses help in regulating the supply of goods.

9. Handling of Exports and Imports:
An efficient system of warehousing is essential for the export of goods. The owners of warehouses sometimes take upon themselves the function of shipping goods on behalf of their clients. They, thus, work as forwarding agents for the exporters.

10. Miscellaneous Functions:
The owner of warehouse is a businessman. In a competitive environment, he wants to get more business by rendering miscellaneous services such as facility of cold storage, purchasing goods on behalf of his clients, collecting market information etc.

Advantages and Importance of Warehouse

1. Seasonal Production:
Goods which are produced seasonally (like wheat, rice, etc.) must be stored so that they are supplied to the consumers throughout the year. In order to supply such commodities to the consumers, their storage is of utmost importance.

2. Seasonal Demand:
Many goods (like woollen cloth, umbrella, rain coats, fans, etc.) are produced throughout the year but their demands are seasonal. Such goods must be stored and preserved until the beginning of the next season. To enable the producers producing such goods to work throughout the year, goods produced by them in off-season must be stored in warehouse.

3. Storage of Perishable Goods:

Perishable goods like vegetables, fruits, eggs, etc. are stored in cold storage to enable the consumers to consume them regularly throughout the year. In the absence of warehouses, the market for the sale of perishable goods will be limited.

4. Production at One Place but Demand at Various Places:

When goods are produced at a distance from the consumers, they must be stored safely in the warehouses near the market as a protection against delays in supply. It enables goods to be made available to the consumers whenever and wherever they are required by them.

5. Stabilisation of Prices:

Prices of goods may oscillate in periods of excess demand and excess supply. During periods of excess supply, if the goods are allowed to flood the markets, the prices would reduce drastically, causing loss to the producers and the farmers. Alternatively during periods of excess demand, warehouses release the goods stored in them to bridge the supply gap, preventing the prices of goods from rising. It is, therefore, necessary to store the goods in the warehouses to avoid violent fluctuations in their prices, especially those goods which are produced during a particular season.

6. Storage of Raw Materials:

It is necessary to store raw materials to ensure continuous largescale production.

7. Production in Anticipation of Demand:

Most of the goods are not produced to meet ready orders but in anticipation of their demand. Therefore, such goods have to be stored until they are demanded.

8. Grading, Packing and Processing:

Warehouses these days provide the facilities of processing, packing and grading of goods. Goods can be graded and packed in convenient sizes as per the instructions of the owner.

9. Financing:

Loans can be raised from the warehouse keeper against the goods stored by the owner. Goods act as security for the warehouse keeper. Similarly, banks and other financial institutions also advance loans against warehouse receipts. In this manner, warehousing acts as a source of finance for the businessmen for meeting business operations.

Types of Warehouses

1. Private Warehouses

These warehouses are owned by the traders or manufacturers to store goods manufactured or bought by them until they are sold out. Since these warehouses are operated for own purposes, their services are not available to other manufacturers. Wholesalers also find it more convenient to deliver goods directly from their own warehouses.

2. Public Warehouses

A public warehouse is the one which operates to store goods of any member of the public in consideration of charges. Public warehouses are held to be public utilities. They are organised to provide storage service and facilities to the retailers, wholesalers, stockist or even general public in return for a storage fee or charge. In order to provide proper storing facilities to the farmers, *General Warehousing Corporation* and *State Warehousing Corporation* have been set up under the Second Five-Year Plan.

The purpose of public warehouses may be enumerated as under:

(a) They provide full safety to the goods and take all possible precautions to prevent them from damage.

(b) They provide transport facility for receiving and shipping the goods both on rail and ship.

(c) They also provide useful services to the businessmen for the sale of products such as packing, branding, etc.

(d) Purchasers can be taken to the warehouse to inspect the goods.

(e) Manufacturers or traders can easily borrow on the security of warehouse receipts.

3. Cold Storages

These warehouses are established and organised for providing storage services and facilities to perishable goods such as, vegetables, fruits, eggs, fishes, etc. They charge storage fee from the traders. In India more and more cold storages are coming into existence.

Advantages of Cold Storages:

(a) They use scientific method for preserving the perishable goods.

(b) They help in preserving the quality of goods.

(c) Because of cold storages, perishable goods are available throughout the year for consumption to public.

(d) They ensure regular and smooth supply of perishable goods.

(e) They also ensure better prices to the farmers.

4. Bank Warehouses or Godowns

Goods pledged to banks against loans advanced by them are kept in such godowns. They are controlled by banks.

5. Railway Warehouses

Railway authorities establish railway warehouses. Goods received by railways are kept in such warehouses till they are loaded in the wagons. Similarly, goods unloaded at the destination are kept in such warehouses till the owners claim them by submitting the railway receipt (R/R).

6. Warehouses of Food Corporation of India

There is a chain of warehouses established under the direct or indirect control of Food Corporation of India, where the food grains procured from farmers are stored for either to be distributed under public distribution system or for exigencies such as natural calamity, which may reduce agricultural supply.

7. Bonded Warehouses

Bonded warehouses are those warehouses which are licensed by the Government to accept imported goods for storage before the payment of custom duties by importers of such goods. These warehouses are situated near the ports. The goods are delivered by the warehouse-keepers only after the payment of import duty. Such warehouses are called 'Bonded Warehouses' and goods stored therein are said to be 'in a bond'.

By storing their goods in such warehouses, importers gain some control over their goods even before they have paid duty on them. Goods which are meant for re-export are also kept in such warehouses.

These warehouses may be owned by the dock authorities or may be privately owned. They have to work under the control and supervision of the custom authorities. A strict watch is kept on these warehouses by custom authorities.

Some Benefits and Services of Bonded Warehouses are as Follows:

(a) The importers are given the facility to keep their goods in such warehouses till they are able to arrange for the payment of import duty.

(b) The goods stored in such warehouses may be taken in parts by paying the proportionate duty.

(c) The warehouse authorities allow the owners of goods to take their customers in the warehouse for the inspection of goods.

(d) The owners of imported goods are allowed to get their goods branded, blended, labelled, etc. in the warehouse.

(e) Goods stored in such warehouses are quite safe and there is no fear of their being damaged.

(f) For the goods imported for re-export, the importer need not first pay the custom duty and later claim it back after exporting the goods. This saves him from a lot of botheration and considerable expenses.

8. Field Warehousing (Custodian Warehousing)

These are centrally-located warehouses from where goods are further distributed to wholesalers and retailers. This is necessary where products from different plants have to be mixed together.

9. Cooperative Warehouses

The ownership of these warehouses is vested in the hands of a few primary Cooperative Societies. They have not been very popular so far in India but if properly organised they will be a boon to the agriculturists.

Lesson at a Glance

- **Warehouse:** A warehouse is an establishment for the storage or accumulation of goods.
- Characteristics of a warehouse: (i) Sufficient space; (ii) Safety; (iii) Proper Supervision; (iv) Near to the Means of Transport; (v) Easy Approach; (vi) Economy.
- **Functions of Warehouses:** (i) Storage of goods; (ii) Sharing the Risk; (iii) Sorting, Packing and Labelling; (iv) Incidental Services for Marketing; (v) Exhibiting and selling

of goods; (vi) Economy in time; (vii) Provision of Market; (viii) Regulation of Supply; (ix) Handling of Exports and Imports; (x) Miscellaneous functions.
- **Advantages/Importance of Warehouse:** (i) Seasonal Production; (ii) Seasonal Demand; (iii) Storage of Perishable Goods; (iv) Production at One Place but Demand at Various Places; (v) Stabilisation of Prices; (vi) Storage of Raw materials; (vii) Production in Anticipation of Demand, (viii) Grading, Packing and Processing; (ix) Financing.
- **Kinds of Warehouses:** (i) Private Warehouses; (ii) Public Warehouses; (iii) Cold Storages; (iv) Bank Warehouses or Godowns; (v) Railway Warehouses; (vi) Warehouses of Food Corporation of India; (vii) Bonded Warehouses.

Project Work

Visit a cold storage or a Bonded warehouse near your town. Prepare a list of commodities that are stored in the warehouse. Ask the warehouse manager about the working of warehouse and the services provided by the warehouse to the traders. Also find out whether that warehouse is managed by a private individual or a Cooperative society.

Assignment

Explain to your class the different forms of warehousing and their benefits.

Questions

A. Short Answer Type Questions:

1. What is a warehouse?
2. Give one definition of warehouse.
3. Write two characteristics of a warehouse.
4. Give three functions of warehouse.
5. List three advantages of warehouse.
6. Write three kinds of warehouses.
7. What is public warehouse?
8. What are bonded warehouses? [ICSE 2020]
   OR
   What is a bonded warehouse? [ICSE 2017]
9. List two benefits of bonded warehouse.
10. How do warehouses helps in price stabilisation? [ICSE 2019]
11. Distinguish between private warehouse and public warehouse. [ICSE 2017]

B. Essay Type Questions:

1. What do you mean by warehousing? What are its characteristics?
2. What do you mean by Bonded warehouse? Describe its importance in trade.
3. Describe the advantages of warehousing.
4. Describe the different types of warehouses.
5. Describe any two kinds of warehouses.
6. Discuss six reasons for the increasing necessity of storage in business.
7. Explain any five importance of warehousing. [ICSE 2017]

CHAPTER-21
Insurance

INSURANCE

Risk and uncertainty are incidental to life. These risk and uncertainties are increasing day by day due to increase in the pace of life. Man may meet an untimely death. He may also suffer from accident, destruction of property from fire, sea, floods, earthquakes etc. Whenever there is uncertainty, there is risk as well as insecurity. It provides a coverage against risk and insecurity.

- Meaning of Insurance
- Objectives of Insurance
- Common Terminology used in Insurance
- Business Risks
- Fundamental Principles of an Insurance Contract
- Advantages and Importance of Insurance
- Types of Insurance

Insurance is a contract between two parties by which one of them undertakes to indemnify the other against a loss which may arise on the happening of some event. The document containing the contract is called the Policy of Insurance, the person insured is called the Assured or Insured, and the party which insures is known as the Assurer, Insurer or Underwriter. In return for the insurer's guarantee to make good a specific loss, the insured undertakes to pay the insurer regularly a sum of money known as the premium. The contingency or happening against which insurance is effected is called the risk.

- *"Insurance is a device for the transfer of risks of individual entities to an insurer, who agrees, for a consideration (called the premium), to assume, to a specified extent, losses suffered by the insured."*
  —W.A. Dinsdale
- *"Insurance is a social device providing financial compensation for the effects of misfortune, the payments being made from the accumulated contributions of all parties participating in the scheme."*
  —D. S. Hansel
- *"Insurance is a contract in which a sum of money is paid by the assured in consideration of insurers incurring the risk of paying a large sum upon a given contingency."*
  —Justice Tindal

To conclude, a contract of insurance is a contract by which a person, in consideration of a sum of money, undertakes to make good the loss of another person, against a specified risk, *e.g.*, fire, or to compensate him or his estate on the happening of a specified event such as accident or death.

Objectives of Insurance

Human life and property are subject to the risk of loss or damage from numerous events. The earning member of a family may die, leaving the family in poverty. The house of a person may catch fire and may be reduced to ashes in no time. The ship of a merchant may be upturned by high waves, lost or damaged. The persons who incur such losses suffer financially and in several cases they are practically ruined.

To safeguard against such risks, the system of insurance has been devised. Insurance in broad terms may be described as a method of protection granted to an individual, institution or indeed the traders, against financial losses that may be caused by the occurrence of risks.

Common Terminology used in Insurance

1. Insured:
One who is covered by an Insurance Company (Individual, Company, Firm, Corporate body etc., with legal status)

2. Insurer:
Party granting the protection under an insurance policy.

3. Policy:
A written contract of insurance between the insurer and the insured, containing all the terms, conditions and warranties of the insurance cover, and as well as the amount of premium, sum insured and the expiry date of the contract among others.

4. Premium:
Non-refundable, small amount of money contributed to the Insurance Company in return for insurance cover.

5. Risk:
It can be defined as the unforeseen element which may impede a person's progress in achieving an objective.

There are two types of risks namely: Insurable risks and Non-Insurable risks.

Insurable risks are those risks that;

(a) can easily be assessed and whose frequency of occurrence can be estimated

(b) can have premiums fairly calculated

(c) have past statistical records

(d) can be accepted for coverage by the insurance company

Examples of Insurable risks include; fire, theft, death, accidents, claims from third parties, damage to property, burglary, bad debts, etc.

Non-Insurable risks are those risks that;

(a) can not be easily assessed and their frequency of occurrence can not be estimated

(b) whose premium can not be fairly calculated

(c) do not have any past statistical record of occurrence

(d) can not be accepted to be covered by the insurance company

Examples of Non-Insurable risks include : bad management, illegal acts such as theft, losses due to change of fashion, natural calamities such as earthquakes, etc.

BUSINESS RISKS

There are multifarious risks in business. The business property is subject to loss by fire, theft, burglary and fraud. The goods are subject to loss by natural causes such as storms, earthquakes, floods, etc. In times of war, the risk is multiplied manifold.

At present, due to industrial revolution and technological changes, risks in business have increased. Business risks can be classified into the following categories:

1. Natural Factors:
Loss by natural causes such as floods, fire, storms, earthquakes, lightening etc., are included in this category.

2. Human Factors:
Losses due to human factors like negligence, incompetence, strikes, riots and civil commotion, lockouts, embezzlement are included in this category.

3. Economic Factors:
Decline in demand or a fall in prices due to changes in economic policy are included in this category.

4. Miscellaneous:
There are so many other factors due to which, risks arise such as changes in government policy, damage caused by insects, pests, rodents, etc., such risks are included in this category.

FUNDAMENTAL PRINCIPLES OF AN INSURANCE CONTRACT

Insurance contracts are governed by Indian contract act, 1872 which states that to be legally valid, following elements should be in order :

(a) Offer and acceptance

(b) Consideration

(c) Agreement between the parties

(d) Capacity of the parties

(e) Legality of the contract

The following are the principles of Insurance:

1. Principle of Utmost Good Faith or Uberrimae Fidei Contract:

Uberrimae Fidei Contract refers to an insurance contract signed on the foundation of utmost good faith on the part of both the insurer and the insured. It is the duty of the person who wants the insurance policy to share all the material facts about the subject to be insured. These facts affect the judgment of an insurance company in assessing the degree of risk and it is imperative that the insured discloses any information or details in good faith to the insurance company. The insurance company assumes that the facts disclosed on the proposal form are reliable and accurate. Consequently, as any loss occurs, the insurance company will check the facts and materials provided by the insured. In case the details provided were inaccurate, then the insured shall not be compensated. For example, a person driving in a drunken state may meet with a car accident, and then claim compensation from his or her insurance company. However, instead of revealing the truth, the insured may fabricate the facts and say that the accident occurred due to the negligence of other driver. In such a case, the insurance company has full rights to reject the contract of insurance on grounds of fabricating the truth and insured will not be entitled for any compensation.

2. Principle of Insurable Interest:

Insurable interest is said to exist when the insured person obtains some benefit from the existence of an insured object or living persons in case of life insurance. The person having insurable interest in an object or person will be subjected to a financial loss by its destruction. For example, a businessman has insurable interest in his shop, and the bank has insurable interest in the life of the businessman till the loan given to him has been repaid.

In case of life insurance policy, the presence of insurable interest must be at the time of taking up the policy. However, it is not necessary that the insurable interest must be present at the time of death also. In marine insurance, insurable interest must exist at the time of loss; it may or may not exist at the time of contract. In case of fire insurance, insurable interest must exist at the time of death as well as loss. In the absence of insurable interest, a contract of insurance becomes a wager or gambling contract; hence, null and void and unenforceable by law.

3. Principle of Indemnity:

The literal meaning of indemnity is 'protection against a loss or other financial burden.' The objective of insurance policy is to restore the insured to the same financial position after incurring the loss as he/she was before facing the loss. The insured is entitled to receive only the amount of the claim or compensation in accordance to the actual loss. Under the principle of indemnity, the insured is not allowed to earn profit out of insurance because the objective of insurance is to cover the perils, and not to be the means for profit-making. For example, Y has insured his factory for ₹ 1,00,00,000. One day, a fire engulfs the property and destroys it. However, Y succeeds in recovering goods worth ₹ 10,00,000 stored in the factory.

Now, Y will be compensated up to ₹ 90,00,000 (*i.e.*, 1,00,00,000-10,00,000). The principle of indemnity is applicable to all types of insurance except life insurance because no amount of compensation is sufficient to make up for the loss of life. The sum insured in case of life insurance is fixed and is payable either on the expiry of the policy or after death of the insured. Therefore, the contract of life insurance could be called a contingent contract, not a contract of indemnity.

4. Principle of Causa Proxima:

Causa Proxima or Proximate Cause means 'that the insurer will consider the immediate and not the remote cause of the loss or liability.' Under this principle, the insurance company pays the claim only if there is a loss of property as per the terms mentioned in the insurance policy. In other words, the insured can claim damages when the loss has been caused due to insured perils (risks), and the cause has been proximate or nearest to the loss. For instance, if sacks of grains kept in a warehouse are destroyed in the rain due to the holes created in them by the rats, then the insurers will ascertain if the cause of loss were the rats or the rain water. If rain water is the primary cause of the loss, then the insurance company will pay the claim even if it all happened due to the holes created by the rats. The losses incurred due to the negligence of the workmen of the warehouse are not covered under insurance.

5. Principle of Subrogation:

According to this principle, after the compensation of losses suffered by the insured, the insurer gets all the rights in the damaged property and the rights of claiming the losses are shifted to the insurer. This principle allows the insurer to pursue legal actions to recover the amount of loss. Suppose an insurance company insures a four-wheeler and the vehicle gets damaged in an accident. If the insurance gives full claim to the insurer for the vehicle, the insurer will become the new owner of the damaged property. The insurer may also choose to sell the scrap of the vehicle to recover money but the insured cannot sell the damaged vehicle to the scrap dealer and earn profit.

Another crucial facet of this principle is that after paying the compensation for the insured loss, the insurance company can rightfully recover the amount from the insured which he or she has received from the third parties for the damage done. For example, A insures his shop against fire for ₹ 70,000. If the shop is set on fire by a jealous rival of A; A will be entitled to receive a claim of ₹ 70,000 from the insurance company. However, if A has recovered a sum of ₹ 40,000 from his rival, he will have to hold this sum as a trustee and return it to the insurance company. The principle of subrogation is applicable to all contracts of indemnity except to life insurance.

The characteristics of this principle are:

(i) The insurance company cannot sue third party in its own name; it can sue them only in the name of the insured.
(ii) The insurance company receives all those rights in property against third parties which were enjoyed by the insured.
(iii) The insured cooperates with the insurance company by taking the side of insurance company.
(iv) The claim recovered by the insured goes to the insurers.

6. Principle of Contribution:

According to this principle, an insurer who paid the insurance claim may rightfully ask other insurers to contribute to the claim he has paid to the insured. If an insured has taken more than one policy on the same subject matter, he will not be getting claim from each insurer more than the proportion of loss for which they are liable. Put together his total claim from all the insurers cannot be more than the total loss suffered by him. The amount of claim is contributed by the insurance companies in the ratio of insured amounts.

This principle is applicable only if four conditions are met, which are :

(i) The insured must be the same person.
(ii) All the policies must cover the same risk.
(iii) All the policies must be in force at the time of loss of property.
(iv) The total amount of compensation under all policies must not exceed the amount of loss.

7. Mitigation of Loss:

This principle implies that the insured should dutifully take measures to minimize the losses in the event of an accident or mishap. The insured should not act under the impression that the insured assets were anyway protected by the insurance cover, and hence, fail to make attempts to protect them from loss. He should take all preventive steps to ensure that the damage is curbed or minimized as much as possible.

ADVANTAGES AND IMPORTANCE OF INSURANCE

Immense are the benefits of insurance to the modern business. The goods may be destroyed due to fire, theft or in transit. The workers are also exposed to various risks which can cause death or permanent disability. Insurance has been helpful in solving these problems of business and private life. Following are the advantages of insurance :

1. Mitigating Fear and Ensuring Employee Welfare:
There is always a fear of sudden loss. Insurance helps to mitigate various types of fear from the mind of the people. Insurance provides security against losses to both individuals and businessmen. The insured feels secured because of the protection of the insurance policy, in the event of some financial loss. It thus creates confidence and eliminates worries which are difficult to evaluate, but the benefit is very real. These days insurance also assures social security by providing unemployment insurance, health insurance, accident insurance, old age insurance etc. These insurance schemes are beneficial to the poor and help in establishing social justice.

2. Protection Against Risks:
The fundamental principle of insurance is to spread risk among a large number of people. Insurance helps in reducing risks by suggesting precautionary measures on one hand and by sharing the losses to a group of people who have agreed to join the common pool on the other hand. Whenever a loss occurs, it is compensated out of funds of a large number of insurers, thus, the loss is spread among multiple policyholders.

3. Removal of Uncertainties:
Insurance company takes the risks of large but uncertain losses. in exchange for a small premium, it relieves the businessman and gives him a sense of security. If all uncertainty could be removed from business, income would be sure. Insurance removes many of these uncertainties and to that extent, is profitable. It improves the efficiency of business operations.

4. Promotion of Saving:
Insurance not only provides protection against risks but it is also a good form of investment. Saving is a device of preparing for the bad consequences of the future. Insurance helps is developing habit of saving money by making regular premium payments mandatory. In case of fixed time policies, the insured gets a lump-sum amount after the maturity of the policy.

5. Capital Formation and Economic Development:
Insurance helps in capital formation and economic development of the nation. Large funds are collected by way of premiums. These funds can be gainfully employed in industrial development of the country. The employment opportunities also increase

because of the large investments made by insurance companies. So insurance has become an important source of capital formation.

Insurer accumulates large resources from the various insurance funds. Such resources are generally invested in the country, either in the public or private sector. This facilitates considerably the over all development of the economy.

6. Promotion of International trade:
Insurance has helped the development of international trade on a large scale. Marine insurance provides protection against all types of sea-risks.

7. Insurance as an Investment:
A life policy is a combination of protection and investment which helps in diminishing the impact of financial losses. These days large variety of policies have been designed for different purposes. Persons, by taking different types of life insurance policies provide for their social and business obligation. The premium that the insured pays go on accumulating in a fund every year. The sum so accumulated by the insurance company earns interest. Under life assurance a person may also invest his capital in a annuity which will pay him an income every year till death. Therefore, insurance may be regarded as an investment.

TYPES OF INSURANCE

There are a number of insurances, but the following types stand out as being of special importance:

1. Life Insurance:

Everyone born on this planet has to die one day but how and when is not known. It is life insurance that covers the risk of loss of life, and offers a sense of security to the insured and his family. Life insurance is not a contract of indemnity as the sum assured is payable to the insured either on his death or maturity of Life Insurance Policy whichever is earlier. Thus, it is also known as 'Life Assurance'. Life insurance is a contract whereby the insurer, in consideration of a premium, undertakes to pay a sum of money or an annuity, either at the death of the insured or on the expiry of a specified period, whichever is earlier. The premium is payable annually or half yearly on a regular basis during the period of the policy. Failure to pay the installment of premium renders the insurance contract as null and void. Once the policy period expires, the insurance company pays the sum assured to the insured. In case the insured dies before the expiry of the policy period, the sum assured is given to the nominated representatives (like the spouse or children) of the policy holder.

The Insurance Act 1938 defines *"Life Insurance as a contract to which the insurer, in consideration of a premium either in gross sum or by periodical payment, undertakes to pay to the person for whose benefit insurance is effected, a sum of money or annuity on the death of the person whose life is insured or upon his attaining a certain age."*

The Life Insurance Corporation of India is the largest Indian state-owned insurance group and investment company, headquartered in Mumbai. Several private sector players like ICICI Prudential Life Insurance, ING Vyasa Life Insurance, Birla Sunlife Insurance, Max HDFC Life Insurance, and Aviva Life Insurance are doing well in the business of life insurance.

Importance of Life Insurance

Life insurance is the most important form of insurance for the numerous benefits it offers. These are:

(a) Protection Against Risk:
Life insurance policy offers protection to the family of the insured from several uncertainties after his demise. If the policyholder dies a premature death, the sum assured could be given to his or her nominees or the dependents of the insured.

(b) Provision for Old Age:
After retirement from work, a person can still remain financially independent by taking a life insurance policy offering pension benefits. Once the policy period gets over, the sum assured goes to the policyholder. Thus, life insurance helps the insured to lead a graceful, independent life even after retirement.

(c) Encourages Saving:
Life insurance helps people develop the good habit of saving money because the premium is paid in installments, which covers the risk and also leads to capital formation. It also enables the policyholder to raise loan against policy, if required.

(d) Tax Savings:
The amount paid as premium of the life insurance policy is allowed as a deduction from income for calculating incomes tax under Income Tax Act. Thus, people can save their taxes by taking a life insurance policy.

(e) Capital Formation:
The funds collected by life insurance firms are channelized into developmental and other industrial projects. It helps in capital formation, which in turn, leads to the economic growth of the country.

(f) Employment Generation:
Life insurance companies offer self-employment opportunities to a large number of people. People from several walks of life such as retired persons, college students, homemakers etc. can work as insurance agents to earn their livelihood, provided they are self-motivated and satisfy the minimum eligibility requirements.

2. Health Insurance:

Health insurance is an insurance risk hedged against the probability that if and when someone, unexpectedly becomes sick, requires expensive treatments, or is at the mercy of a chronic condition, which requires long-term care, will not fall into dire financial state. It is an effective tool to cover the costs of diseases or accident, thereby saving people from financial hazards resulting from illness or accident. The financial loss from diseases or accidents arises from loss of income and medical expenditure. Individual and group health insurance helps in dealing with these losses. The medical expenses up to a certain amount are paid by the insurance company to the hospital. In case of health insurance, insurable interest must be present at the time of taking the policy. Health insurance mostly covers the consultation fee of the doctor, cost of medicines and hospitalization expenses. There are various types of health insurance policies such as:

(a) Mediclaim Insurance:
Mediclaim is the most preferred insurance policy these days. Under this policy, the insured can even get cashless treatment from the specified hospital which means

that the bills are directly paid to the hospital or the insured can pay the bills in the specified hospital and get a reimbursement after submission of bills to the insurance company.

(b) Disability Insurance:

This insurance provides periodic payment if the insured becomes disabled or incapable of working as a result of an illness or accident. The insured is compensated on the basis of the kind and level of disability.

(c) Long-term Hospitalisation:

It covers the treatment expenses of specified serious illnesses like heart problems, cancer, and kidney failure among many others. This insurance policy asks for heavy premium to be paid by the insured.

(d) Maternity Health Insurance:

It covers the expenses associated with maternity and other additional expenses .The policy covers pre and post-natal care, delivery of babies (normal/cesarean), physician fees, hospitalisation, etc.

Importance of Health Insurance

Health insurance is important for the following reasons:

(a) Huge Coverage at Small Cost:

Health insurance helps the insured in avoiding significant expenses involved in hospitalization for serious conditions like heart ailments, cancer, kidney problems etc. By paying regular premium in small amounts, the insured can get beneficial coverage against health risks.

(b) Tax Savings:

The premium paid for health insurance is allowed as a deduction up to a certain amount from taxable income under the Income Tax Act.

(c) Controls Emergency Hospitalisation Expenses:

If the insured is hospitalised urgently, his or her family does not need to bear the expenses of unexpected hospitalisation.

(d) Economic Development and Social Welfare:

Health insurance contributes remarkably to the economic and social development of the people by making the people healthy.

3. Fire Insurance:

Fire insurance is a contract of indemnity under which the insurer undertakes to indemnify any loss of insured on the event of the subject matter getting destroyed by accidental fire. Generally, a fire insurance policy is taken for a year.

As per the Fire Insurance Act, 1938, *"In addition to other insurances, fire insurance is that insurance which takes place against fire and such other risks which are mentioned in the fire insurance contract."*

Fire insurance is a contract of indemnity. The policyholder has the right to get compensation of actual loss due to fire, not the insured sum. Fire insurance is only meant for safety and not as a means of earning money. In order to claim, the insured must compulsorily assure the damage of insured property. The claim is not paid more than the actual loss suffered. The insurable interest in goods must exist at the time of taking the policy as well as at the time of loss by fire.

An insurance company is liable to pay for compensation of loss caused to insured due to fire only if the following conditions are satisfied:

(a) There must be fire or ignition in reality. Loss of property due to smoke or heat is not covered under fire insurance. Loss by electricity, lightning or explosion is not covered unless it results in fire which damages the property.

(b) The fire should be accidental, not intentional or planned. Loss resulting solely by the negligence of the insured person is covered. However, if the loss is caused due to the malicious intentions of someone it is not covered.

Importance of Fire Insurance

Fire can cause major losses to the property of a person. It may gut down the office or warehouse of a business person, thereby destroying the source of income of the victim and the staff. Fire insurance comes to bailout people by providing the impenetrable and protective shield against fire, and placing the insured person in the same financial position as he or she was before the loss by fire had occurred.

4. Marine Insurance:

Marine insurance is a contract of indemnity under which the insurance company promises to compensate for the loss or damage to the ship or cargo or freight on account of marine travel. The risks covered under marine insurance are sea storms, fraud by ship captain, collusion of ships, fire, sea piracy, political upheavals, natural disasters etc. Marine insurance provides protection against these risks to importers, exporters and shipping companies.

Section 3(IA) of Marine Insurance Act, 1963 defines marine insurance as, *"The business of affecting contracts of insurance upon the vessels and items of any description including cargo, freights and other interests which may be legally insured."*

Marine insurance policy can be taken either for a particular time period or for a particular trip. The insurable interest must exist at the time of signing the policy as well as at the time of marine loss. In marine insurance, there are mainly three implied warranties–(a) seaworthiness of the vessel, (b) non-deviation from the route, and (c) legality of the venture.

Importance of Marine Insurance

Marine insurance plays a key role in decreasing sea perils (risks) and thus supporting foreign trade. It protects the insurer against Jettison or throwing off the good over board in the middle of the sea to avoid sinking of the ship. It also safeguards the insurer against breach of duty on part of the captain or staff. As the time taken for goods to reach the destination is long, the chances of their damage are also high. The owners of ship usually take hull insurance policies to insure the ship against the risk of loss or damage during voyage. Similarly, cargo insurance provides security cover to the shipment freight (or bulk goods) against possible perils. In addition, when freight is supposed to be paid at the port of destination, the shipping company may not receive the freight if the goods are lost in transit. Therefore, the shipping company may choose to insure the freight to be received. This is known as freight insurance.

Lesson at a Glance

- **Insurance:** Insurance is a contract between two parties by which one of them undertakes to indemnify the other, against a loss, which may arise on the happening of some event. Insurance in its technical sense is a social device which employs the use of pooling technique to eliminate uncertainty.
- **Objectives of Insurance:** Insurance is a useful commercial device for protecting people from financial losses.
- **Common Terminology used in Insurance:** (i) Insured; (ii) Insurer; (iii) Policy; (iv) Premium; (v) Risk. Risks are of two types: (a) Insurable risks; (b) Non-Insurable risks.
- **Business Risks:** (i) Natural factors; (ii) Human factors; (iii) Economic factors; (iv) Miscellaneous.
- **Principles of an Insurance Contract:** (i) Principle of utmost good faith; (ii) Principle of Insurable Interest; (iii) Principle of Indemnity; (iv) Principle of Causa Proxima or Proximate Cause; (v) Principle of Subrogation; (vi) Principle of Contribution; (vii) Mitigation of Loss.
- **Importance of Insurance:** (i) Mitigating Fear and Ensuring Employee Welfare; (ii) Protection against risks; (iii) Removal of uncertainties; (iv) Promotion of saving; (v) Capital formation and economic development; (vi) Promotion of international trade; (vii) Insurance as an investment.
- **Types of Insurance:** (i) Life Insurance; (ii) Health Insurance, (iii) Fire Insurance; (iv) Marine Insurance.

Project Work

Students are advised to ask their parents about the Insurance cover they have chosen for themselves and their family. Also try to find out the objectives for the choice of particular type of insurance.

Assignment

Explain to your class the different forms of business risks and the importance of insurance.

Questions

A. **Short Answer Type Questions:**
1. What do you mean by Insurance? [ICSE 2020]
2. List two principles of Insurance.
3. What do you mean by Insurable interest?
4. What do you mean by indemnity?
5. Write two importances of Insurance.
6. Give a proper definition of Insurance.

7. Briefly explain the principle of utmost good faith of insurance. [ICSE 2020]
8. What do you understand by 'Health Insurance'? [ICSE 2019]
9. Explain 'Contribution' as a principle of insurance. [ICSE 2018]
10. Mention any two main advantages of group life insurance to employees and employers. [ICSE 2017]

B. Essay Type Questions:

1. What do you mean by Insurance? Give proper definition of insurance.
2. Discuss briefly the principles of an insurance contract.
3. "Insurance is a contract of indemnity." Explain
4. Differentiate between insurable and non-insurable risks.
5. What are the advantages of insurance?
6. Explain the Principles of Insurance:
   (i) Doctrine of subrogation.
   (ii) Mitigation of loss.
7. What do you mean by Group Life Insurance? Explain three main features of Gorup Life Insurance.
8. Explain any five Principles of Insurance.

CHAPTER-22
Banking

Banking is an important aid to business. Banks facilitate trade, mobilise savings and provide much needed finance to businesses and industries. Finance is the foundation of every business activity which is provided by banks of different types. Banks are thus, regarded as indispensable spokes of the wheels of commerce.

- Meaning of Bank
- Kinds of Bank
- Central Bank or Reserve Bank of India
- Functions of Reserve Bank of India or Central Bank
- Commercial Banking in India
- Functions of Commercial Banks
- Difference between Central Bank and Commercial Bank
- Internet Banking

BANK

Bank is an institution which deals in money and credit. It is often described as a credit institution which accepts deposits from the public and lends money. On deposits, the bank pays interest and for lending money, it charges higher rate of interest. The difference between these two rates of interest is the profit of the bank.

According to Banking Regulation Act, 1949, *"Banking means the accepting, for the purpose of lending or investment, of deposits of money from the public repayable on demand or otherwise, and withdrawal by cheque, draft, order or otherwise."*

Thus, a bank is an institution which accepts deposits from the public and in turn advances loans by creating credit. It is different from other financial institutions in the sense that they cannot create credit though they may be accepting deposits and making advances. Hence, it may as such be defined as an institution which purchases and sells money, and transacts other businesses of like nature.

Kinds of Bank

1. Commercial Banks:
Commercial Banks are those banks which perform all kinds of banking functions, such as accepting deposits, advancing loans, credit creation, and agency functions. They are also called joint-stock banks because they are organised in the same manner as joint-stock companies. They are meant to finance the internal trade of a country. Some of the commercial banks in India are Andhra Bank, Canara Bank, Indian Bank, Punjab National Bank, Axis Bank, HDFC Bank, Yes Bank, etc.

2. Exchange Banks:
Exchange Banks are a type of commercial banks whose main function is financing foreign trade. They are also called foreign exchange banks. They are incorporated

outside India but conduct foreign exchange business in India. Exchange banks work under the direct guidance of Reserve Bank of India.

They provide services such as discounting of foreign bills of exchange, facilitating foreign remittances, financing internal trade through regular banking methods, etc.

3. Industrial Banks:

Industrial Banks are those banks which provide medium-term and long-term finance to industries for the purchase of land, machinery, etc. They underwrite debentures and shares of industrial undertakings and also subscribe to them.

Functions of these banks may be summarised as follows:

(a) Providing long-term loans to industries requiring block capital for their schemes of expansion, modernisation, etc.;

(b) Subscribing directly to shares and debentures of industrial undertakings;

(c) Underwriting of shares and debentures issued by industrial concerns;

(d) Promoting new industrial ventures;

(e) Providing technical guidance in the management of industries;

In India, there are a number of financial institutions which perform the functions of Industrial Banks, such as Industrial Development Bank of India (IDBI), Industrial Finance Corporation of India (IFCI), Industrial Credit and Investment Corporation of India (ICICI), etc. Each State in India has its own State Financial Corporation. These institutions are also known as Development Banks. The loans provided by these institutions are both in Indian and foreign currency.

Agricultural Banks Or Land Mortgage Banks: Agricultural Banks are those banks which provide credit to farmers for short-term, medium-term and long-term needs. In India, commercial banks, regional rural banks and agricultural co-operative banks provide short-term loans to farmers. Land Development Banks give long-term loans to farmers on the mortgage of their land. The National Bank for Agriculture and Rural Development (NABARD) provides refinance facilities to all types of banks which give loans to agriculturists.

4. Co-operative Banks:

Co-operative Banks are those financial institutions which are organised on the principle of co-operation. They provide short-term finance to farmers and small-scale industrial units. They also encourage thrift among their members. In rural areas, there are agricultural co-operative banks which accept deposits and give loans to agriculturists, rural artisans, etc. In urban areas, co-operative bank perform the functions of ordinary commercial banks but give loans to their members only.

5. Indigenous Bankers:

Indigenous bankers in India play a very significant role in financing trade and industry. They carry on banking business as a hereditary occupation. They are known as Mahajans, Seths, Sahukars, etc. They carry on the business of financing along with their usual commercial activities. They issue, negotiate and discount hundies, etc., as commission agents. However, they charge a higher rate of interest on loans advanced by them than what is charged by the commercial banks.

6. Export-Import Bank (EXIM):

The Export Import Bank of India (Exim) was launched on 1st January, 1982, with a view to promote, finance and facilitate export and import of goods and services so as to promote the country's international trade and commerce by way of expert advice, viability studies, coordination with bankers of the world, and quick supply of information.

7. Central Bank:

Central Bank of a country is an institution which acts as the leader of the banking system and the money market. It regulates money and credit in close cooperation with the Government. It also controls and regulates all the commercial banks of the country. It occupies a central position in the banking structure, but its operations are not guided by profit motive. In our country, the Reserve Bank of India acts as the Central Bank.

THE CENTRAL BANK OR RESERVE BANK OF INDIA

The bank that controls the operations of the banking system in a country and carries out its monetary policies, is referred to as the Central Bank. Central Bank is the apex institution of the banking system.

According to Vera Smith, *"The primary definition of Central Banking is a banking system in which a single bank has either a complete or a residuary monopoly in the note-issue. It was out of monopoly in the note-issue that were derived the secondary functions and characteristics of modern Central Banking."*

R.S Sayer has differentiated the central bank from a commercial bank by remarking that, *"The business of a Central Bank as distinguished from a Commercial Bank is to control the commercial banks in such a way, as to promote the general monetary policy of the state."*

Thus, the Central Bank may be defined as the apex banking and monetary institution whose main function is to control, regulate and stabilize the banking and the monetary system of the country in the national interests.

The Central Bank in our country is called the Reserve Bank of India. It was established in the year 1935 under the Reserve Bank of India Act of 1934. In the beginning it was a shareholders' bank with a share capital of ₹ 5 crores, divided into 5 lakh shares of ₹ 100 each. The Reserve Bank of India was nationalized in the year 1949 and its entire share capital was acquired by the Government of India.

Functions of Reserve Bank of India or Central Bank

The functions of Reserve Bank of India are the same as performed by the Central Banks of various countries of the world. But these functions are basically different from those performed by the Commercial Banks. It is because like other Central Banks, the Reserve Bank of India also plans and acts particularly to promote and stabilize the economy of the country. It also tries to solve the balance of payments and foreign exchange problems.

The main functions of Reserve Bank of India have been described below:

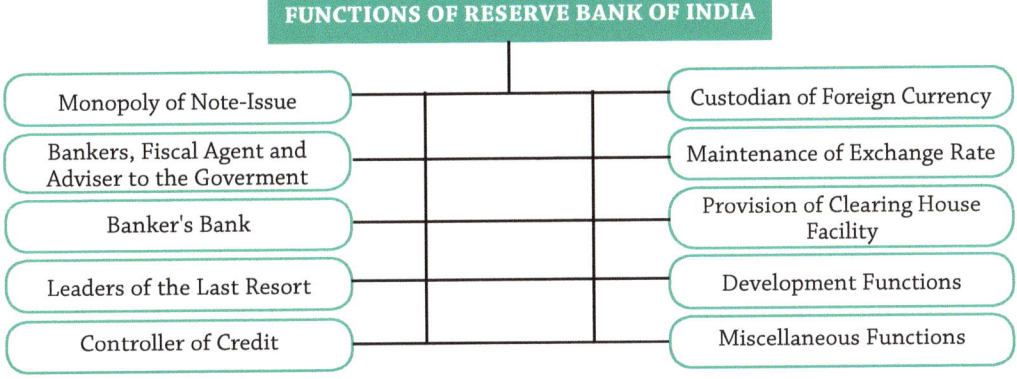

1. Monopoly of Note-Issue:
The Central Bank has the monopoly to issue currency notes. For issuing notes, the Central Bank keeps reserves of gold, silver and foreign securities in fixed proportions to inspire confidence among the people in the paper currency. The Reserve Bank of India issues all the currency notes from ₹ 2 to ₹ 5, ₹ 10, ₹ 20, ₹ 50, ₹ 100, ₹ 200, ₹ 500 and ₹ 2,000.

2. Banker, Fiscal Agent and Adviser to the Government:
The Central Bank is the Government's bank. It acts as a banker, agent and adviser to the Government. The Central Bank makes and receives payments on behalf of the Government. It floats and manages public debts for the Government. It acts as the fiscal agent of the Government in matters relating to monetary and banking policies. The Central Bank also acts as a representative of the government in international conferences on monetary and economic matters.

3. Bankers' Bank:
The Central Bank is the bank for all the commercial banks of the country. Legally or conventionally, commercial banks have to keep a certain proportion of their deposits in the form of cash, as reserve with the Central Bank. These reserves facilitate the Central Bank to control the issue of credit by commercial banks and, thus, keep the credit system elastic. As a bankers' bank, the Central Bank also provides the facilities of short-term loans, discounting bills, etc., to commercial banks. Further, the Central Bank also advises commercial banks on various matters concerning their business.

4. Lender of the Last Resort:
In times of emergency, Commercial Banks may have to borrow from other banks. But other banks, sometimes, may not be in a position to help the bank in trouble. In such situations, the Central Bank is the lender of the last resort. Central Bank helps Commercial Banks either by granting loans or by buying their securities. The RBI extends this facility to protect the interest of the depositors also.

5. Controller of Credit:
Credit control is the most important function of the Central Bank. A country can have a stabilized economy only when the Central Bank of the country exercises its

strict control on the credit granting capacity of the banking structure. Fluctuations in the level of credit available cause fluctuations in the price level, business and level of employment which destabilizes an economy. The Central Bank, therefore, exercises control, qualitatively as well as quantitatively on the credit-granting capacity of Commercial Banks.

6. Custodian of Foreign Currency:

This is one of the most important functions of the Central Bank. The Central Bank is the sole custodian of gold and reserves of foreign exchange of a country. It collects and preserves the gold and foreign currency reserves of the country, in order to utilize them for making payments to foreign countries. If the country's balance of payment is favourable (exports of goods, services and capital > imports of goods, services and capital), then it will earn foreign exchange. However, if the balance of payment is unfavourable (exports of goods, services and capital < imports of goods, services and capital), then foreign exchange goes out of the country. RBI keeps a close watch on external value of its currency and undertakes exchange management control. It also buys and sells foreign currencies at international prices. Further, it fixes the exchange rates of the domestics currency in terms of foreign currencies.

7. Maintenance of Exchange Rate:

The Central Bank keeps a watch on the exchange rate of the home currency in relation to foreign currencies. An exchange rate of two currencies is the rate at which one currency will be exchanged for another. The Central Bank makes every effort to maintain a stable exchange rate by buying and selling foreign currencies at the rates fixed by it.

8. Provision of Clearing House Facility:

The Central Bank performs 'The-Clearing-House Function' for the commercial banks. This means, it settles the claims of commercial banks and enable them to clear their dues by a process of book entries. as such, the daily balances between the commercial banks can be adjusted conveniently by means of debit and credit entries in their respective accounts in the Central Bank. This can be explained by an example; Suppose, the Union Bank of India has to pay an amount of ₹ 5 lakhs to the Syndicate Bank. In this case, the only thing the Union Bank of India has to do is to issue a cheque of this amount to the Syndicate Bank. By means of this cheque, the Union Bank of India's account will be debited by ₹ 5 lakhs, and the account of the Syndicate Bank will be credited by ₹ 5 lakhs. This process has several advantages. Firstly, it facilitates settlement between different commercial banks by a very simple operation, *i.e.*, making entries in the book. Secondly, it eliminates the use of money in these operations. Finally, it helps to stabilise the banking system of the country, as it reduces the possibilities of cash withdrawals during the period of economic crisis. Here, it is important to mention that the Reserve Bank offices are not at all places in India. As such, in those places, where there is no branch of the Reserve Bank, the State Bank of India has been empowered to conduct these settlements.

9. Development Functions:

The above mentioned functions are performed by the Central Banks of all the countries, whether they are developed or underdeveloped. These are known as the traditional functions of the Central Bank. These functions, as such have become regulatory in nature. But in underdeveloped countries, the Central Bank also performs many developmental and promotional functions. For example, it creates special financial institutions for promoting economic developments in different sectors of the economy. In our country, the Reserve Bank of India has a special department of agricultural credit. This department provides long-term credit for agriculture to the farmers and coordinates the activities of the cooperative societies, cooperative banks, and land mortgage banks in rural areas. The Reserve Bank also provides loan facilities to special agencies, like Industrial Finance Corporation, Industrial Development Bank of India, etc., for financing various kinds of industries. Thus, in underdeveloped and developing countries, the main task of Central Bank is to make adequate funds available to finance developmental programmes in respect of agriculture, industry, transport and trade.

10. Miscellaneous Functions:

Besides the above functions, the Central Bank also performs several optional functions. These are called optional functions because they are not regulatory and the Central Bank may or may not perform them. Some of these functions are as follows:

(a) The Central Bank studies different economic problems of the country and compiles data and information, and publishes reports and periodicals for the use of banks and the public. The Reserve Bank of India bulletin is one of them.

(b) It acts as an agent to international institutions, like the International Monetary Fund, the World Bank, etc., on behalf of the Government.

COMMERCIAL BANKING IN INDIA

Progress of Commercial Banking in India: After Independence, the Indian banking system has recorded a rapid progress. This was due to planned economic growth, increase in money supply, growth of banking habits, control and guidance by the Reserve Bank of India and above all, nationalisation of banks in July 1969. After the economic reforms of 1991, a number of private banks and foreign banks have started their operations in India. Recently, Reserve Bank of India has approved the setting up of payments bank and small finance banks for financial inclusion of the poor people as well as of the people living in rural and unbanked areas.

Payments banks are expected to reach its customers mainly through their mobile phones rather than traditional bank branches. These banks can accept a restricted deposit, which is currently limited to ₹ 1 lakh per customer. These banks, however, cannot issue loans and credit cards and cannot accept term deposits. Examples of payment banks are Airtel Payment Bank and India Post Payment Bank.

Small Finance Banks can accept deposits and lend to people who typically won't be served by commercial banks. These people include small farmers, unorganised workers, small business units, etc. They were set up with the twin objectives of providing an institutional mechanism for promoting rural and semi-urban savings and for providing credit for viable economic activities in the local areas.

FUNCTIONS OF COMMERCIAL BANKS

Banks perform numerous functions which throw light on the variety of services they render to the modern society. They have been termed as the 'nerve centre' of the modern world.

Some of the most important functions of Commercial Banks have been discussed below:

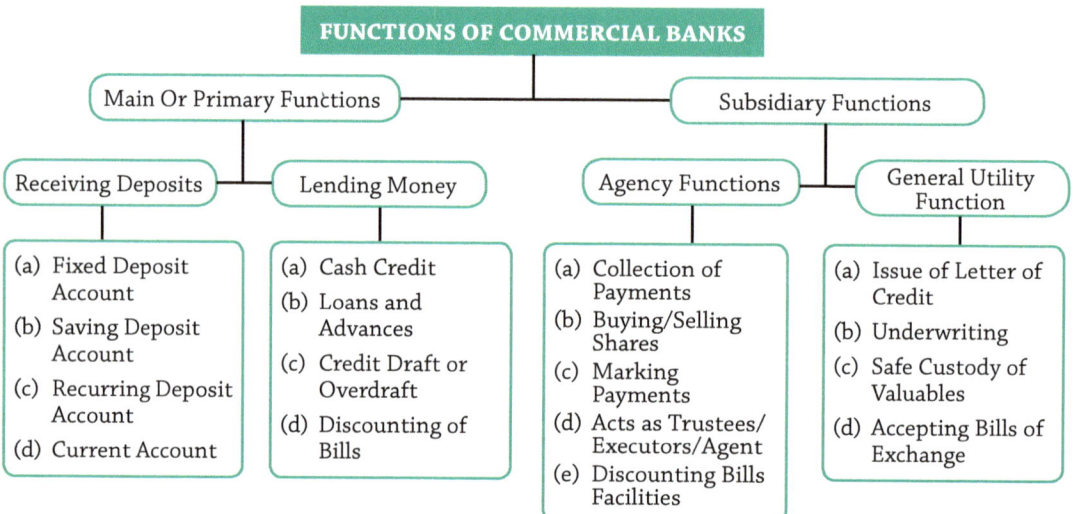

(A) Main or Primary Functions

(i) Receiving Deposits:

Receiving deposits is the primary function of a Commercial Bank. A Commercial Bank accepts deposits from the people for the purpose of making investments and providing loans. People deposit their money for the sake of safety and also for the sake of interest, which is paid by the bank. Commercial banks accept deposits from individuals, firms, industries and institutions. As borrowers, Commercial Banks pay interest on the balance of deposits and undertake to repay them in full legal tender money as and when demanded by the depositors. The banks by accepting the deposits become indebted to the depositholders to the extent of the credit balance indicated by the depositholders' accounts.

Deposits are accepted by these banks in the form of Fixed Deposits, Saving Deposits, Recurring Deposits and Current Deposits.

(a) Fixed Deposit Account: Fixed deposits are made for a specified period and cannot be withdrawn before the expiry of the period for which they have been deposited in the bank. These deposits are repayable after the expiry of the fixed period. It is also known as Time Deposit or long term deposits. Higher rate of interest is offered to attract such deposits. However the interest varies with the duration of the deposits.

(b) Saving Deposit Account: Saving deposits are those deposits an which bank pays a contains rate of interest to the depositors but places certain restriction on their withdrawals. This account is opened with the small amount. The main aim of the saving account is to develop the habit of saving among the common people.

(c) Recurring Deposits Account: This deposit account has been started to encourage those people to save who cannot give large deposit in lump sum. This account can be opened with small amount and the depositor keeps on depositing a certain amount of money every month for a specified period of time. After the expiry of the specific period the depositor get back his money along with interest.

(d) Current Account: It is generally operated by business houses under this account the depositor can withdraw money from this account by cheque at any time during the working hours of the bank. There is no restriction to limit the number of withdrawals subjected to minimum credit balance to be kept on per rules of the bank.

(ii) Lending Money:

Lending money is the most important function of a Commercial Bank. The bank lends out the money which it gets as deposits from the public. A Commercial Bank lends money to traders, businessmen, agriculturists, artisans, etc., to finance their need for capital. Commercial Banks usually lend money in the following ways:

(a) Cash Credit: Cash Credit is an arrangement by which the bank advances cash loans of a specified limit to the customers against a bond or other securities. When the cash loan is granted, the borrower opens a cash credit account which is similar to current account, with that amount in the bank. The borrower has the right to withdraw the full amount of loan. Interest is charged on the amount actually utilised by the borrower and not on the whole amount granted to him.

(b) Loans and Advances: A loan is a lump sum advance repayable wholly after an agreed period or in installments. The borrower may withdraw the whole amount at once or draw as and when he needs. Interest, however, is charged on the entire amount of the loan. When the loan is granted for a period not exceeding one year, it is known as short-term loan. When the period of the loan ranges from 5 to 7 years, it is called medium-term loan. Loans for more than 7 years are called long-term loans. Usually a loan is granted against the securities of assets or the personal security of the borrower.

(c) Credit Draft or Overdraft: A Commercial Bank allows the facility of overdraft only to its depositors who have current accounts in the bank. Under this arrangement, a depositor is allowed to withdraw more than what he has deposited. But, this extra withdrawal has to be repaid by the customer within a short period, along with the interest charged by the bank on the extra amount withdrawn. The rate of this interest may be somewhat more than the interest rate charged on loans. Banks, however, give overdraft facility only on the security of some assets or on the personal security of the customer.

(d) Discounting of Bills: Banks provide financial help to their customers (the businessmen, the merchants, the exporters, etc.) by way of discounting their bills of exchange.

A bill of exchange is an instrument in writing containing an unconditional order, signed by the maker, directing a certain person to pay a certain sum of money only to the bearer of the instrument.

When a customer (say, an exporter) comes to the bank with a bill of exchange, the bank pays him the amount of the bill after deducting the usual discount (interest) charges. The bank, thus assists its merchant customers considerably by accepting their bills of exchange and by providing them cash in return to meet their short term capital requirements. After a few months or weeks, when the bill matures (a bill generally matures in 90 days), the bank presents it to the acceptor (say, an importer) and gets back its full amount. In this case, a bill of exchange is of great benefit, both to the importer and the exporter. By using bill of exchange, the exporter gets the amount from the bank and the importer does not have to pay anything to the exporter immediately. Importer pays the amount only when he has funds in his hands. In case the payment is not received on due date, the bank recovers this amount from the customers (that is, the exporter in this case).

(B) Subsidiary Functions

(i) Agency Functions:

Commercial Banks render several services as the agents of their customers. These services are known as their agency functions. Some of the most important agency functions are as follows:

(a) Collection of Payments: Commercial Banks collect the payment of the bills of exchange, promissory notes, cheques, etc., on behalf of their customers. They also collect dividends, interest on shares, debentures, rent, etc., on behalf of their customers.

(b) Buying/Selling Shares: Commercial Banks buy and sell shares and securities on behalf of the customers as per their instructions.

(c) Making Payments: They transfer funds from one branch of the bank to another and from one place to another as per the instructions of their customers. They make payments of loan installments, interest, insurance premiums, taxes, etc., on behalf of their customers.

(d) Act as Trustees/Executors/Agents: Commercial Banks act as trustees or executors and deal with the financial matters, relating to other institutions, for their customers. They act as the agents or representatives of their customers for other banks and financial institutions, inside the country and abroad.

(e) Discounting Bills Facilities: Commercial Banks offer discounting facilities in respect of foreign and local bills of their customers.

(ii) General Utility Functions:

Besides the above mentioned functions, Commercial Banks also perform several general utility and miscellaneous services not only to their customers but to the public in general as well. These are described below:

(a) Issue of Letter of Credit: Commercial Banks issue letters of credit like circular notes, drafts and provide credit card services and travellers cheques which facilitate the customers in purchasing goods in distant places.

(b) Underwriting: They give references about the financial position of their customers, when it is so required. The banks also undertake to sell shares and debentures of companies on behalf of their customers for which they charge a specified commission.

(c) Safe Custody of Valuables: They provide safety vaults or lockers for the safe custody of jewellery, valuable documents and other precious possessions of their customers.

(d) Accepting Bills of Exchange: Letter of credit represents an undertaking by the banker that bills drawn by the exporter will be duly honoured as per terms of credit specified in the letter. Letter of credit opened by a bank at the request of the importer authorises its branch or correspondent bank in the exporter's country to pay the Bills of Exchange drawn by the exporter relating to specified transactions.

Differences between Central Bank and Commercial Bank

Basis of Comparison	Central Bank (Reserve Bank)	Commercial Bank
Meaning	The Central Bank is the apex institution of the monetary and banking structure of the country.	The Commercial Bank is one of the organs of the money market. It accepts deposits and lends money to individuals, firms and industries.
Status	It is a banker to the Government and does not engage itself in ordinary banking activities.	It is a banker to the general public.
Profit Motive	It is non-profit institution which implements the economic policies of the Government.	It is a profit-making institution.
Ownership	It is owned by the Government.	It is owned by shareholders.
Monetary Authority	It has the monopoly of issuing note.	It can issue only cheques.
Advancement of Loans	The Central Bank is the banker's bank. As such, it grants assistance to commercial banks in the form of rediscount facilities, keeps their cash reserves, and clears their balances.	It advances loans and accepts deposits from the public.
Credit Control	It controls credit in accordance with the needs of business and economy.	It creates credit to meet the requirements of business.
Number of Banks	Every country has only one Central Bank with its offices at important cities of the country.	There are a number of Commercial Banks with hundreds of branches within and outside the country.
Foreign Currency	It is the custodian of the foreign currency reserve of the country.	It is the dealer of foreign currencies.

Designation	The chief executive of the Central Bank is designated as "Governor".	The chief executive of the Commercial Bank is called "Chairman".
Governing Statute	Reserve Bank of India Act, 1934.	Banking Regulation Act, 1949.
Deals With	Banks and government	General public

INTERNET BANKING

Internet banking or on-line banking is basically virtual banking which is done through the use of Internet. Internet banking refers to systems that enable bank customers to access accounts and general information on bank products and services through a personal computer (PC) or other intelligent devices.

Internet banking products and services can include wholesale products for corporates and businesses as well as retail products for consumers. The products and services obtained through Internet banking is same as offered by banks through physical delivery channels.

Some examples of wholesale products and services include: Cash management, Wire transfer, Automated clearing house (ACH) transactions, Bill presentation and payment. Examples of retail products and services include: Balance inquiry, Funds transfer, Downloading transaction information, Loan applications, etc.

Numerous factors such as competitive cost, customer service, and demographic considerations are motivating banks to provide Internet banking facilities to their customers. Competitive pressure is the chief driving force behind increasing use of Internet banking technology. Banks see Internet banking as a way to keep existing customers and attract new ones to the bank. Internet banking technology and products can provide a means for banks to develop and maintain an ongoing relationship with their customers by offering easy access to a broad array of products and services. Banks can deliver banking services on the Internet at transaction costs far lower than traditional brick-and-mortar branches. Internet banking also allows expanded customer contact through increased geographical reach. In fact, some banks are doing business exclusively via the Internet, that is, they do not have traditional banking offices and only reach their customers on-line.

Modes of Transferring Money:

1. NEFT:

NEFT stands for National Electronic Funds Transfer. NEFT is a nation-wide payment system facilitating one-to-one funds transfer. It is one of the most prominent ways of transferring money since its inception in the year 2005.

Under this scheme, individuals, firms and corporates can electronically transfer funds from any bank branch to any individual, firm or corporate having an account with any other bank branch in the country participating in the scheme. There is no limit – either minimum or maximum – on the amount of funds that could be transferred using NEFT. However, maximum amount per transaction is limited to ₹ 50,000/- for cash based remittances within India.

The NEFT system takes advantage of the core banking system in banks. Accordingly, the settlement of funds between originating and receiving banks takes places centrally at Mumbai, whereas the branches participating in NEFT can be located anywhere across the length and breadth of the country.

Presently, NEFT operates in hourly batches - there are twelve settlements from 8 am to 7 pm on week days (Monday through Friday) and six settlements from 8 am to 1 pm on Saturdays.

2. RTGS:

The acronym 'RTGS' stands for Real Time Gross Settlement, which can be defined as the continuous settlement of funds transfers individually on an order by order basis. 'Real Time' means the processing of instructions at the time they are received rather than at some later time; 'Gross Settlement' means the settlement of funds transfer instructions occurs individually (on an instruction by instruction basis). Therefore, under RTGS, the funds transfer takes place on a real time basis, or in other words, at the time the request is received. It is one of the fastest inter bank money transfer facility available through banking channels in India.

The RTGS service window for customer's transactions is available to banks from 9:00 hours to 16:30 hours on week days and from 9:00 hours to 14:00 hours on Saturdays.

The RTGS system is primarily meant for large value transactions. The minimum amount to be remitted through RTGS is ₹ 2 lakh. There is no upper ceiling for RTGS transactions.

The difference between NEFT and RTGS is that NEFT is an electronic funds transfer system that operates on a Deferred Net Settlement (DNS) basis which settles transactions in batches whereas in RTGS, the transactions are settled individually and beneficiaries are expected to receive the funds in real time as soon as funds are transferred by the sender.

Both NEFT and RTGS systems are maintained by the Reserve Bank of India and they can be used for transferring money only within the country.

3. IMPS:

Immediate Payment Service (IMPS) is an instant interbank electronic fund transfer service which is carried out through mobile phones. It was launched in the year 2010. Unlike NEFT and RTGS, the service is available 24 × 7 throughout the year including bank holidays. Thus, IMPS is an emphatic tool to transfer money instantly within banks across India through mobile, which is not only safe but also economical both in financial and non-financial perspectives. It is managed by the National Payments Corporation of India (NPCI) and is built upon the existing National Financial Switch network.

4. Mobile Wallets:

Mobile wallets are digital wallets which act as the user's real wallet. Mobile wallets help the users to store their payment card information on the application and to pay or receive payments through their smartphones.

How mobile wallets work
1. Download the mobile wallet application on your smartphone.
2. Add your credit card or debit card information to the mobile wallet.
3. When making purchases at participating merchants, access the mobile wallet and choose your card. If you're making an in-store purchase, just hold your mobile device at the terminal to make payment. Paytm, MobiKwik, Oxigen are a well known mobile wallets in India.

Lesson at a Glance

- **Bank:** Bank is an institution which deals in money and credit. It accepts deposits from the public and lends money to individuals, firms and governments.
- **Various Kinds of Bank:** (i) Commercial Banks; (ii) Exchange Banks; (iii) Industrial Banks; (iv) Agricultural Banks; (v) Cooperative Banks; (vi) Indigenous Bankers; (vii) Export-Import Bank (EXIM); (viii) Central Bank.
- **Central Bank:** Central Bank in our country is called the Reserve Bank of India. It is the apex institution whose main function is to control, regulate and stabilise the banking and the monetary system of the country.
- **Functions of Reserve Bank:** (i) Monopoly of note-issue; (ii) Banker, fiscal agent and adviser to the government; (iii) Banker's bank; (iv) Lender of the last resort; (v) Controller of credit; (vi) Custodian of foreign currency; (vii) Maintenance of exchange rate; (viii) Provision of clearing house facility; (ix) Development functions; (x) Miscellaneous functions.
- **Functions of Commercial Banks:** (i) Receiving Deposits; (ii) Lending Money; (iii) Agency functions; (iv) General utility functions.
- **Internet Banking:** Internet banking refers to systems that enable bank customers to access accounts and general information on bank products and services through a personal computer (PC) or other intelligent devices.

Prepare a list of banks located in your city/town and categorise them into public sector banks and private sector banks.

You have to explain to your class the relationship of central bank and commercial banks.

A. **Short Answer Type Questions:**
   1. What is a Bank?
   2. Explain Industrial Banks.

3. Explain Exchange Banks.
4. Name two types of banks.
5. Explain Commercial Banks.
6. Give the meaning of Central Bank.
7. State two functions of the Reserve Bank of India.
8. Name the Central Bank of our country.
9. Give two major functions of the Central Bank of our country.
10. "A Central Bank is a banker's bank." Explain in brief. [ICSE 2020]
11. State two agency functions performed by commercial banks.
12. What are the two main functions of a commercial bank?
13. What is 'National Electronic Fund Transfer'? [ICSE 2019]
14. What is RTGS?
15. What is IMPS?
16. What is a Mobile Wallet?
17. What are indigenous banks?
18. Mention any two agency functions of commercial banks.
19. A Commercial Bank serves as an agent for its customers. Justify.
20. The Central Bank is the lender of the last resort. Explain.
21. Distinguish between Central Bank and Commercial Bank. [ICSE 2020]
22. Explain:
    (i) NEFT   (ii) RTGS   [ICSE 2020]
23. Distinguish between Central Bank and Commercial Bank. [ICSE 2019]

B. Essay Type Questions:
1. Define Bank. Explain different types of banks.
2. What is a Central Bank? What are its important functions? Which of these functions are more important in a country like India?
3. What is meant by the term 'commercial bank'? Explain the functions of a commercial bank.
4. Give in detail the functions of a Bank in modern time.
5. Explain the five functions of the Central Bank of India.
6. What is Internet Banking? What are the different modes of Internet Banking?
7. Explain five differences between a central bank and a commercial bank.
8. What do you understand by Agency services of a commercial bank? Explain any four agency services of a commercial bank.
9. Explain the 'Clearing House Function' of the Central Bank. [ICSE 2019]

CHAPTER-23
Banking Transactions

A bank is an institution which accepts deposits from the public and in turn advances loans by creating credit. Banks create credit by advancing loans on cash credit basis or by an overdraft arrangement and by purchasing securities and paying for them with its own cheques. Banks are different from other financial institutions in the sense that other financial institutions cannot create credit though they may be accepting deposits and making advances. Hence, a bank may as such be defined as an institution which purchases and sells money, and transacts other businesses of like nature.

- *Types of Deposit Accounts*
- *Cheque*
- *Parties to a Cheque*
- *Advantages and Disadvantages of Payment by Cheque*
- *Pass Book*
- *Bank Drafts*
- *Traveller's Cheque*
- *Bill of Exchange*
- *Promissory Note*
- *Hundies*
- *ATM*
- *Advantages and Disadvantages of ATMs to Customers and Bankers*
- *Credit Card*
- *Debit Card*
- *Types of Debit Card*
- *Difference between Debit Card and Credit Card*
- *Cautions to Be Taken While Using Debit Card and Credit Card.*

TYPES OF DEPOSIT ACCOUNTS

Banks receive deposits in various forms. the different types of Bank Deposits or Bank Accounts are as follows:

(i) Fixed Deposit Account
(ii) Savings Deposit Account
(iii) Recurring Deposit Account
(iv) Current Deposit Account.

(i) Fixed Deposit Account:
Deposits are made in this account for a specified period and cannot be withdrawn before the expiry of the period for which they have been deposited in the bank. These deposits are repayable after the expiry of a fixed period, *e.g.*, one year, five years or any other period. These are also known as 'Time Deposit' or 'Long-Term Deposit'. Higher rate of interest is offered to attract such deposits. However, the rate of interest varies with the period of deposit. The longer the period of deposit, the higher will be the rate of interest. No Pass Book or Cheque Book is issued for fixed deposits. Only a fixed deposit receipt is issued containing the name and address of the depositor, the amount and period of deposit etc. This receipt is signed by the Bank Manager. The depositor is entitled to claim back his money on producing the receipt on the due date.

(ii) Savings Deposit Account:
Savings deposits are those deposits on which the bank pays a certain rate of interest to the depositors but places certain restrictions on their withdrawals. For savings

deposits, an account is opened with the bank which is called savings account. This account is opened with small amounts. The main aim of these accounts is to develop the habit of saving among common people. Such an account can also be opened by two persons in joint names. Overdraft facilities are generally not allowed to the operators of these accounts. The accountholders are allowed to withdraw money by cheque or by withdrawal form subject to the condition that they maintain a minimum balance in their accounts. Withdrawals are limited to two or three times a week to discourage the habit of frequent withdrawals. In order to deposit the money, a pay-in-slip is filled in. A Pass Book is also issued in which transactions relating to the account are recorded from time to time. Interest is paid on minimum monthly balances and credited to the respective accounts on a yearly or half yearly basis. In order to tap small savings, banks have introduced various schemes, such as daily home collection scheme or door-to-door collection scheme, to encourage the habit of thrift to mobilise savings.

(iii) Recurring Deposit Account:

This deposit account has been started to encourage those people to save who cannot give large deposit in lump sum. Recurring deposit account can be opened with small amount and the depositor keeps on depositing a certain sum of money every month for a specified time period. The number of monthly installments may be 12, 24, 36, 48, 60 and so on. After the expiry of the specified period, the depositor gets back his money along with interest thereon. A Pass Book is issued to the depositor showing the installments deposited by him from time to time. Cheques cannot be drawn to withdraw money from a recurring deposit account.

(iv) Current Deposit Account:

Current Account is one into which money may be deposited and withdrawn at any time. Current account is generally operated by the business houses. Most banks agree to open current account with a minimum deposit of ₹ 5000. Under this account, the depositor can withdraw money from his account by cheque at any time during the working hours of the bank or any working day. There are no restrictions to limit the number of withdrawals, subject to the minimum credit balance to be kept as per the rules of the bank. The bank does not pay any interest on current deposits but infact makes a small charge (bank charge) from the operators of this account according to the number of transactions. The bank also grants overdraft facilities in case of need to the operator of this account.

Distinction Among Different Types of Bank Accounts

Basis of Distinction	Current Deposit Account	Fixed Deposit Account	Savings Deposit Account	Recurring Deposit Account
Objective of the Banks	To provide facilities to account-holder to deposit and with-draw the money as and when they need.	To attract savings for a longer period of time.	To cultivate habit of saving and thrift.	To accumulate small savings.

Period of deposit	No fixed period.	Fixed period.	No fixed period.	One year to five years.
Number of deposits	No limit to the number of deposits that can be made.	Deposit can only be made once at the time of opening Fixed deposit account.	No limit to the number of deposits that can be made.	Deposits are made every month
Time and number of withdrawals	Withdrawals can be made as many times in a day as one pleases.	Withdrawal can be made only after the expiry of the fixed period.	Withdrawals can be made once or twice a week according to the rules of the banks.	No withdrawals are allowed before the due date.
Rate of interest	No interest or a very low rate of interest is allowed.	A high rate of interest is allowed as compared to other accounts.	Small rate of interest is allowed.	A comparatively low rate of interest is allowed.
Operation by cheques	It is normally operated by cheques.	Cheques are not used.	It is normally operated by cheques and withdrawal form	Cheque facility is not allowed.

CHEQUE

The most important negotiable instrument is the Cheque. Payment by issue of cheques is a easy and convenient method of making payments. It avoids the risk of carrying cash from one place to another. The cost involved is very small and it is a documentary evidence for payment made.

It can be defined as a signed document by which money is transferred from the account of one person to the account of another person. A cheque can be said to be an instrument in writing containing an unconditional order signed by the maker, directing a banker to pay on demand, a certain sum of money to the bearer of the instrument. Cheques are printed by banks on a special type of paper.

Parties to a Cheque

There are three parties to a cheque:
(i) The first one is a drawer or maker who is the person or depositor who writes it.
(ii) Second comes the drawee or banker on whom the cheque is drawn. In other words, drawee is the bank of the drawer which pays money to the payee.

(iii) Last comes the payee. Payee means the person named in the cheque to whom the money is to be paid. Sometimes, the drawer makes the cheque in his own favour by writing the word 'self' in place of writing any name. In such a condition, he is both a drawer and payee. In case the payee is a fictitious person, the cheque may be treated as payable to its bearer.

Advantages and Disadvantages of Payment by Cheque

Advantages:
1. The cheque provides an easy and inexpensive means of transferring money. It may be drawn for any sum within the limit of the drawer's current account balance. The cost of transmission is the same for any amount, namely the cost of postage.
2. Payment by cheque eliminates the need for counting and checking bank notes.
3. The cheque, excepting the bearer cheque, acts like a receipt. It is a proof once it has been cleared, that the money has been received.
4. The cheques avoids risks involved in carrying cash from one place to another.
5. It increases the credit worthiness of a business concern.
6. There is no need to keep large amounts of cash in office or at resident.
7. It saves frequent use and handling of government currency.

Disadvantages:
1. Cheques are not legal tender and a creditor may refuse to take a cheque in payment.
2. Unless a cheque is carefully drawn, it may be altered by a dishonest person.
3. A cheque for a big sum is of the same dimensions as a cheque for a small sum and can be just as easily mislaid or lost without the loss being noticed immediately. Such a risk in the use of cheques makes it necessary to handle them with great care.
4. Receiving payment by cheque may be inconvenient for those who have no bank account.

PASS BOOK

A pass book is a book issued by the banker to customer to record the entries simultaneously in the bank account and in the book, to tell about the position of the account on any given date or at any point of time. This book contains only the true copy of the entries made in the bank account. It acts as an information card to the customer to know the position of his account maintained with the banker. When the cheques are credited, a credit entry will be made in the pass book and when the debit is made for payment or withdrawal of cash, the debit entry in the pass book is also made. The balance is shown for the information of the customer. As the book passes from banker to customer, it is called pass book.

BANK DRAFTS

A bank draft is a type of cheque, drawn by a bank either on its own branch or on another bank. It is the most convenient and the cheapest method of remitting money from one place to another. For remitting money by a bank draft, a person first obtains the bank draft from the bank by paying the amount he wants to remit and the prescribed commission. He, then, sends the bank draft to the receiver by post. When the receiver receives the bank draft, he goes to the concerned bank and gets it encashed. The draft is payable only at demand. In many respects bank drafts are similar to cheques as both are dated and both can be crossed.

TRAVELLER'S CHEQUE

The tourists and travellers have to carry adequate money with them. It is always risky to carry large sums of money while travelling from one place to another. There are possibilities of theft, pick pocketing, misplacement or overspending. Ordinary cheques may be carried out but they are not accepted everywhere as they may even get dishonoured. To avoid these difficulties, traveller's cheques are issued by the State Bank of India or leading commercial banks for the convenience of the travelling public.

Traveller's cheques are issued in different denominations printed thereon, *e.g.*, 50, ₹ 100 or ₹ 500. A person can buy any number of traveller's cheques. However, he will have to deposit equivalent amount of money with the issuing bank. A person without a bank account may also purchase it. The purchaser will have to sign on the traveller's cheque at the prescribed place. To convert the cheques into cash, he has to sign again in the presence of the authorised officer of the State Bank of India or some leading Commercial Banks. The cheques are valid until use, unused cheques can be returned and the cash is received from the issuing bank. Thus, traveller's cheques make the journey safe and comfortable.

Specimen of A Traveller's Cheque

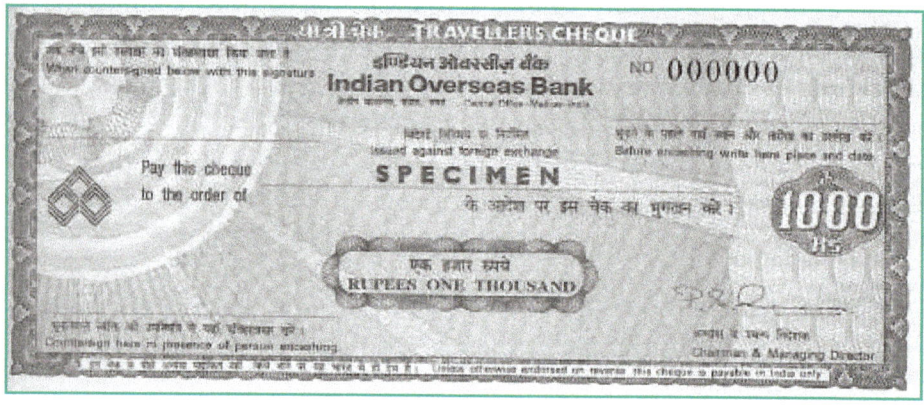

BILL OF EXCHANGE

A bill of exchange is an instrument in writing containing an unconditional order, signed by the maker, directing a certain person to pay a certain sum of money only to, or to the order of, a certain person, or to the bearer of the instrument. The important characteristics of a bill of exchange are:

1. It must be an unconditional order to pay.
2. It must be in writing.
3. It must be signed by the maker.
4. The maker must direct a certain person to pay money.

5. The payment must be of a certain sum of money only.

Bill of Exchange

> ₹ 500/-   Mumbai
>   January 19, 2008
> Stamp
>   Three months after date please pay to me or my order a sum of Rupees Five Hundred only, for value received.
>   Miss Liza Rey
>   18, Villey Parle Scheme, Mumbai
>
> To,
> Mr. Merry Desouza
> 4300 Crooked Tree , SW- 6, Wyoming,
> Michigan - 49509

Parties to the Bill of Exchange

A bill of exchange has three parties to it:

1. The drawer, *i.e.*, the person who makes the order,
2. The drawee, *i.e.*, the person on whom the order is made, and
3. The payee, *i.e.*, the person who will collect the money on the due date.

The bill may be issued by an exporter of goods (or an inland seller) upon the buyer, requiring the buyer to pay the stated amount, that is, the price of the goods through a named banker.

PROMISSORY NOTE

A promissory note can be said to be an instrument in writing with unconditional undertaking signed by the maker to pay a certain sum of money only to, or to the order of a certain person, or to the person having the possession of the promissory note.

Following are the essentials of promissory note:

1. It must be in writing.
2. It should contain an unconditional promise to pay, *i.e.*, the promise to pay must not depend upon the happening of a certain event.
3. The amount promised to be paid must be a certain sum of money only and not shoes or clothes or any other thing.
4. It must be signed by the maker.
5. It must be payable to the bearer of the instrument.

Essential Parties to a Promissory Note: There are two parties to a promissory note:

1. Maker, *i.e.*, the person who signs the note and thereby undertakes to pay.
2. Payee, *i.e.*, the person to whom money is to be paid.

Specimen of Promissory Note

> ₹ 700/-
>
> Mumbai
> March 1, 2008
>
> Stamp
>
> Three months after date, I promise to pay Mr. S. Henry or order the sum of Rupees Seven Hundred only, for value received.
>
> For Smith & Co.
> Liza Rey
> Manager

A promissory note contains a promise to pay money either on demand when it is called a demand promissory note, or after a fixed period, when it is known as a time promissory note.

A promissory note may be made by an individual or by two or more persons. The Promissory Note made by a single individual is called Single Promissory Note. The Promissory Note made by two or more persons may be either Joint Promissory Note or Joint and Several Promissory Notes.

A promissory note is prepared on stamped paper.

Distinction between Promissory Note and Bill of Exchange

Promissory Note	Bill of Exchange
A promissory note has two parties *i.e.*, maker and payee.	A Bill of Exchange has three parties, *i.e.*, Drawer, Acceptor or Drawee and Payee.
In a promissory note, the debtor himself creates the instrument.	In a bill, the creditor usually originates it by directing the debtor to pay.
The liability of a maker of promissory note is primary and absolute because he himself is the main debtor.	The liability of the drawer of a bill is secondary and conditional, *i.e.*, drawer will be liable only if the bill is presented to the drawee and is dishonoured by the drawee.
It does not need any acceptance for its legal validity.	It has to be accepted by the drawee to enforce his liability on it.
Notice of dishonour need not be given to the maker of a promissory note.	Notice of dishonour has to be given to the drawer of the bill to make him liable.

HUNDIES

A hundi is an Indian bill of exchange which has been in use in our country from time immemorial. It is indeed the oldest surviving form of credit instrument in this country. It may be defined as a written order, usually unconditional, drawn by one person on another for payment, on demand or after a specified time, of a certain sum of money, to a person named therein. A bill of exchange, is always unconditional. But a hundi is sometimes, conditional, *e.g.*, a Jokhami Hundi. Such a conditional hundi is not, strictly speaking, a bill of exchange.

AUTOMATED TELLER MACHINE (ATM)

An ATM is a device located on or off the bank's premises to receive and give out cash round the clock and to provide, other banking services. It is a specialized terminal connected to a bank's central computer via public telephone network. ATMs allow access to a range of banking transactions by inserting a magnetic strip plastic card called ATM card containing account details and keying in a personal identification number (PIN).

Various useful services provided by an ATM are as follows:

1. ATMs allow round the clock cash withdrawal.
2. Mini statements can be issued using ATMs.
3. ATMs allows one to request for a cheque book.
4. To ensure safety, ATMs allows one to change his PIN whenever needed.
5. Pay credit card bills: Credit card bills can be paid through the ATM using a debit card. However, this facility can be availed only if the customer's credit card and debit card are of the same bank.
6. Pay utility bills: Electricity bills, telephone bills, insurance premium etc. can be paid through ATMs. This helps in saving both time and money.
7. Recharging mobiles: Prepaid services of most mobile operators can be recharged from at ATM.
8. Transfer funds: Banks allows you to transfer funds from one bank account to another bank account using an ATM. These accounts should however be linked to your ATM/Debit card.
9. Income tax payment: Some banks offer the convenience of paying income tax using ATMs. This includes advance tax, self-assessment tax as well as tax due after regular assessment. However, to avoid this service, one needs to register for the facility on the bank's web site or branch first.
10. Book air and railway tickets: Air and railway tickets can be booked using an ATM only if one's banks ATM has this option or has a tie up with a particular airline company or the Railways. At present, SBI, PNB and Bank of Baroda and Karur Vysya Bank offer this facility.
11. Open or withdraw a fixed deposit: Fixed deposit can be made in one's bank using an ATM. For this, one has to select the option 'Open Fixed Deposit' on the ATM menu, select the duration, enter the amount and confirm the other necessary details.

Advantages of ATMs to customers

1. It gives round the clock service and thereby banking time is saved.
2. Service is quick and efficient and free from errors.
3. The cardholder can access cash and services at any place, where an ATM is located.
4. Funds can be transferred easily to any branch of the banks.
5. Withdrawals can be made at any time and hence it can be called as anywhere banking facility.

Advantages of ATMs to Bankers

1. Crowd at the bank counter is considerably reduced.
2. It is an alternative to extend banking hours and new branches and therefore the operating expenses are reduced.
3. Help bank employees to focus on the analytical and innovative work.
4. It increases the volume of banking business by placing ATMs at the central places.
5. It avoids the cash transportation and cash handling.

Disadvantages of ATMs to Customers

1. Presence of Various Constraints:
Banks have a very few or no branches in rural areas in India and even if banks make some efforts to introduce ATM services in the country side, various constraints like illiteracy of the villagers, security concern, lack of commuting facilities etc., may obstruct smooth functionality of ATMs.

2. Limitation on Cash Withdrawals:
There is a limitation on the amount of cash that can be withdrawn from the ATMs in one transaction and also in a day. For example, many banks do not permit withdrawal of more than ₹ 10,000 at a time.

3. Possibility of Fraud:
ATM card, if misplaced, lost or stolen, may be misused by unscrupulous persons. Criminals can fit skimming devices and small cameras inside ATMs. These machines record account details and personal identification numbers of the customers using the ATMs. These criminals can later use these details to withdraw amount from the customers' accounts.

4. Loss of Personnel Touch With the Banks:
Customers lose personal touch with their bankers when they start using ATMs for nearly all transactions.

5. Operational Issues:
ATMs located in busy locations may not have adequate funds for busy holiday weekends when large numbers of people are taking out cash.

6. Fees:
Banks and machine owners draw a huge source of revenue from ATM fees. Cardholders can usually withdraw cash for free from ATMs owned by their bank, but typically have to pay to use machines owned by other banks.

CREDIT CARD

A Credit card, issued by the customers' bank, is a small plastic card entitling the holder to buy goods and services on credit. The name, account number of the holder and the validity period are marked on the card. The specimen signature of the cardholder are given on the reverse of the card. The cardholder is sanctioned a limit by the bank. The cardholder can buy products and services at specified outlets by swiping the card, within the limit sanctioned by the bank.

The seller of goods or services, at the specified outlets verify the validity of card, cardholder's identity and credit limit before selling the goods or services to the customers.

Thereafter a credit card voucher showing the details of purchases is prepared. The image of card is transferred on the voucher by means of an imprinter and signatures of the cardholder are obtained on the voucher.

The card issuing bank release payment to the seller on the basis of these vouchers. The cardholder is required to make payment to the bank in due course of time.

Some banks also allow cash withdrawal facility to the cardholders. For this cardholder has to pay service fees/interest.

DEBIT CARD

A debit card (also known as a bank card) is also a plastic card that provides an alternative payment method to cash when making purchases. Functionally, it can be called an electronic cheque, as the funds are withdrawn directly from either the bank account, or from the remaining balance on the card. In some cases, the cards are designed exclusively for use on the Internet, and so there is no physical card.

The use of debit cards has become widespread in many countries and has overtaken the cheque, and in some instances, cash transactions by volume. Like credit cards, debit cards are used widely for making purchase on telephone and Internet.

A point of sale terminal electronically tied to the bank computer automatically transfers the money from customer's account to seller's account.

The debit cardholder can make purchases only to the extent of availability of funds in his account.

Types of debit card

Debit cards can also be used as ATM card for withdrawing cash. Merchants can also offer "cashback"/"cashout" facilities to customers, where a customer can withdraw cash along with their purchase.

There are currently three ways in which debit card transactions are processed: (i) On-line Debit Card (also known as PIN Debit); (ii) Off-line Debit Card (also known as Signature Debit) and (iii) Electronic Purse Card.

(i) On-line Debit Card:
On-line debit cards require electronic authorization of every transaction and the debits are reflected in the user's account immediately. The transaction may be additionally secured with the personal identification number (PIN) authentication system and some on-line cards require such authentication for every transaction, essentially becoming enhanced automated teller machine (ATM) cards. One difficulty in using on-line debit cards is the necessity of an electronic authorization device at the point of sale (POS) and sometimes also a separate PIN pad to enter the PIN, although this is becoming common place for all card transactions in many countries. Overall, the on-line debit card is generally viewed as superior to the off-line debit card because of its more secure authentication system and live status, which alleviates problems with processing lag on transactions that may have been forgotten or not authorized by the owner of the card. Banks in some countries, such as Canada and Brazil, only issue on-line debit cards.

(ii) Off-line Debit Card:

Off-line debit cards have the logos of major credit cards (*e.g.* Visa or Master Card) or major debit cards (*e.g.* Maestro in the United Kingdom and other countries, but not the United States) and are used at the point of sale like a credit card (with payer's signature). This type of debit card may be subject to a daily limit, and/or a maximum limit equal to the current account balance in the account from which it draws funds. Transactions conducted with off-line debit cards require 2-3 days to be reflected on users' account balances. In some countries and with some banks and merchant service organizations, a "credit" or off-line debit transaction is without cost to the purchaser beyond the face value of the transaction, while a small fee may be charged for a "debit" or on-line debit transaction (although it is often absorbed by the retailer). Other differences are that on-line debit purchasers may opt to withdraw cash in addition to the amount of the debit purchase (if the merchant supports that functionally); also, from the merchant's standpoint, the merchant pays lower fees on on-line debit transaction as compared to off-line debit transaction.

(iii) Electronic Purse Card:

Smart-card-based electronic purse systems are those in which value is stored on the card chip, not in an externally recorded account, so that machines accepting the card need no network connectivity. These are in use throughout Europe since the mid-1990s.

The Differences between Debit Card and Credit Card

Debit card	Credit card
Transactions are made with the available funds in the current or savings account of a customer.	Transactions are made on credit even when there are no available funds in the customers' account. The payment is made by the bank to the seller on behalf of the customer.
Interest is earned on the deposits in the account.	Interest is charged on the amount taken on credit by the customer from the bank.
Need to be connected to a savings or checking account.	Need not to be connected to any savings or checking accounts.
Nothing to repay as no money is borrowed.	Repayment is required by the borrower to the bank with the interest within the due period.

CAUTIONS TO BE TAKEN WHILE USING DEBIT CARD

1. Memorise your PIN and do not write it down anywhere. Also, do not share your PIN with anyone.
2. You may receive fake calls asking for your bank details. Do not share any such information on calls as the bank will never ask for your bank details as they already have them.
3. After completing your transaction in the ATM, always press the cancel key.
4. If you lose your debit card, report to the bank immediately and get your card blocked.

5. Change your PIN numbers as often as possible.

CAUTIONS TO BE TAKEN WHILE USING CREDIT CARD

1. Always keep your card private and do not reveal your credit card number to anyone.
2. Do not give your credit card details over phone unless you get the call from the trusted bank.
3. Keep a regular track of your credit card statements and reports.
4. Contact your bank immediately when you lose your credit card or when you suspect a deceptive activity.
5. Make your passwords complex using with both letters and numbers.

Lesson at a Glance

- **Types of Deposit Accounts:** (i) Fixed Deposit Account; (ii) Saving Deposit Account; (iii) Recurring Deposit Account; (iv) Current Deposit Account.
- **Cheque:** The most important negotiable instrument is the cheque. It is a signed document by which money is transferred from the account of one person to the account of another person.
- **Pass Book:** A pass book is a book issued by the banker to customer to record the entries simultaneously in the bank account and in the book, to tell about the position of the account on any given date or at any point of time.
- **Bank Drafts:** A bank draft is a type of cheque, drawn by a bank either on its own branch or on another bank. It is the most convenient and the cheapest method of remitting money from one place to another.
- **Traveller's Cheque:** Traveller's cheques are issued in different denominations printed thereon, e.g., ₹ 50, ₹ 100, or ₹ 500. A person can buy any number of travellers' cheques. However, he will have to deposit equivalent amount of money with the issuing bank.
- **Bill of Exchange:** A bill of exchange is an instrument in writing containing an unconditional order, signed by the maker, directing a certain person to pay a certain sum of money only to, or to the order of, a certain person, or to the bearer of the instrument.
- **Parties to the Bill of Exchange:** (i) The drawer; (ii) The drawee; (iii) The payee.
- **Promissory Note:** It is an instrument in writing with unconditional undertaking signed by the maker to pay a certain sum of money only to or to the order of a certain person, or to the person having the possession of the promissory note.
- **Hundies:** Hundi is a written order, usually unconditional, drawn by one person on another for payment, on demand or after a specified time, of a certain sum of money, to a person named therein.
- **Automated Teller Machines (ATM):** An ATM is a device located on or off the bank's premises to receive and give out cash round the clock and to provide other banking services.
- **Credit Card:** It is a card entitling its holder to buy goods and services on credit based on the holders promise to the bank to pay for these goods and services on a later date.

- **Debit Card:** A debit card is a plastic card that provides an alternative payment method to cash when making purchases.
- **Types of Debit Card:** (i) On-line debit card; (ii) Off-line debit card; (iii) Electronic purse card.

Project Work

Visit a nearby bank and record the formalities which are to be fulfilled for opening a savings account and a current account.

Assignment

Explain to your friend the various types of bank accounts that can be opened in a bank

Questions

A. **Short Answer Type Questions:**
  1. What do you mean by bank deposits?
  2. Name the accounts that can be opened in a bank.
  3. What is Fixed Deposit Account?
  4. What is Current Account?
  5. What is Recurring Deposit Account?
  6. What is Hundi?
  7. What is Pass Book?
  8. What do you understand by Bank draft?
  9. What do you understand by a Cheque?
  10. What is traveller's cheque?
  11. What purpose is served by a Bank draft?
  12. What is a Savings Account?
  13. What are the different parties of a cheque?
  14. What is the Bill of exchange?
  15. Write any two advantages and disadvantages of a cheque.
  16. Who is the drawee on a bill of exchange?
  17. What is a promissory note?
  18. Differentiate between promissory note and bill of exchange.
  19. What is a bank account called in which a depositor can deposit and withdraw amount at will?
  20. State two features of current account.
  21. What is credit card?

22. What is debit card?
23. Name two types of debit card.
24. Distinguish between debit card and credit card.
25. What is an ATM?
26. Distinguish between a bill of exchange and a promissory note.
27. What is 'Discounting of bills of exchange'? [ICSE 2019]
28. State any two precautions while using an 'ATM'. [ICSE 2019]
29. Distinguish between Saving Account and Current Account. [ICSE 2018]
30. State any two advantages of Traveller's Cheques. [ICSE 2018]
31. Distinguish between Over Draft and Cash Credit. [ICSE 2017]

B. Essay Type Questions:
1. What are the different types of deposit accounts that can be opened in a commercial bank? Briefly explain them.
2. What is the bill of exchange? Distinguish between a Bill of Exchange and a Promissory Note.
3. Define a promissory note. What are the essential parties to a promissory note?
4. What do you mean by a cheque? List down the various parties to a cheque.
5. What is credit card? Differentiate between credit card and debit card.
6. "Your journey becomes safe and comfortable by taking traveller's cheque." Explain clearly.
7. What is a cheque? What are the advantages of a cheque?
8. Differentiate between:
    (i) Savings Deposit and Current Deposit.
    (ii) Fixed Deposit and Recurring Deposit.
9. What are the precautions to be taken while using Debit card and Credit card?
10. Write short note on:
    (i) Bank draft; (ii) Traveller's cheque; (iii) Recurring Deposit Account; and (iv) The importance of a cheque.

CHAPTER-24
Financial Fraudulent Practices

FRAUDULENT PRACTICES

Fraudulent practices are any act or omission, including a misrepresentation, that knowingly or recklessly misleads, or attempts to mislead, a party to obtain a financial or other benefit or to avoid an obligation. The example of fraudulent act is forging a document or signature or altering a document.

- *Fraudulent Practices*
- *Types of Fraudulent Practices*
- *Credit card Frauds*
- *Insurance Fraud*
- *Intellectual Property Fraud*
- *Internet and Cyber fraud*
- *False Accounting*

Omission

An "omission" is the act of knowingly and deliberately failing to disclose any fact to take the advantage, for example, that a contractor has been debarred, to obtain an improper benefit or avoid an obligation.

Misrepresentation

A misrepresentation is the act of giving a false statement of facts or manipulating some fact to get undue advantage.

Generally, a fraudulent practice relates itself with illegal methods to obtain financial gain. This can happen in various ways. Sometimes the motto behind the frauds can be simple hatred for the individual or company but mostly it is because of the next level financial gain that it would bring.

Types of Fraudulent Practices

Since the main motive of fraudulent practices is financial gain, fraudsters can commit fraud in many ways. Some of the ways are discussed below in detail:

1. Credit Card Fraud
2. Insurance Fraud
3. Intellectual Property Fraud
4. Internet and Cyber Fraud
5. False Accounting

Credit Card Fraud:

This type of fraud is most common in recent times due to ease of access makes it one of the most committed fraud of recent times. A wide range for theft and fraud has been committed involving a credit card or a debit card which is the source of funds in a particular transaction. The main motto for this type of fraud can be to purchase goods without paying through on-line payments, or to obtain unauthorized funds from an account of any person.

One can access the account and retrieve cash from the account at any point if he or she has the PIN number of the debit or credit card. This particular type of fraud can also be termed as cyber fraud where fraudsters call up a consumer at random claiming to be from the bank and take their details, withdrawing cash from them at a later point. The fraudsters can also make clone of the card to withdraw money.

Insurance Fraud:
Any act that is committed keeping a fraudulent outcome from an insurance process in mind falls under this category. If the claimant attempts to obtain some benefit or advantage for which the claimant is not entitled or when the insurer denies the due benefit, an insurance fraud is committed.

Fake insurance agents visit the houses of the consumers to commit these frauds. Enticing the consumer with lucrative options, they take the deposit cheque and then pick up the money from the bank.

Intellectual Property Fraud:
This type of fraud is committed when the fake counterfeit products and pirated products which are no longer original, are passed to customers as being original. The industries that usually fall under this category of frauds are–health, fashion, films and music where piracy and theft are very common.

Counterfeit goods have lower safety standards, which can pose health and safety risks to the consumers. They also damage the reputation of the companies who produce the legitimate products as it creates negative perception about the company.

Piracy is one of the best examples that can be given for this type of fraud. Original design or work is copied and then a fake product made based on the design for selling it at a cheap rate. Piracy is punishable and a person who is caught with a pirated version of any good is also punishable under the law.

Internet and Cyber Fraud:
Cyber fraud is one of the most committed frauds which are gaining fast recognition in today's time. As per the FBI statistics of Internet Crime Complaint Centre, 2014's, there were around 2,69,422 complaints were filed. The numbers of complaints are increasing in recent times. This fraud is a threat to people across the world as everything is managed by computers. In today's world, it is mandatory to increase the awareness among the people so that they can be careful against these frauds. Hacking, is the example of the most common cyber frauds.

An experienced unethical hacker can actually hack the on-line account and commit frauds. Sometimes frauds are committed if we click on a link while browsing which turns out to be a spam and downloads malware into the system, gaining access to every data in your computer. This not only affects the Internet security but also increases the chances of having access to an individual's banking details. The main motto of this fraud can be harassing the individual or financial gain.

False Accounting:
Deception is common in today's world. The easiest way of deception now-a-days has to be through the accounting. False accounting is done by changing the figures of the accounts books, records or presenting false information in the accounts of a company is a punishable offence. All this is done to gain money through unfair means.

It is, thus, advised to be very careful while handling the finance or accounting statements of any company or entity and every person should be aware of the types of frauds committed.

Raising awareness also helps in decreasing the rate of frauds happening in the country.

LESSON AT A GLANCE

- **Fraudulent Practices:** Fraudulent practices are any act or omission, including a misrepresentation, that knowingly or recklessly misleads, or attempts to mislead, a party to obtain a financial or other benefit or to avoid an obligation.
- **Types of Frauds:**

  1. Credit Card Fraud: Done through the misuse of the financial transaction cards

  2. Insurance Fraud: Done through fake agents on the phone or by visiting the house

  3. Intellectual Property Fraud: The major medium being Piracy

  4. Internet and Cyber Fraud: Some through dangerous malware, spam links, Hacking

  5. False Accounting: Done through false digits in the financial account statements

PROJECT WORK

Find out the different types of frauds that are happening in your locality, citing examples of each.

ASSIGNMENT

Write a report of 1000 words on the most committed fraud in 2017 with proper statistics.

QUESTIONS

A. **Short Answer Type Questions:**
   1. Define Fraudulent Practices.
   2. State the different types of frauds that take place.
   3. Explain in brief a credit card fraud? [ICSE 2020]
   4. What do you mean by Internet and cyber fraud? [ICSE 2019]
   5. What is False Accounting?

B. **Essay Type Questions:**
   1. Mention the different types of financial Fraudulent Practices with examples of each.
   2. What are the ways that one can commit false accounting fraud and how do you think it can harm a company?
   3. State examples of intellectual property frauds along with its definition.

CHAPTER-25
Government Initiatives in Environment Protection

ENVIRONMENT PROTECTION

- *Environment Protection Act, 1986*
- *Central Pollution Control Board and its functions*

We live within the walls of our environment. The environment is our mother and it supports the life of each and every living thing on earth. We depend on our environment to sustain our life. If we protect our environment we can get better health, better food, and better quality of air to breath. The environment protection is the steps taken to protect and preserve the natural environment by reducing the overuse of natural resources and reducing the pollutants that can degrade the quality of the environment. Individuals and organisations have to play their part to conserve the environment for the benefit and existence of the human life.

Over consumption, technology advancement, population exceeding the permissible limit is some of the reasons which have adverse effect on our environment. The degradation of the environment has been acknowledged by the government and a lot of steps have been taken to protect the environment from further degradation. The major step that has been taken by government in this direction is the implementation of Environment Protection Act, 1986.

ENVIRONMENT PROTECTION ACT, 1986

Government of India enacted the Environment Protection Act of 1986 under Article 253 of the Constitution. This Act was passed in March 1986 and comes into force on 19 November 1986 for the protection and the improvement of the environment and for matters connected there with.

Under this Act "environment" includes water, air and land and the inter-relationship which exists among and between water, air and land, and human beings, other living creatures, plants, micro-organism and property.

Features of the Environment Protection Act, 1986:

The Act gives the powers to the Central Government for controlling environmental pollution:

1. Take all necessary steps to protect the quality of the environment.
2. Coordinate the actions of States, officers and other authorities under the Act.
3. To make the list of standards to be maintained for the discharge of the pollutants in the environment.
4. Plan and execute a nationwide programme to prevent and control the environmental pollution.

5. Empower any person to inspect, take samples and perform any kind of tests to find out the level of pollution.
6. Appoint any kind of government analysts.
7. Restrict areas under which any industry, operation may not be carried out without safeguards.
8. Lay down safeguards for prevention of accidents and take remedial measures in case of such accidents.
9. Lay down procedures for handling hazardous substances.
10. Form a committee of people having the right to exercise powers and control.
11. Issue directions to any person, officer or authority including the power to direct closure, prohibition or regulation of any industry, operation or process.
12. Delegate powers to any officer, authority or state.
    - The Act makes it compulsory for any person who is in charge to inform the authorities with regards to any accidental discharge of the pollutant when there's an excess of prescribed standards.
    - The Act makes sure of charging penalties in case of violation of the provisions of it.
    - The Jurisdiction of civil courts is barred under the policies of the Environment Protection Act, 1986.

CENTRAL POLLUTION CONTROL BOARD

The Central Pollution Control Board (CPCB) of India is a statutory body established in 1974 under the Ministry of Environment, Forest and Climate Change (MoEF&CC). It coordinates and control the activities of the State Pollution Control Boards by providing technical assistance to them. It is the apex organisation in country in the field of pollution control, and works as a technical wing of MoEF.

It is responsible for maintaining and monitoring of water and air quality in the country. It advises the Central Government and assist in the formulation of strategies to prevent and control water and air pollution. CPCB along with the State Pollution Control Boards (SPCBs) are responsible for implementation of legislation relating to prevention and control of environmental pollution.

Functions of the Central Pollution Control Board

CPCB functions fall under both national level and as State Boards. CPCB, under the Water (Prevention and Control of Pollution) Act, 1974, and the Air (Prevention and Control of Pollution) Act, 1981, aims for prevention, control and abatement of water pollution, and to improve the quality of air in the country by controlling air pollution.

1. Air Pollution Check:

The Central Pollution Control Board ensures that the vehicles run at a proper speed and do not emit the harmful smoke in case of overheating or over speeding. Regular monitoring of the four pollutants (Sulphur Dioxide, Nitrogen Oxide, Suspended Particulate Matter and Respirable Suspended Particulate Matter) is done by the CPCB.

2. Water Pollution Check:
Fresh water is a warehouse for agriculture, propagation of fisheries etc. Water quality monitoring is done on a quarterly basis so as to make sure that there is no pollutant in the water and it remains fresh for consumption.

3. Noise Pollution Check:
Places where sound is high is kept under the monitoring system so that the sound limit doesn't exceed the decibel level for the safe and protected living of the elderly, children and the animals.

4. Urban Area Programs:
Various programs have been set up in urban areas as those areas have been identified as the major problem areas.

5. Municipal Solid Waste Rules:
MSW rules, 2000 is taken into consideration for the collection, storage, transportation, disposition of the solid municipal waste. The necessary information collection is CPCB's duty.

6. Environment Data Statistics:
The maintenance of the data related to air, water and noise pollution is also one of the main functions of the CPCB.

Lesson at a Glance

- **Environment Protection:** The environment protection is the steps taken to protect and preserve the natural environment by reducing the overuse of natural resources and reducing the pollutants that can degrade the quality of the environment.
- **Environment Protection Act, 1986:** The Environment Protection Act, 1986 was set up by the government as an act to provide for the protection and the improvement of t he environment and for matters connected there with.
- **Central Pollution Control Board:** The Central Pollution Control Board (CPCB) of India is a statutory body established in 1974 under the Ministry of Environment, Forest and Climate Change (MoEF&CC). It is responsible for maintaining and monitoring of water and air quality in the country. It advises the Central Government and assist in the formulation of strategies to prevent and control water and air pollution.
- **Functions of the CPCB:** (i) Air Pollution check (ii) Water Pollution check (iii) Noise Pollution check (iv) Urban Area Programs (v) Municipal Solid Waste Rules (vi) Environment Data Statistics.

Find out the sources which are creating environment pollution in your society. Implement at least one activity that helps to improve the quality of environment. Note your observations from it with proper pictures.

Write an essay stating how would you control and change the system and what steps would you have taken as the Chairman of the Central Pollution Control Board to control the pollution.

A. Short Answer Type Questions:
1. What do you mean by Environment Protection?
2. Define the Environment Protection Act, 1986.
   OR
   Explain any two feature of Environment (Protection) Act, 1986. [ICSE 2019]
3. What are the ways by which the environment gets degraded?
4. What is the Central Pollution Control Board?

B. Essay Type Questions:
1. State the features of the Environment Protection Act, 1986.
   OR
   Explain any five features of Environment Protection Act. [ICSE 2020]
2. What are the functions of the Central Pollution Control Board? [ICSE 2019]
   OR
   Explain briefly any five functions of 'Central Pollution Central Board.
3. Explain any five rights enjoyed by consumers as per the Consumer Protection Act, 1986. [ICSE 2019]

www.ingramcontent.com/pod-product-compliance
Ingram Content Group UK Ltd.
Pitfield, Milton Keynes, MK11 3LW, UK
UKHW051659240426
12048UKWH00046B/692